Understanding Ignorance

The Surprising Impact of What We Don't Know

Daniel R. DeNicola

The MIT Press
Cambridge, Massachusetts
London, England

This book was set in ITC Stone Sans Std and ITC Stone Serif Std by Toppan Best-set Premedia Limited. Printed and bound in the United States of America.

Library of Congress Cataloging-in-Publication Data

Names: DeNicola, Daniel R., author.
Title: Understanding ignorance : the surprising impact of what we don't know / Daniel R. DeNicola.
Description: Cambridge, MA : MIT Press, [2017] | Includes bibliographical references and index.
Identifiers: LCCN 2016053943 | ISBN 9780262036443 (hardcover : alk. paper)
Subjects: LCSH: Ignorance (Theory of knowledge) | Knowledge, Theory of.
Classification: LCC BD221 .D46 2017 | DDC 153.4--dc23 LC record available at https://lccn.loc.gov/2016053943

10 9 8 7 6 5 4 3 2 1

For my teachers and my students, who have given me, in the interplay of knowing and not knowing, a joyful life

Contents

Preface

Over the years, I have occasionally taught a seminar for first-year students titled Secrets and Lies. During our discussions about the ethics of seeking, withholding, and revealing information, I became drawn to the epistemological issues, the ways in which we trade in knowing and not knowing within an epistemic community. Early thoughts about the multifaceted nature of ignorance coalesced in "Intimations of Ignorance," a talk given to Gettysburg's Phi Beta Kappa chapter in 2009. Later that year, I devoted a Senior Seminar to an exploration of the topic. I had intended to discuss ignorance in the book that became *Learning to Flourish* (2012), but soon realized it was too large, complex, and rich for anything but a peripheral inclusion. Ignorance required a front-and-center discussion. It took until 2015, and a sabbatical granted by Gettysburg College (for which I am thankful), before a first draft was completed.

Many of my intellectual debts are of course reflected in the bibliography, but some of the most significant are not. My home department, an exemplary epistemic community, has continually offered encouragement: I am grateful to my colleagues—Steve Gimbel, Gary Mullen, Lisa Portmess, Kerry Walters, Vernon Cisney, Paul Carrick, and Gary Ciocco—for their engagement with my preoccupation and for their thoughtful responses. At Lancaster University (UK), where I was a visiting scholar in 2012, I had numerous helpful conversations with faculty members and doctoral students. All were first rate, but I owe special thanks to Neil Manson for a memorable lunchtime discussion of "epistemic restraint." I benefited from interchanges with many at both institutions who attended my research colloquia. There are also people with whom I had a quite brief conversation that proved significant—though they would not have known it then. I recalled with new resonance nearly forgotten interchanges about ignorance with mentors Israel Scheffler and John Rawls; though both are now gone, they have my gratitude. I thank Catherine Elgin and Amelie Rorty for their quick enthusiasm for my project; Timothy Williamson for his immediate, astute response to an out-of-the-blue email query; and Jennifer Logue and Tyson Lewis for sidebar discussions inspired by their conference papers. The anonymous reviewers engaged by the MIT Press improved this book—even when they differed. One later agreed to divulge his identity to give me access to his many perceptive annotations to the text: Michael McFall, I thank you. MIT's editorial staff is excellent, especially Chris Eyer and Judith Feldmann, and the book simply would not have appeared without the steady support of Senior Acquisitions Editor Philip Laughlin.

It is my wonderfully good fortune to have, every day and always, the loving support of my wife, Sunni. I have regularly called upon her indulgence as a listener; her fine, editorial sense of the reader's needs; and her tolerance of precarious piles of books. *Grazie, luce del sole della mia vita.*

An acknowledgment: the epigraph for part 2 is from "The Outcry," a poem by Abu al-Qasim al-Shabbi, as translated by Atef Ashaer, and is reprinted here with permission of Taylor & Francis. It appears on page 396 of Ashaer's article, "Poetry and the Arab Spring," in the *Routledge Handbook of the Arab Spring: Rethinking Democratization*, edited by Larbi Sadiki (New York: Routledge, 2014), 392–407.

Four decisions shaped the writing of this book. I chose: (1) to attempt a comprehensive study that would examine many facets of ignorance; (2) to integrate perspectives drawn from contemporary studies in many disciplines; (3) to structure the discussion using four spatial metaphors for ignorance—place, boundary, limit, and horizon; and (4) to write a rather nontechnical, occasionally broad-brush text. (Even so, I am likely to try the patience of some readers.) The public importance and interdisciplinary nature of ignorance have led me to reach for a readership beyond epistemologists, beyond philosophers—*beyond*, but not *without*, I hope, for the issues and conclusions are also of philosophical relevance.

This book is about ignorance, but it is sure to exemplify it as well. If I knew the where or how, I would have made it better. But *ignorance* is both a charge and an excuse. To the former, I can only offer the latter—and the hope that it exemplifies understanding, as well.

Daniel R. DeNicola
Gettysburg, 2017

I   Images of Ignorance

If I were given carte blanche to write about any topic I could, it would be about how much our ignorance, in general, shapes our lives in ways we do not know about. Put simply, people tend to do what they know and fail to do that which they have no conception of. In that way, ignorance profoundly channels the course we take in life.

—David Dunning

1 The Impact of Ignorance

Knowledge is a big subject. Ignorance is bigger. And it is more interesting.
—Stuart Firestein

Ignorance abounds. It is ubiquitous, and to doubt that fact is to risk becoming another case in point. In the familiar metaphor, our ignorance (whether individual or collective) is a vast, fathomless sea; our knowledge but a small, insecure island. Even the shoreline is uncertain: both the history of the human race and psychological research suggest that we know even less than we think we do. Indeed, our ignorance is extensive beyond our reckoning.

Ignorance endures. It persists. Oh, we may be lulled by its apparent fragility, as in the oft-quoted Oscar Wilde quip: "Ignorance is like a delicate exotic fruit; touch it and the bloom is gone."[1] It wilts and vanishes at the merest touch of learning. But, its evanescence notwithstanding, ignorance is not endangered. Its blooms may be delicate, but the species is as hardy as kudzu. Despite the spread of universal, compulsory education; despite new tools for learning and great advances in knowledge; despite breathtaking increases in our ability to store, access, and share a superabundance of information—ignorance flourishes.

One might wonder *why* this is so. Does ignorance thrive because, well, we are so ignorant? Might we simply lack enough knowledge—or the right knowledge—to roll back the tide of ignorance? Perhaps its persistence is a reflection of our fallen state, a shameful weakness of will, or a sin of epistemic laziness. Is ignorance like the dirtiness of the world, which stubbornly resists our most industrious efforts to cleanse it thoroughly, and which will be with us eternally? Or, worse, is it possible that more learning actually increases our ignorance—like daubing a stain that only spreads further with every attempt to eradicate it? The idea has become cliché: the more we know, the more we know we don't know. Could we really be the creators of our own ignorance? Such ruminations, like all questionings, express a desire to understand, that, ironically, can arise only within and from ignorance. Ignorance is both the source and the target of such questions.

Pictured in this way, there is a mysterious grandeur, even a sublimity, in the dark profusion of our unknowing. It has overwhelmed some since ancient times, reducing them to a skepticism in which knowledge is out of reach and learning is ultimately futile. Others, like the anonymous fourteenth-century author of *The Cloud of Unknowing*, have been moved to a courageous surrender, abandoning the pretense of knowledge to seek a mystical transcendence. But those of us who resolutely affirm the human capacity for genuine knowledge, even those who would enshrine knowledge or understanding as the highest of goods, may still be awed by the vast surround of impenetrable and imperishable ignorance.

Ignorance devastates. Every one of us—however intelligent and knowledgeable—is bedeviled by our ignorance. Indeed, our personal and collective ignorance exacts a fearful toll every day. The morning news brings word of a friend who has died from a disease for which we know no cure; of a horrible crime enabled by a church that unknowingly put a pedophile in charge of children; of the financial ruin and angry despair of unsuspecting victims defrauded in a phony investment scheme; of a politician's secret that has blown up in shame and heartbreak for his unknowing and innocent family and friends; of a nation in turmoil because its citizens do not know whether their votes were fairly counted; of the pain of those whose loved ones are missing after a natural disaster, their fate unknown, perhaps forever. Our ignorance weighs on us: it can be exasperating, as when we have forgotten a password or the combination to a lock; humiliating, as when it is revealed to peers that we do not know something we should; haunting and distressing, as when someone simply disappears without explanation, or when we are told that the cause of a friend's death will never be known.

Ignorance is implicated in nearly all our suffering; it enables our errors and follies. It can threaten anything and all we value. Is ignorance not our woeful plight, a mighty scourge, and a profound conundrum?

Public Ignorance

We live, we are told, in a "knowledge society" during the "Information Age." Indeed, we carry small devices that give us access to an enormous portion of human knowledge and allow us to share information, virtually instantaneously, with people around the globe. But our era has also been called the "Age of Ignorance." Thoughtful observers decry the contemporary "culture of ignorance"—especially, but not solely, in the United States. The contradiction is troubling and puzzling. Ignorance, it seems, is trending.

The sort of ignorance sparking concern is what might be termed *public ignorance*, by which I mean *widespread, reprehensible ignorance of matters that are significant for our lives together.* Functional illiteracy and innumeracy are examples. Such ignorance might once be explained, if not excused, by lack of educational opportunity; but that seems obtuse when applied to countries with rich educational resources. Besides, the rate of functional illiteracy may be higher in today's America that it was in colonial New England.[2] Stubbornly high rates of illiteracy and innumeracy are a public shame, no doubt. This is remediable ignorance. The need is for learning—except that many such forms of ignorance thrive *despite* years of schooling.

Among young students, whose schooling is incomplete, a certain lack of basic knowledge is unsurprising. The evidence can be ruefully comic (picture knowing teachers chortling over hilarious student errors). But when the individuals are schooled adults, our surprise becomes shock and our amusement fades. Gross historical misunderstanding, witless anachronisms, appalling geographical mistakes, quantitative and literary obtuseness—these are, as depressing surveys regularly inform us, widespread.[3]

Political ignorance, especially in an advanced democracy, is especially disturbing. Tyrants and other advocates of authoritarian systems have long appreciated the advantages of an ignorant constituency. Claude Adrien Helvétius, the eighteenth-century philosopher, observed: "Some politicians have regarded ignorance as favourable to the maintenance of a prince's authority, as the support of his crown and the safeguard of his person. The ignorance of the people is indeed favourable to the priesthood."[4] By contrast, democracies—at least in theory—rest on the pillar of an enlightened citizenry. Unfortunately, the problem of political ignorance in the United States is now so severe that the ideal of an informed citizenry seems quaint.

It goes far beyond not knowing the names of one's congressional delegation: in a survey conducted by the National Constitution Center, a third of respondents could not name any First Amendment rights, and a majority of the remainder could identify only free speech; 42 percent thought the Constitution explicitly states that "the first language of the United States is English"; and a quarter believed that the Constitution established Christianity as the official national religion. In a second survey, 41 percent of respondents did not know there are three branches of government; 62 percent could not name them all; and 33 percent could not identify even one.[5]

Faced with dismal surveys like these and the intractability and extent of political ignorance, some scholars see the need to revise democratic theory in response. A few have argued that capitalism actually *prefers* widespread ignorance to informed citizen-consumers. If extensive ignorance of political matters is now the "new normal," argues one theorist, we are left with an imperative for smaller, more localized, less significant government[6] (as though, I might note, a reduction in the scope and agency of government would reduce in parallel our public interests and real problems of living).

Language, our strongest medium of communication, is another arena of public ignorance. In the United States, all too many have felt embarrassed and resentful over their inability to master a second language (often despite years of instruction). With disturbing frequency, this inability is coupled with hostility toward "foreign" speech. All of this is on display in a recent, widely reported incident. A Vermont eighth-grader studying Latin proposed that her state should have a historically resonant Latin motto to accompany its English motto, and a state legislator agreed to advance her proposal. The proposed motto was: *Stella quarta decima fulgeat* ("May the Fourteenth Star Shine Bright")—an allusion to Vermont's place in joining the Union. When her idea was floated on social media, the benighted replied in force: "I thought Vermont was American not Latin? Does any Latin places have American mottos?" "No way! This is America, not Mexico or Latin America. And they need to learn our language ..." and "ABSOLUTLY NOT!!!! sick and tired of that crap, they have their own countries." Sadly, these are typical of the angry postings.[7] Below some threshold, ignorance does not recognize itself.

False beliefs structure networks of ignorance that incorporate other false beliefs and erroneous actions. A 2014 study, using a national sample of over 2,000 Americans, polled citizens' views about the proper response of the United States to the conflict in Ukraine.[8] It also asked respondents to locate Ukraine on a world map. Though about one in six correctly located Ukraine, the median response was 1,800 miles off target. Many respondents placed it in Asia or Africa, some even in Latin America or in Canada. As bad as this is, the correlation that emerged is more alarming: the less the respondents knew about the location of Ukraine, the more likely that they would urge the United States to intervene in the conflict.

All forms of ignorance are especially dangerous when allied with arrogance or bigotry. As Goethe commented, "There is nothing more frightening than ignorance in action." It can be truly horrifying: in 2012, six members of a Sikh temple in Wisconsin were fatally shot by a man who apparently thought they were Muslims—one of hundreds of cases of hate crimes misdirected against Sikhs in the United States since 9/11.[9]

A Culture of Ignorance

There is more to a culture of ignorance, however, than abominable public ignorance. In a culture of ignorance, appalling ignorance not only flourishes, it is flaunted, even celebrated. It becomes an ideological stance.[10]

The tenacious strain of anti-intellectualism in American life is well documented. Disparagement of "book-learning," wry skepticism about establishmentarian views, trust in "common sense" over expertise, and rural suspicion of urban life and values—these have long characterized a populist strain in American public life. Whatever portion of thoughtful skepticism may motivate this outlook, it is soured by those who take a perverse pride in their ignorance. Sometimes, the attitude may be a matter of class envy turned to spite, a poke in the eye of intellectuals; but often it is merely a defensive pose adopted for religious or political reasons. ("I am not a scientist," say politicians who wish to avoid any public acknowledgment of climate change or evolution—as though such pleas of comfortable ignorance are excusable or commendable.)

Frequently, a disdain for commonly accepted knowledge is buttressed by claims of private, special insights into "the real truth"—insider knowledge of conspiracies, information available only to the initiated, or truths "revealed" to individuals. But such claims to esoteric knowledge by the supposedly savvy are merely forms of ignorance in elaborate disguise.

Today, their number is legion. They are not benignly eccentric; they shape public discourse. As a nation, we have to spend too much time, energy, and capital battling willful ignorance: "Vaccinations cause autism." "The Earth is 4,004 years old and Neanderthals roamed with dinosaurs." "The wild winter in my state disproves global warming." "President Obama is Muslim." "The Sandy Hook massacre never happened." "Massive voter fraud allowed Hillary Clinton to win the popular majority." Such claims represent a refusal to know and a denial of the possibility of error. Their proponents assert their "right to believe"—a silly claim that carries no acknowledgment of responsibility for their beliefs. Many simply deny any evidence that falsifies a cherished belief about policies, practices, and people. Currently, there is an Internet slang term for this phenomenon: *derp*. When such ignorance is influential, it becomes difficult not only to solve social problems, but even to acknowledge them as problems. Who weeps for the truth?

In cases like these, it is hard to separate ignorance from stupidity and unreason, though their meanings are quite distinct. *Ignorance* is, in common usage, a lack of knowledge.[11] *Stupidity* is a mental dullness that indicates an inability to learn or a sustained disinterest in learning.[12] Although stupidity is surely a contributing factor, to make rife stupidity the single, simple explanation for this culture of ignorance is cheaply reductionist and unfairly dismissive. *Unreason* refers to any type of irrationality, such as intentional but self-defeating actions or the affirmation of contradictory beliefs. Ignorance can be remedied; stupidity is intractable. One can be ignorant without being stupid or irrational, though stupidity is sure to produce ignorance across an impressive front. Irrationality seems less a matter of not knowing than of acting contrary to what one knows—though willful ignorance may indeed be irrational.

What is going on in today's culture of ignorance is complicated. It is more than widespread, reprehensible ignorance; it involves the distrust of mainstream sources of information and the rejection of rationally relevant factors in forming beliefs. It seems to abandon institutions and hard-won standards of knowledge that have served us since the Enlightenment, that have brought us the living conditions we enjoy today. Blindly and oddly, individuals will couple the rejection of scientific knowledge with the use of technology it has produced. Evidence and conclusions are accepted selectively, usually to fit some intractable ideological commitment. This culture discounts the value and authority of expertise in favor of shared opinion. The empty "right to believe" (a claim I will discuss in chapter 7) is linked to the right to be heard. We are left to wonder, with Scott Adams's cartoon character Dilbert, "When did ignorance become a point of view?"[13]

Social critics suggest many possible precipitating conditions of this culture: the thrall of fundamentalist religion and partisan political ideology; postmodern deconstructions of institutions and ideals, including truth and reason; the conflation of news and entertainment and misdirected attempts to offer "balanced" coverage by the media; the seduction of virtual reality; the corruption of pure science by "sponsored" research and profit motives; "the silence of the rational center";[14] and many other ingenious and plausible candidates. Today, our ignorance can be sustained by "user-preference" technology. Whatever our beliefs, we may enjoy a cozy informational cocoon in which we hear only the news, opinions, music, and voices we prefer. Ideas that might challenge our views never reach us. Whatever its causes, the culture of ignorance reflects an elevation of will over reason, the loss of a credible concept of objectivity, and a radical change in democratic epistemology. To be sure, its participants would deny that ignorance is involved. But when you undermine the concept of knowledge, you undermine ignorance as well.

Knowledge over Ignorance

Perhaps this assessment seems harsh and presumptuous. In common parlance, when I call someone ignorant, it is an insult. I implicitly claim a kind of superiority: I know that which they do not, plus I know that they do not know it. All too frequently, ascriptions of ignorance and stupidity have been used to deprecate and further marginalize minorities or unpopular groups.[15] Saying "He is ignorant" can be verbal epistemic shaming and a subtle assertion of power. So, yes, the sometime arrogance of the knower should be a cautionary image when one asserts the ignorance of others.

The term *ignorance* gets its harshness from its negative value, particularly in historic Western culture. There is no doubt that the Classical strain of Western culture embraced the idea that knowledge is good and ignorance is a defect that requires remedy. Socrates and Plato took the extreme view that every vice and all societal evil ultimately derive from ignorance. Over the centuries, education (the formal pursuit of knowledge) has evolved from a merely private to a public good, from an elite privilege to a human right. As individuals—especially as students, parents, and educators—and as a society, we invest so much in education. Is not the point of learning or inquiry to remove the bane of ignorance? Therefore, the burden of argument usually falls on the advocate of ignorance; the champion of knowledge carries a positive presumption and the burden only of rebuttal.

True, we often encounter the cliché that "ignorance is bliss"; but it is usually offered as a context-relative witticism, not as a serious, general prescription for a fulfilling life. Yet, also true is that, especially given the state of our postmodern world, we all may sometimes doubt whether learning really leads to happiness; wonder whether some knowledge is not dangerous; or harbor qualms about the certainty of what we know. Would life be best if everyone knew everything (an admittedly impossible perfection)? I have said ignorance abounds, persists, and devastates; it is an ominous, ascendant presence in our lives—but might it also, at times, have a positive value? These doubts, as we shall see, reflect a different strain of Western thought. But either way, we ignore ignorance at our peril.

Calling ignorance by its name can be good. Acknowledging one's ignorance and the possibility of being wrong is the first step to an open mind. It is cognitively healthy: it prepares us for learning, directs our curiosity, and takes us into the real world. Pursuing the truth takes intellectual courage. Finding the truth is often difficult. Accepting the truth may be the hardest part.

Understanding Ignorance

This book is an attempt to *understand* ignorance—at first glance, a quixotic quest sprung from a paradoxical idea. Professing to write a whole book on ignorance reeks of clever irony and invites sarcasm. Isn't ignorance by definition *beyond my knowledge*? Am I not launching a discourse on something I know nothing about—or, perhaps, on *everything* I know nothing about? How can the unknown become known—and still be the unknown? Must not any attempt to understand ignorance alter it, and any successful attempt, destroy it? It is as though I propose to shine a spotlight on my shadow in order to see it better.

But this is a merely superficial paradox, as we shall see, though it points to the genuine and profound question of what we can and cannot come to know about our ignorance. There is indeed a point at which the possibility of understanding ends, and one is left, at best, with intimations. Nonetheless, I think there is a great deal we might learn about our ignorance before we reach that point. I believe that ignorance is far more than a mere void or lack, and that it has dynamic and complex interactions with knowledge. A rich account of what it is to know or to be learned must also comprehend what it is *not* to know or to be *un*learned. Any adequate theory of knowledge or philosophy of education must incorporate an understanding of ignorance. For those fields, it poses an alteration in theoretical perspective that, once absorbed, would be transformative.

Ignorance is neither a pure nor a simple concept; it has a multiplex structure and many forms. In its house are many mansions. It is both an accusation and a defense. Its practical import ranges from the inconsequential to the momentous, from the benign to the fatal, from the excusable to the unforgivable. It is a scourge, but it also may be a refuge, a value, even an accompaniment to virtue. Or so I will argue. In short, ignorance is a many-splendored thing.

The Study of Ignorance

Strangely, until quite recently the usual practice was to leave our ignorance of ignorance undisturbed: full-frontal studies of ignorance were relatively rare, even among otherwise curious philosophers with a keen interest in understanding what it is to know.

A brilliant German of the fifteenth century, Nicholas of Cusa, thought the understanding of our ignorance to be the most fundamental and significant we can acquire. Renowned for his learning and accomplishments as a philosopher, theologian, mathematician, astronomer, and jurist, he nonetheless made ignorance the subject of his greatest work, *De docta ignorantia* (*On Learned Ignorance*)—one of the few treatises with this focus. At the outset of that work, he explains: "Our natural desire to know is not without purpose: hence its first object must be our own ignorance. If we can gratify this natural desire fully, then we shall be in the possession of learned ignorance. There could be nothing, in fact, more efficacious to even the most avid scholar than his being learned in just that ignorance which is peculiar to him; and the more profoundly a man knows his own ignorance, the greater will be his learning."[16] He cites the iconic example of Socrates, who claimed to know only that he was ignorant—an ironic self-awareness that entitled him to a reputation for wisdom.

Nicholas himself, however, aims much higher than self-awareness alone. He projects a true knowledge that goes far beyond mere acknowledgment of one's ignorance: he attempts to reveal the limits of human understanding, to explicate them as a contrast between the finite and the Infinite, and to demonstrate the implications of understanding our own ignorance for cultivating lives of learning. Understanding ignorance is, for Nicholas, fundamental to understanding the human condition. I concur.

Yet, for centuries, serious studies of ignorance were scarce. Few scholars followed Nicholas's ambitious lead. An important exception is the nineteenth-century Scottish philosopher, James Frederick Ferrier, who gave ignorance a central role in his *Institutes of Metaphysic*. Ferrier was well aware of the inattention given to the topic: "There have been many inquiries into the nature of knowledge: there has been no inquiry into the nature of ignorance."[17] Next to the vast literature on knowledge—texts on learning and education, studies in the sociology and social history of knowledge, analytical works of epistemology, accounts of the scientific method and its self-correction, and so on—the literature on ignorance is remarkably slim.

One reason for this dearth is found in the traditional preoccupations of Western philosophers engaged in epistemology—the "theory of knowledge," to use its brief-form definition. The analytical focus has been on the sources, structure, and justification of knowledge, along with its distinction from mere belief. Certainty has seemed the only safe standard in the face of withering skepticism, yet ignorance has infrequently been mentioned directly. It is truly remarkable how seldom the word *ignorance* occurs in the indexes of books on epistemology. Thus, ignorance has had no special interest; it was simply a negative, an absence. Formally, it has been just the denial of the proposition, "*S* knows that *p*." It has been assumed that, by theorizing knowledge, one would capture all that was relevant about its lack.

Within the last few years, however, the concept has generated notable scholarly interest: several monographs and anthologies on aspects of ignorance have appeared, emanating from many disciplines, including sociology, anthropology, psychology, economics, education, environmental studies, science studies, women's studies, and philosophy.[18] The term is appearing in titles of conference papers in the social sciences and humanities with increasing frequency. Although the conceptual frameworks vary widely in these studies, and differ in scope, purpose, and rigor, they are promising and pioneering studies that reflect the naturally wide-ranging and multidisciplinary nature of the subject. I have benefited from many of them in forming my own thoughts, and I will draw upon all of these approaches in this book.

Within this recent literature, the grandest proposal I have encountered is that ignorance should define an emerging field of systematic study: an incipient discipline to be baptized *agnotology*.[19] Some scholars, less sanguine about the prospect of a discipline, have called the topic of ignorance studies *agnoiology*.[20] One cannot legislate usage, of course, but if in what follows I do not adopt these terms, it is not because I reject the idea outright. Both are heuristically useful, and the notion of a special field is provocative, for we do need to accelerate the study of ignorance. Rather, it is because I prefer ultimately to support a stance that *integrates* ignorance and knowledge and explores their interactions.

My approach is broadly philosophical. In the pages that follow, I hope to engage you in an exploration of the intricacy and impact of what we do not know. To structure the discussion, I use four spatial images or metaphors: ignorance as place or state, as boundary, as limit, and as horizon. Though the treatment is comprehensive, including ethical and practical issues, it is neither exhaustive nor tightly systematic. Nor, unfortunately, does it provide a solution to our current culture of ignorance. While this study has implications for mainstream epistemology, it is not intended as a technical work of epistemology; but I will reserve for an epilogue a summary of those implications.

2 Conceiving Ignorance

The deprivation of anything whose possession is consistent with the nature of the Being which wants it, is a defect. But ignorance is the deprivation of something which is consistent with the nature of intelligence: it is a deprivation of knowledge. Therefore ignorance is an intellectual defect, imperfection, privation, or shortcoming.
—James Frederick Ferrier

The aim of this chapter is to sketch the contours of the concept of ignorance. The task is not simply a matter of consulting the dictionary and reviewing common usage; because it reveals contested and subtle issues, it requires doing philosophical work and taking positions on these issues. The analysis inevitably entails argument. At this early stage, precision is less important than evocativeness; elaboration and refinement will continue through the book. First, however, we must deal with the quirkiness of the concept.

Despite its ubiquity and importance, whenever we try to think seriously or talk insightfully about ignorance, especially about our own ignorance, we step into a muddle. We encounter two conceptual peculiarities that may lead to frustration, irony, or futility. Together, they suggest that any attempt to understand ignorance is impossible and to pursue the topic is folly.

The first arises from the negativity of the concept; the second concerns the implicit paradox in understanding our ignorance. Neither is as problematic as it first might seem, but the wise course is to confront both at the outset. As you might guess, I will conclude that neither concern should dissuade us.

Negative Concepts

Privatives, or negative concepts, are those that indicate an absence, deficiency, or loss of something. Our use of them is a tribute to our capacity for abstract thought, and they can be philosophically complex and deceptive. *Ignorance* is a privative: it is, at its core, a *lack* of knowledge or understanding (though I will argue it is not merely this). We will need, therefore, to examine an absence, a privation, a deficiency, a negative state or property. Talking about an absence seems to turn it into a presence, in the way that talking about nothing seems to transform it into a something: nothingness. At first glance, this is only linguistic sleight-of-hand, an illusion of syntax that results from treating all nouns equally. That trick, however, can ensnare the unwary in metaphysical tangles.

The traditional concern is a fallacy of reification: the error of taking what is merely a negation to be a real entity. In some contexts, that mistake is blatant to the point of silliness. For example, if I were to say, "I saw no one in the office," it would be ridiculous to ask whether "no one" was sitting or standing. If I tease a child by saying, "You may eat the donuts, but be sure to leave the holes," the reification is deliberate and funny, like the playful nonsense of Lewis Carroll. I too would be exploiting the fallacy to perplex or delight.

But this might take a more serious turn: my little joke might lead to musings about just what sort of thing a donut hole is, how this one differs from that one, and what it might mean for a hole to be gone. There are grounds for taking holes to be real, if nonmaterial, entities: we perceive them; we can locate, count, and measure them; we often create and use them; we can distinguish actual from possible holes—and yet they are a kind of negativity, an emptiness. What is ontologically proper, what holes really are, is difficult to discern.[1]

Moreover, there is a baffling array of such negativities, from those that have a physical locus to those that are quite abstract: we speak of the crack in the sidewalk, the holes in Swiss cheese, the vacuum in the pump, the shortage of family physicians, or a deficiency of vitamin D. Many of these negativities may be interpreted alternately as denoting a missing property or as the absence of a particular state of affairs: incongruence, for example, may be thought of as a negative property (the lack of congruence) or negative state (the absent state of being congruent). Negative concepts even appear to function causally, as when the cause of a diver's death is determined to be lack of oxygen, or the cause of crop failure is the dearth of rainfall, or the absence of a quorum forces cancelation of a meeting. These ascriptions and the common uses we make of them in reasoning need not be fallacious.

Furthermore, from a phenomenological perspective, we do sometimes experience an absence as a kind of presence, as when a loved one is gone and we are aware of a vacant chair, not merely of an extra chair; or when the sudden loss of a charismatic leader is felt as a gap and leaves followers in disarray. In such cases, what is present to us is not a generic absence, but a quite specific one. To use Jean-Paul Sartre's example: when he arrived late for his appointment with Pierre at the café, Sartre saw the absence of Pierre, not the absence of Wellington or Valéry.[2]

What sort of negativity does ignorance have? Basic analytic epistemology would say that "Sascha is ignorant of p" means that the proposition "Sascha knows that p" is false. In other words, ignorance is simply a logical negation. Ignorance occurs when the requisite for genuine knowledge is absent. This quickly directs attention toward the substantive question of what is required for knowledge claims to be true—which has been the dominant direction and debate in epistemology for centuries. (One might wonder: if we do not yet know what knowledge is, how can we presume to know what its lack is?)

This traditional view has both narrow and broad implications: it affirms that *ignorance* has no conceptual content beyond the negation of propositions about knowledge; yet on this account, even a bowling ball is ignorant, because the proposition "A bowling ball knows that p" is false. The innovative epistemologist Timothy Williamson interprets knowledge as *the mental state of knowing*. Either the state is present (one knows) or it is not (one doesn't know). One's claims to knowledge are true when one possesses the mental state of knowing.[3] So, what then is ignorance? For Williamson, ignorance is simply the absence of the state of knowing, and thus, again, sticks and stones and bowling balls are all ignorant, for they do not possess the state of knowing.[4]

My view is that calling a bowling ball ignorant, metaphorical possibilities aside, is *a category mistake*; that is, it ascribes to an object of a certain category something that is logically inappropriate for objects of that category. It is similar to calling an idea purple or a stone condescending. It is not merely by linguistic convention that we don't assert such pointless (though true) claims. More than conventions of language are involved: indeed, I think it is conceptually significant that *ignorance implies the capacity to learn.* It is thus a category mistake to apply the term to things that do not have such a capacity. Moreover, ignorance, *not-knowing*, may be manifested as a distinctive mental state, or more accurately, a cluster of related states.[5] This means that the concept has discernible content; it is more than a mere absence or negation; its negativity may be substantive. I agree with literary critic Shoshana Felman, who concludes: "Ignorance is thus no longer simply *opposed* to knowledge: it is itself a radical condition, an integral part of the very *structure* of knowledge."[6]

In short, the negativity possessed by the concept of ignorance is not emptiness. It does not render otiose the attempt to study ignorance. Yes, caution is required regarding the sort of reality we give negative concepts. But it is wrong to think that, if we understand knowledge and identify its necessary and sufficient conditions, we will automatically understand all there is to know about ignorance. Would we expect to understand everything about drought simply by understanding rainfall?

It is true that we bestow an intuitive primacy on positive concepts and affirmations; their correlative negative concepts and denials seem wholly parasitic on them. But not all conceptual polarities are fixed; many may be reversed, as with a figure–ground reversal. We can view silence as the absence of sound, or sound as the absence of silence, depending on context and on our desires and purposes. The same is true of ignorance and knowledge.

Paradox

The concept of ignorance carries a second, compounding peculiarity. I noted this paradox earlier: *How can I know that which I do not know? Must not any attempt to understand ignorance alter it, and any successful attempt, destroy it?* Ignorance seems necessarily to defy understanding. It is opaque, a blank label for the unknown; as a signifier, it merely points to what we do not understand. Won't ignorance vanish before our eyes as we learn about it?

There is, of course, an elementary confusion in play in this paradox: the confusion between understanding the *concept* of ignorance and understanding *that which we do not understand.* Coming to understand the former (alas!) does not vanquish the latter. But that clarification does not completely resolve the problem. In trying to understand ignorance, we hope for more than definitional clarity: we hope to understand the shape of what-we-do-not- know, its varieties, something of its qualities, and its impact on our lives.

The question is how much we can learn about what we do not know. We can progress by tactics such as distinguishing the particular from the general, invoking metalevels of discourse, and parsing different types of ignorance—essentially by identifying with greater precision the particular ignorance to which we refer. We can take into account the perspectives of different knowers and the relation of epistemic events in time. All these techniques will be used in the pages that follow, but for the moment, two specifications may be helpful.

First, *ignorance* refers not only to the *state of not-knowing*; it also designates *that which we do not know.* In that respect, *ignorance* has what philosophers call *intentionality*: it takes an object. To be ignorant is to be ignorant *of something.*[7] Objects of ignorance, like objects of knowledge, can vary enormously in scope. What one is ignorant *of* may range from a specific, fine-grained fact to whole fields of knowledge. This means that an individual may be knowledgeable and ignorant simultaneously—but in regard to different matters. Furthermore, *ignorance* may also be used sweepingly to refer to *all that we do not know*, as in the statement, "My ignorance is vast." In such usage, the implied object is comprehensive but unspecified or unspecifiable. Our apparent paradox exploits the ambiguity of these usages. *Coming to know X* vanquishes only *the ignorance of X*—and leaves all our other ignorance untouched.[8]

We can, therefore, gain knowledge about ignorance; we are not limited to clarifying definitions. Just as one can make precise claims about vagueness, so one can make cognitive claims about ignorance without self-contradiction ("Ignorance abounds," for example). We can, as I hope to show, learn many significant and specific things about our ignorance and the way it functions in relation to our knowledge.

Second, it is important to specify *whose* ignorance we have in mind, because the possibilities for affirming knowledge and ignorance shift with perspective. The constraints I encounter in trying to delineate my own ignorance are not the same as those I experience when discussing the ignorance of someone else (although clearly my own ignorance will always be in play). When *I* talk about *your* ignorance or *someone else's* (making second- or third-person ascriptions), I may know thoroughly that which you or they don't. But when the ignorance I discuss is mine (a first-person ascription), my epistemic constraints are tighter, and what I can affirm is correspondingly limited. Moreover, one may ascribe ignorance to individuals, groups, large-scale populations, or even the whole human race. This progression of enlarging scope introduces interesting notions of individual, shared, collective, and distributed ignorance. And when we sweepingly refer to universal human ignorance, we designate that which *no one* knows. If I include myself in any of these plural referents (I am necessarily included in "the whole human race"), I again feel the epistemic constraints of the first-person perspective.

Years ago, I heard the venerated Kant scholar, William Henry Werkmeister, deliver a paper with the cleverly punning title, "Der unbekannte Kant," or, as he translated it, "The Kant Nobody Knows." As he began, a wag in the audience immediately asked if "nobody" included the speaker. That backed "Werkie" (his affectionate nickname) into either admitting that even he did not know this Kant, or making the more likely, but slightly off-putting claim that this Kant was known to *nobody else* except Werkie himself. Or perhaps, that this Kant was known to *no one present* in the audience except him. But before he could make his painful choice, another wit in the audience asked whether "nobody" also included Immanuel Kant himself. Werkie had not even passed the announcement of his title, and surely the next question would be: "And how do *you know* that *nobody* knows this Kant?" Instead, he joined the laughter and quickly began to read. The gentle fun of that moment derives from play on the varying epistemic constraints of first-, second-, third-person, and universal ascriptions of ignorance. The interchange also displays the difference between claiming one's own knowledge or ignorance, and claiming to know that someone else has knowledge or ignorance.[9]

The point is fundamental: in the same general way in which questions arise from a perspective of ignorance, assertions or claims derive from a perspective of knowledge (or presumed knowledge). Therefore, all ascriptions of ignorance are necessarily made from a perspective of presumed knowledge: *it requires knowledge to identify ignorance.* All sincere cognitive claims (assertions that are true or false), even those made about ignorance, declare one's presumption to knowledge and operate with a norm of truth.[10] All attempts to understand ignorance will necessarily build from what is (thought to be) known. To assert that "ignorance abounds" is to assert that I know it to be so—or at least that I believe (I know) it to be so. This explains why, at some level, ignorance doesn't recognize itself: it does not have the cognitive wherewithal. I stress this basic point because, as we shall see (in part 2), it has troublesome implications.

Because we are capable of learning, claims about ignorance are also affected by temporal reference. One may make a wider range of claims about one's past ignorance based on current knowledge than one may make about one's current ignorance. "I thought he was trustworthy, but I did not know his treachery" is, sadly, a judgment that can only be made in hindsight.

This trio of specifications—*who* is ignorant of *what* and *when*—serves to structure epistemic space, opening up room for the understanding of ignorance. It also provides axes for the structure of ignorance.

To summarize: what we initially encounter as paradox does not derail a study of ignorance at the start. The study of ignorance is not disqualified by insinuations of conceptual vacuity or logical impossibility. We do have the realistic, tantalizing possibility of studying ignorance purposefully to gain substantive insights about our lack of knowledge. A caveat is that, however far we may journey toward an understanding of ignorance, when we go beyond the context of our knowledge—particularly when we speak of our own current ignorance or of what no one knows—our grasp will necessarily be oblique or indirect. Our most precious insights are, beyond that point, only intimations.

The Language of Ignorance

The etymology is straightforward: *ignorance* is descended ultimately from the Latin *ignorantia*, which has the same core meaning; it is a compound of *ig-* (not) and *gnarus* (knowing or known). Latin, however, gives us two different verbs: *ignoro*, which means *to be unaware of*; and *ignosco*, which means *to overlook, refuse to take cognizance of, disregard*, or even *to forgive*. Interestingly, English has not retained those distinct formulations.[11] In contemporary usage—and for centuries previous—the English verb, *to ignore*, has had the latter meaning, not the former. So for example, when I ignore an annoying pet or someone's bad manners, it does not imply that I am ignorant of them. On the contrary, one might even say that I must, on some level, know that the annoyance or the faults are manifest in order to ignore them. Oddly, however, we have in English no cognate transitive verb meaning *to be ignorant of.* The English noun and verb have long gone their separate semantic ways.[12]

I have accepted as an initial account the standard one: *ignorance* means *a lack of knowledge or understanding*, though I noted it is not a full or final account.[13] Earlier, I remarked that ignorance is neither stupidity nor irrationality, though they are understandably entangled in practice. Neither should ignorance be confused with error. *Error* is a negatively normative concept; it marks an action or a judgment or ascription as having failed in relation to some cognitive standard (accuracy, validity, truth, etc.) or performance standard (efficiency, effectiveness, elegance, etc.). One "makes" or "commits" an error, whether by omission or commission. Ignorance, by contrast, requires no action.[14] There is, nonetheless, a relationship: ignorance is a frequent cause of error—though there are plenty of others, such as overconfidence, carelessness, and interference. Moreover, we are always ignorant of our errors as we make them, assuming they are unintentional. ("Intentional errors" are, in a deeper sense, not really errors at all: they are deceptions.) And, for better or worse, we may well remain ignorant of our mistakes, once we have made them.[15]

Is ignorance similarly a normative concept? It is conceptually negative, but is it normatively negative as well? Is ignorance essentially bad? Common usage may suggest that it is. It is true that the flat ascription, "Max is ignorant," has harsh connotations to our ears; the judgment seems derisive and decisive about Max's capacity or character. Notice, however, that the harshness lessens as the object of the ascription becomes more narrowly particular. Consider this progression: "Max is ignorant"; "Max is ignorant of poetry"; "Max is ignorant of the poetry of Santayana"; and "Max is ignorant of Santayana's first draft of that poem." The last is certainly a weaker condemnation than the first—if it is a condemnation at all. Now consider another set of ascriptions: "Fred is ignorant of his wife's dalliance, of his mother's last will, of his son's password, of his daughter's whereabouts, of his neighbor's fantasy life, of his sister's true parentage, of his cousin's bank account, of his dog's fate." Poor Fred? Bad Fred? Well, perhaps, but we would need to hear more of the soap opera to know whether, in each case, we should judge Fred or his ignorance good or bad, and to what degree. These varying resonances hint at hidden presumptions regarding our expectations or even obligations to know certain things, and our sense of when not knowing is blameworthy, excusable, justifiable—or perhaps even preferable.

Ignorance does denote a lack, but it does not presume that lack is a bad thing. If it is a "negative concept," it is so only in a logical sense, not in a normative sense. That platitude of fecklessness, "Ignorance is bliss," may have its times and places. "Knowing too much" is a meaningful phrase. Nevertheless, as I acknowledged earlier, our default assumption is that ignorance is normatively negative. Our "epistemic presets" are these: gaining knowledge is a worthy achievement accomplished by vanquishing ignorance; knowledge has intrinsic worth; and ignorance is debilitating.

It would, however, beg important questions to build this default of negative normativity into the very definition of *ignorance* itself. I do not want to foreclose at the outset the possibility that particular types or instances of ignorance might be useful or epistemically valuable or morally good. Scrutinizing this presumption and sorting out these questions are parts of the task at hand, so we need to preserve a neutral, descriptive sense of the concept. Going forward, I will take the disvalue of not knowing to be a matter of normal contexts and implications, not of definition. We may find value in what we do not know and in the not-knowing of it, but claiming it will require accepting the burden of explanation and justification that falls on anyone who would advocate ignorance, anyone who would claim that it is ever preferable not to know.

Ways of Knowing and Not Knowing

Being ignorant of seems to be the opposite of *knowing*, but philosophers have distinguished three ways knowing: *knowing that*, *knowing how*, and *knowing by direct acquaintance*.[16] *Knowing that* refers to factual knowledge expressible in propositions ("*S* knows that *p*"), such as knowing that "today is Saturday," "the atomic number of beryllium is 4," or "John Stuart Mill's godson was Bertrand Russell." This form of knowing requires the retention and purposeful retrieval of systematically related vocabularies, concepts, propositions, facts, and conventions. It also limits the range of knowledge to facts that can be given propositional form. The opposite, *not knowing that*, is the conventional case of ignorance. This formulation requires that what one does not know (designated as *p*) is a specific fact that can be formulated as a proposition. But specification and propositional form are not possible for many kinds of ignorance: for example, one who is ignorant of trigonometry is not merely ignorant of a fact, or even of a set of facts. Propositional knowledge is but one form of knowledge; it is too restrictive to be exclusive.

Knowing how refers to skills, such as knowing how to jump rope or knowing how to play the pipe organ. This form of knowing requires abilities, techniques, and a competence in performance that is typically earned through practice. Is *not knowing how* a type of ignorance? The question is not easy, because the answer seems intuitively to turn on the sort of skill we have in mind. When an activity has a relatively low cognitive component, we are less likely to say that not knowing it constitutes ignorance. For instance, we are not apt to think of a person who is unable to jump rope or whistle as ignorant of rope-jumping or whistling; she is simply *unskilled*. Knowing how to play a pipe organ, however, is more complex. It requires difficult subsidiary skills (such as knowing how to move one's feet deftly to play the pedalboard) as well as esoteric propositional knowledge (such as the meaning of *diapason* and the difference between the Choir, Swell, Great, and Solo manuals). In such cases, *not knowing how* does seem to entail ignorance. In short, it appears that we apply the term *ignorance* to *not knowing how* when referring to a complex skill in which are entailed significant cognitive, *knowing that*, elements. In such cases, one is both *unskilled* and *ignorant of* certain relevant knowledge. Gaining propositional knowledge alone will not, of course, make one skilled.

I should acknowledge, however, that some philosophers believe that *knowing how* is fully reducible or translatable into *knowing that*. If this reduction were successful, it would mean that skills are merely matters of knowing certain facts, which admittedly may be complex and involve sensitivity to context and minute actions. To be preemptive: I do not believe that project can succeed.[17] A more plausible suggestion, however, is that jumping rope, whistling, organ-playing, and perhaps any other skill, always involve *tacit* knowledge, things the competent rope-jumper or whistler or organist must know but cannot verbalize. What exactly is tacit knowledge? One might interpret it as a type of *knowing that* in which one is unable to formulate the relevant proposition, or perhaps even recognize it. Or, tacit knowledge might be interpreted as the cognitive infrastructure of a *knowing how* that cannot in principle be reduced to propositional knowledge—such as our know-how in recognizing familiar faces. Under either interpretation (I will say more on tacit knowledge later), not possessing relevant tacit knowledge would constitute a genuine case of ignorance—even for activities seemingly low in cognitive content.

The third form of knowing refers to unmediated experience, as in "knowing the taste of pineapple" or "knowing Mr. Zorian"; such knowledge requires the experience and memory of immediate contact or direct sensation. One may *know of* Mr. Zorian and one may *know* a lot of facts *about* him, but that is not the same as *knowing* him. Similarly, you may know many facts about pineapples, and you may even have laid eyes and hands on dozens of them, even read about their taste, but if you have never tasted one, you do not (in this sense) "know the taste of pineapple."[18] Would we say you are *ignorant* of that taste? Our senses provide knowledge by acquaintance, but would we call a blind person ignorant of color? Perhaps, but our reluctance may be more about the harshness of the word and its entangled association with stupidity.

Though it is difficult to generalize about knowledge by acquaintance, the label we apply may depend on the nature and context of the missing experience. The ascription of *not knowing by direct acquaintance* is sometimes interpreted as *not knowing what something is like* or as not knowing *qualia*;[19] it shades into *never having experienced* and thence into *being innocent of*, which (as we shall see in chapter 4) are states related to but not identical with ignorance.

Understanding is a term we often use when the first and third forms of knowing are combined, coupled with epistemic justification, and placed in a broader, coherent, cognitive context. "Understanding Heidegger's thought," for example, involves many elements of *knowing that* and of *knowing by direct acquaintance* various texts; but it requires still more. Moreover, I may know Heidegger and many things about him, but still not understand him. To understand something implies the possession of an insight epistemically deeper than merely "having knowledge of" that thing, but it does also entail such knowledge.[20] If I am ignorant of X, I don't understand X; and if I understand X, I am not ignorant of it. But although *not understanding* might be a matter of ignorance, it also might result from a lack of imagination or empathy, or from a dearth of experience. If I complain that

I do not understand how people in some cultures can eat dogs, my problem may not be a lack of knowledge; one cannot be sure that more knowledge would make me understand.

There are other terms for qualities or states for which knowledge is a necessary component. *Wisdom*, for example, seems to presuppose relevant knowledge; achieving wisdom would be thwarted by ignorance. *Expertise* requires specialized knowledge and often great skill. Again, there can be no true expert in *X* who is ignorant in regard to *X*. Being a *cultured* person has a similar cognitive dynamic, requiring pertinent knowledge and social skills. The Greeks had a term, *amousos* (literally, "without the Muses"), which meant "uncultured," specifically "unmusical," "graceless," "boorish," and "ignorant." Appreciating music (in the broad Greek sense of the arts and humanities) was thought to be essential in forming a noble soul. It suggests an interesting conception of ignorance as *not being cultured*, lacking certain knowledge and precious skills and the understanding and character these would bring.[21] The concept suggests that ignorance as much as knowledge shapes or reflects one's character.

All these forms of *not knowing* and *not understanding* may be removed or annihilated by *learning*, though different modes of learning may be necessary. The range of learning is as wide as the range of remediable ignorance. When we learn the meaning of the Italian word *falegname*, we replace our ignorance with knowledge (or at least the information) that the word means "carpenter." When Bill learned to jump rope, however, it is dubious that he was remediating his ignorance. Consider also this case: when she moved into a new house, Jenny formed the habit of placing her keys on a hook she found inside the door. She did indeed learn something—a new behavior pattern—but her learning did not replace anything one would normally identify as ignorance. We would not say that Jenny had been ignorant of this convenient habit beforehand. What we normally take to be required for ignorance is a cognitive deficiency, a lack of knowledge or understanding, and this was not Jenny's previous situation. So, if ignorance is not the lack of a skill or of a particular experience, neither is it the lack of specific behavior patterns or habits—though we may indeed learn all these things.

I have been painting this conceptual picture rapidly and with a broad brush, so let me offer a summary. We distinguish at least three ways of *not knowing*: being *ignorant of*, being *unskilled in*, and being *unacquainted with* (or *not knowing what it is like*). *Ignorance* does not indicate lack of ability, skill, experience, or specific behavior *simpliciter*; nor is it a matter of error. Rather, *ignorance* refers centrally to a *lack of knowledge* (even when knowledge is bound up with skills), which can also result in a lack of *understanding*. It may be removed, when possible and practical, only by *learning*, by *coming to know or understand*.

This does not mean that all ignorance is removable or remediable. There are limits to knowledge, both practical and theoretical. On the practical level, learning may be incidental or intentional; when intentional, the effort required varies from easy and instantaneous to difficult and lifelong, fading into the practically impossible, with significant individual and group differences in the placement of those limits. Beyond that, there are theoretical limits to knowledge as well. In part 4, we will discuss these limits, but for now it is enough to mark the point that ignorance in general or of a specific matter, may not always, even in theory, be eliminable.

Metaphors of Ignorance

Many of our images of ignorance devolve from naturally privileging the sense of sight as the source of knowledge and light as its medium; most are normatively negative. The ignorant are "in the dark," "blind," "benighted," and "unenlightened." The images are drawn from situations in which knowledge and its benefits escape us: we are "in a fog" and "clueless."

The descriptor *oblivious* is interesting. Its contemporary meaning is "unaware or unmindful of something" or "ignorant of something that is relevant to one's situation." This was once considered erroneous usage. The original meaning is "forgetful" or "producing forgetfulness," derived from the Latin *oblivion* ("forgetfulness"). The Latin term is itself metaphorical, though what metaphor is involved is controversial: *Webster's Third International Dictionary* says its root components (*ob* + *levis*) literally meant "to smooth over"; the *Oxford English Dictionary* (*OED*) states that it is ultimately derived from a root (*lividus*) that meant "livid," a dark or purplish black. In either case, if we once knew something but have forgotten it, it has been smoothed over or gone dark, and we no longer know it. We are, consequently, ignorant of everything we have forgotten.

But this raises a provocative question: do things we have forgotten and things we have never learned have the same epistemic status? They both are things I do not know, yet they seem cognitively different: relearning is different from learning for the first time. Plus, there is the lurking potential that something we have forgotten might one day be remembered. Plato famously taught that all learning is remembering, and he constructed an elaborate myth to explain why all of us had forgotten everything we knew before birth.[22] For him, to be ignorant is simply *not to remember*, to have forgotten. The poetic beauty of this doctrine aside, it is useful to distinguish the "once known" from the "not yet known" in exploring forms of ignorance.

I think of this book as an extended, exploratory essay. As I announced earlier, I have chosen to organize it around four images of ignorance, four spatial metaphors (parts 2–5). Spatial language is commonplace in discourse about knowledge: we speak of "domains" or "fields" of knowledge, "areas" of research or specialization, disciplinary "boundaries," and so on. My four guiding images are: ignorance as *place, boundary, limit,* and *horizon.* They embody clusters of ideas that reflect the ways in which we experience ignorance; revealing the architecture of ignorance, they point to different aspects of the human condition.

II   Ignorance as Place

O people, how come I see you dwelling in ignorance as an abode?
—Abū al-Qāsim al-Shābbī

3 Dwelling in Ignorance

Now I believe I can hear the philosophers protesting that it can only be misery to live in folly, illusion, deception and ignorance, but it isn't—it's human.
—Desiderius Erasmus

We are all well acquainted with ignorance: it is our native state. We begin our lives in ignorance and in need. Human beings are, to a dramatic extent when compared with other creatures, born in an "unfinished" condition, incapable even of survival without a long period of nurturance under the protective guidance of elders. As Rousseau declared, "We are born weak, we need strength; we are born entirely destitute, we need help; we are born stupid, we need understanding. All that we lack at birth and need in maturity is given us by education."[1] Fortunately, we are also uncommonly keen learners. Through the processes of human development, socialization, and education, we rapidly discover and construct the world in which we live and move and have our being. The imperative to learn is primal: not only to thrive, but simply to survive, we must escape the profound ignorance that shrouds us at our birth. No wonder we fear ignorance.

But fear is not the only possible reaction. Ignorance is our first place, and we may recall it with nostalgia. Knowledge carries costs, and we are forever changed by our knowing. When, with curiosity or compassion, we reflect on what it would be like to dwell in ignorance or in some similar state, our thoughts may lead in different directions. Indeed, our imaginings may diverge sharply: our "places of ignorance" may be as far apart as hell and heaven.

Ignorance as Hell or Heaven

The state of ignorance may be envisaged as a dark and terrible place. Ignorance is a swamp that harbors superstition, confusion, and fear, that breeds error and prejudice. It is the horror we must escape to survive. Only adult care and interaction, reason, and a proper education can dispel this miasma, illumine our path, pull us from this quagmire to the *terra firma* of knowledge and understanding, and equip us to find the bedrock of truth. In the Enlightenment, this heroic view gave rise to the "new learning" of science and to social reforms that established ever more inclusive and extensive schooling. Just as learning liberates us from our individual ignorance, so do universal education and scientific progress free us from our collective ignorance.

In such accounts, ignorance is never merely a neutral place, a mere locus; it is a plight, a predicament, a trap. These are charged images, and their suspenseful negativity invokes a positive possibility: an escape to a better place.

The contrasting vision is bright and shining. Ignorance can be imagined rosily as a place of sweet innocence, as a condition or time before we were sullied by knowing things that have left us worldly and jaded. In such a place, there are no worried, fearful brows; no hollowed and wearied souls drained by the burdens and toxins of knowledge. Rather, there is purity, freshness, goodness. It is a precious place—a golden valley, a magical garden, a paradise. It is also unavoidably a delicate and endangered place, which forewarns of a tragedy, a fateful fall, a despoiling of innocence. Idle curiosity and the restless, ruthless pursuit of knowledge are seductively corrupting. We must protect such unknowing innocence, for knowledge is indelible. Be forewarned: as Glen MacDonough lyricized Toyland, "Once you pass its borders, you can ne'er return again."[2] You would be left only with a sense of loss and remorse, a searing nostalgia, and a chastened and wistful exile. Better to dwell secure in ignorance and protect the thrall of innocence.

These contrasting, dramatized visions of ignorance are mythically profound. Do they really represent two different places? How exactly do they differ, or might they be the same place? What is it like to dwell in ignorance—not just to look back on it, yearn for it, or recoil from it—but to *dwell within* it? How and why would one depart from such a place? To explore these places of predicament and paradise, I turn inevitably to reconsider two of the oldest and most familiar places of ignorance in the Western heritage: Plato's Cave and the Garden of Eden. The spelunking will occupy this chapter; in the next, we'll cultivate the garden.

In Plato's Cave

The most memorable image of ignorance occurs in what is probably the most famous passage of all philosophy: Plato's Allegory of the Cave in the *Republic*.[3] Recall the scenario: human beings dwelling in the darkness of an underground cavern, bound at the legs and neck so that they cannot move, even to turn their heads. They have no other memory of life, since they have been imprisoned in this way since childhood. Before them, they see only moving shadows that are cast by objects unknown to them, illumined by a flickering fire that we are told lies somewhere behind them. They know nothing of this except the shadows and hear only echoes from the voices of their keepers, whom they have never seen. In such a benighted state, they pass their days.

This place of ignorance is not only a dark cave; it is a prison, a deprivation chamber. As we imagine this predicament, what we are likely to feel acutely is an epistemic claustrophobia, the absence of freedom in any meaningful sense, and the numbness and despair that would set in from such a deprived routine. Freedom is primordially the ability to move our body. Beyond being our basic capacity for meeting our needs, bodily movement, including change of place, leads us to new experiences, permits learning, and generates perspective. But confined in such profound ignorance, the world of experience is severely restricted. Plato regards such a plight as worse than imprisonment, worse than servitude, more like death: he says, quoting the *Odyssey*, "Better to be the humble servant of a poor master and to endure anything, than to live and believe as they do"—and the Homeric reference here is to the dead who dwell in Hades.[4] As Plato expects, we feel deep sadness at the absence of any chance to understand anything, to achieve anything of value, or to experience anything of beauty. *The horror of ignorance is incapacity.*[5]

This account of their predicament is not, of course, one that the prisoners themselves would—or could—offer. They do not and cannot understand their situation, since all of life's experiences are but shifting shadows and echoes. Plato says that the "prisoners would in every way believe that the truth is nothing other than the shadows." Indeed they would not suspect that the things they see are but shadows, nor even have the concept of a shadow. They pass the time in trivial games of shadow-prediction, unaware of their keepers, the fire, or the parade of objects behind them. Though they are troglodytes *in extremis*, they do not feel claustrophobic or deprived. The actual circumstances of their confinement in the dark cavern, the possibility of a way up and out, and indeed the notion that there may be an incandescent world of wonders to ascend to, are unknown and unsuspected. Life is what it is, what it has always been; they do what they do and feel what they feel because they know nothing else. They are ignorant. But *we* know ... and it is terrifying. Because Plato has, through his narrative, given us privileged knowledge of their situation, we know what they do not; we can affirm their ignorance.

The Cave is a fiction, of course. With a shudder, we gratefully distance ourselves and our lives from that bizarre place and its "strange prisoners." We breathe deeply the air of the sunlit world. But then, almost off-handedly, comes Plato's stark and chilling statement: "They're like us."

Recognizing Ignorance

Are we like these cave dwellers? Is this gloomy cave the image of the womb from which we were all thrust unknowing into the light? But do we not then quickly overcome this primal oblivion—or do we all still dwell in a place of such abysmal ignorance? To think this through, I want to reverse Plato's approach: rather than describing how we may know the truth, let us consider *how we recognize ignorance*.

Obviously, no one is born educated; and every educated person is, at any given moment, ignorant about many things. Often, it is easy to pinpoint our ignorance quite precisely. Though you may have acquired considerable knowledge about a subject, say, automobiles, you may not know a particular arcane fact—for example, the number of carburetors that were standard in a 1955 Singer roadster. You simply lack a piece of information. In this common form of factual ignorance, should the question arise, you are able to specify exactly the datum you lack. Based on what you already know, you comprehend fully what you need to learn, even before you learn it—you know what to "look up" or to search for. And you even already know the sort of fact that will constitute the answer—"one" or "two," for example, and not "one hundred" and certainly not "red" or "mammalian" carburetors.

Suppose, however, that you had never heard of the Singer automobile. Despite your familiarity with antique automobile manufacturers and models, you might be surprised to learn of a make or model that had escaped your notice. Or, imagine that you, somewhat less expert, only knew the names of a few sports car manufacturers. In either case, you would have some sense of what acquiring such new knowledge would be like; you could specify its parameters beforehand. You would grasp in a general way what learning about an unfamiliar auto maker would entail; and given that possibility, you could identify what it is you do not know—albeit with less precision than in the first case. Such factual ignorance can be delineated in this way because you possess other general, relevant knowledge (in this case, knowledge about cars, their manufacturers, the meaning of "roadster," and so on). In these ordinary situations, it is the knowledge we possess that serves to awaken and focus our sense of our own ignorance.

Our world is vast, however. There are whole realms of knowledge of which each of us is ignorant, though the list, if we could make one, is different for each person. You may be unusually well educated, perhaps possessing expertise in several fields, and yet, when it comes to, say, ichthyology or Chinese porcelain or deltiology or Sanskrit grammar, you are lost. In such cases, our sense of what we don't know isn't as sharp; we are less sure that we understand what it would mean to know such things. Nevertheless, if we know the meaning of the relevant terms, if we are familiar with parallel or related subjects, we may have some sense of what such missing knowledge would involve. (If you know English, Latin, and Greek grammar, for instance, you will have a clearer idea of what it would mean to learn Sanskrit grammar than if you had never studied any grammar.) Of course, you might really have no desire to learn about such facts or fields; indeed, you might ignore them, avoid them, or even resist attempts to be informed or taught about them. Or, you might decide to master them or to learn more about them. In these cases also, we can identify what we have not learned, at least to some level of specification.

So, let us pause to amend a fundamental point made earlier: *ignorance may be recognized and ascribed only from the perspective of knowledge, and the knowledge we possess determines the degree of specificity of the ignorance we recognize and serves to characterize the ignorance and its importance.* This is why we readers of Plato can recognize that cavern as a place of profound ignorance, lacking in truth and sustained by deception.

Utter ignorance, however, for which the dictionary offers the term *ignoration*, is yet more profound: the prisoners in Plato's Cave do *not* know *what* they do not know; they do not even know *that* they do not know. They dwell in ignorance, but cannot recognize it. Ignoration is thus a predicament, a trap—one that is not comprehended by those who are caught in it and dwell there. In a sense, they are not in a place at all: theirs is rather a placelessness in which one doesn't even know one is lost.

Fortunately, this trap, like a Chinese finger puzzle, has a simple solution: learning. And yet, it is remarkable that an escape occurs—how does one come to learn what one does not know one does not know? After all, the prisoners have no ability to free themselves; more to the point, they have no motivation to escape, since even that desire would presuppose a sense of possibility they lack. Their bondage seems natural to them; it is their form of life; nothing better calls to them. They cannot see their ignorance *as* ignorance. As the influential Muslim philosopher Al-Ghazzali put it: "Heedlessness is an illness which the afflicted person cannot cure himself."[6]

In Plato's account, the unenlightened must rely on accident or the beneficent intervention of others for the critical first step: a prisoner is released from his bonds by happenstance (*phusei*)[7] or by an implied other—"one of them was freed." What follows his release is not a swift and purposeful escape motivated by eager anticipation of the waiting outside world; it is only the slow, hesitant, gradual, painful process of learning itself. The newly released prisoner is hardly keen for enlightenment: he is "compelled to stand up, to turn his head," and he is "pained and dazzled and unable to see the things whose shadows he'd seen before." He is stupefied and wants to return to life as he knew it. Plato asks, "And if someone dragged him away from there by force, up the rough, steep path, and didn't let him go until he had dragged him into the sunlight, wouldn't he be pained and irritated at being treated that way?" Who the "someone" is doesn't matter at this point (except that it cannot be another prisoner), but it is clear that this is an educational intervention: it is necessary for finding the truth, it is initiated from without, and it is initially coercive, requiring the forceful overcoming of the learner's resistance. "He'd need time to get adjusted before he could see things in the world above," Plato acknowledges. But eventually, as understanding flows into him, "he'd count himself happy for the change and pity the others." He finally comes to know the sunlit world of wonders; and then he understands, with horror, what his condition was in the Cave. And, as we have heard, he would rather undergo anything than return to that place of ignorance.

Plato thus legitimates the claim of educational paternalism, the infamous, age-old dictum that parents say to their children and teachers repeat to their students regarding all sorts of coerced activities: "You will thank me for it one day, because then you will understand." His justification rests on the distinctions between knowledge, mere belief, and ignorance, and on the transformation of the soul that learning can produce. Regardless of the likelihood of later gratitude, however, if accident or intervention or coercion is required to start one on the path of learning, then the escape from utter ignorance is not self-motivated.[8] And that does not seem surprising. Would it be reasonable to pursue a goal that one does not possess and cannot envision? A self-initiated escape would not be a reasonable decision or even a live option.

But that explains only why the prisoner would not seek to escape. What explains his resistance to freedom and the need for coercion? One factor is that, in general, human beings tend to prefer cognitive comfort, the reinforcement of the familiar, to an encounter with the unknown. Learning may disrupt our cognitive comfort; it *dis*places us. Education requires us to revise or abandon our routines, recipes, and rituals—life as we know it—and to do so we must overcome a kind of natural cognitive inertia. A place of ignorance can be a sturdy nest of cognitive comfort for those who dwell within.

Plato's benighted Cave dwellers believe they already know the important truths.[9] *We* know, of course, that their "knowledge" is not worthy of the name; it is no more than pointless familiarity with contrived images. And when forced to widen their experience and confront their illusory situation, they are nonplussed, irritated, and even pained. We understand. It is painful for any of us to accept the revelation that our precious "knowledge" is false, that we have been deluded, and to confront the radical implications: assumptions discarded, insights misguided, principles betrayed, relationships undone, lives altered, and worlds shattered. False knowledge can be sticky; it is difficult to remove it and all it implies from our worldview— even when we acknowledge its falsity. Belief can be a bulwark against learning. The ignorance that hides in false knowledge is disguised as the very learning it defies.

These considerations may cause us to question whether Plato's Cave is, after all, a place of *utter* ignorance. It may indeed be home to deep ignorance, but the prisoners have beliefs about the shadows, make cognitive claims, and seem confident that what they believe is true—however deluded they may be. Actually, some of their beliefs are confirmed by their experience— some prisoners are adept at identifying shadows and remembering the sequences of their appearance.[10] Perhaps it is impossible to describe a human situation of complete and total ignorance, ignoration so abysmal that no thin shaft of understanding penetrates it. One wonders how beings in such a situation could survive without any knowledge, without a single belief that is true. And one wonders what a mental state of ignoration would be: a *tabula rasa*—the hypothetical blank slate of the mind before it receives outside impressions? Consciousness without memory? Awareness without conceptualization? Prenatal mind? Analytic epistemology would interpret utter ignorance in this way: "S is completely ignorant if and only if there is no p such that S knows that p." There is nothing S knows, including the fact that S knows nothing. Some would claim that bowling balls are *utterly* ignorant, but if any human being fits this description, it surely would be an odd case.[11]

To ascribe ignorance as a mental state is to imply a capacity for learning, which in turn implies a capacity for knowing. A potential for knowledge is embedded in ignorance. Moreover, the ascription of ignorance is relational; it is made from the vantage point of someone's knowledge about the lack of knowledge in an otherwise knowing creature. Ignorance and knowledge are concepts that cannot stand alone: they presuppose each other. It seems as convoluted to describe absolute and complete ignorance as is to describe absolute and complete knowledge. Ignoration and omniscience are comprehendible only as limiting concepts.[12]

We will revisit the issues of resistance to learning and preference for ignorance later on, but at the moment I need to return to the still unanswered question: *are* we like Plato's Cave dwellers—not just in infancy, but throughout our adult lives? It seems we are, at least in one important way: I refer to the unsettling fact that we too are haunted by things we do not know we do not know; and we cannot imagine how drastically those unknowns would alter our lives and our view of the world.

A Basic Typology from Rumsfeld to Žižek

One clear-cut typology of ignorance has become a meme in popular culture: the famous parsing by Donald Rumsfeld. Secretary of Defense during the presidency of George W. Bush, Rumsfeld enjoyed acerbic interactions with reporters who frequently pressed him to reveal information. But at one news conference, in a typically barbed response, he gave a pithy and now widely quoted mini-lecture: "There are known knowns; there are things we know we know. We also know there are known unknowns; that is to say, we know there are some things we do not know. But there are also unknown unknowns—the ones we don't know we don't know."[13]

To identify something as a known unknown, I must be able to specify with accuracy the object of my ignorance (as in my earlier automobile examples). But it is the contents of that third category, the "unknown unknowns," that bedevil all our plans—which was Rumsfeld's point. They seem to make ignorance the place we cannot escape. *That* there are such truths seems obvious, though *what* those truths are we cannot say—we cannot, by definition, even offer a single example. Rumsfeld's assertion that there are things "we don't know we don't know" is true but *noninstantiable*: it is logically impossible to specify an instance (except in referring to oneself retrospectively, by which point it is known); any attempt to do so results in a self-contradiction.[14]

Nevertheless, our confidence that there are unknown unknowns is well grounded. Hindsight regarding our own life histories convinces us about our personal cluelessness: our lives are full of surprises, serendipities, shocks, discoveries, and comeuppances. And we know enough of the history of the human race to be convinced of the point regarding our collective knowledge, as well: think how each epoch brings events and inventions that were not only unknown, but could not have been imagined, in earlier periods. We can generalize about our unknown unknowns; but merely to observe that they likely include facts, concepts, relationships, and so on provides no cognitive advance because we cannot cite an instance. Whether "we" refers to ourselves, someone else, a group existing at a given time, or all humanity, "we" are always and by necessity ignorant of the full content and the extent of our own ignorance. And in that respect, we are indeed like Plato's Cave dwellers.

A reader of Plato's Allegory might protest that surely we are quite different from the prisoners in that our knowledge is much greater. Granted; however we might go about comparing our knowledge with theirs (and tricky as this may prove to be), it seems obvious that our knowledge is much greater—richer in concepts, more comprehensive in scope, deeper in its network of epistemic explanations, wider in the range of activities and technology it supports, and so on. Conspicuously, we know important facts about their situation that they do not. But it is the entirety of our ignorance that we cannot compare, because *we have no valid method of assessing the extent of our ignorance*; there is no way to take the measure of what we do not know we do not know.

The Rumsfeldian parsing introduces a second-order level of discourse or *metacognitive* perspective. This distinction was well known years before Rumsfeld, of course, and most scholars recognize that there are actually four categories, not just three:

(1) *known knowns*: what I know I know;
(2) *known unknowns*: what I know I don't know;
(3) *unknown unknowns*: what I don't know I don't know; and
(4) *unknown knowns*: what I don't know I know.

These four categories were summarized in a paper by philosopher Ann Kerwin nearly a decade before Rumsfeld's quote.[15] She labels the four types as follows: (1) *Known knowns* are "explicit knowledge." (2) *Known unknowns* comprise our "conscious ignorance." (3) *Unknown unknowns* she calls "meta-ignorance." (4) *Unknown knowns* are forms of "tacit knowledge."

One can group these four possibilities in several ways. While the first is the category of certified knowledge in the fullest sense, the other three involve ignorance (*not knowing*) in various ways. Together, the first two categories mark epistemic self-awareness, while the last two mark obliviousness. The first and fourth categories refer to knowledge that is, in some way, possessed. The second and the third involve substantive ignorance. Incorporating metalevel states not only introduces valuable conceptual distinctions, it also defines and differentiates epistemic mental states. It does not, however, explicate the meaning of "known" or "unknown"; indeed, it doubles the problem—or perhaps triples it, if one includes their relationships.

The fourth category—the category omitted by Rumsfeld[16]—seems odd and perhaps self-contradictory, since it requires that I don't know something that in fact I know. What could it mean to say that I know something, but not know I know it?

This missing fourth category was also noted by Slavoj Žižek, who interpreted it as that which we willfully refuse to acknowledge that we know ("the Freudian unconscious, 'the knowledge which doesn't know itself'"), and who therefore found Rumsfeld's omission psychologically significant.[17] Žižek's analysis suggests that the sense of "knowing" is different on the two levels. One might know something unconsciously or dimly, but have forgotten it or buried it in a willful denial. (Willful ignorance is a focal topic of chapter 6.) Others, however, who deny any degree of elasticity to the conditions for knowledge, may think that one cannot really know something without knowing that one knows it—and therefore rule out the fourth category as an impossible null set. Perhaps Rumsfeld is among them.

I agree that because these terms function differently on the two levels of cognition, there is no direct contradiction. But I prefer Kerwin's interpretation of the fourth category as tacit knowledge. Tacit knowledge and willful ignorance are quite distinct. Ignorance that is willful involves ignoring, the suppression or denial of what one knows, or the refusal to learn. Tacit knowledge is knowledge one may possess and apply successfully without being able to articulate it or even recognize its correct formulation. Contrasted with explicit knowledge, such tacit knowledge is, as I noted earlier, usually identified as a component of skills in which we seem to "know more than we can tell." Famous examples of tacit knowledge are the principles by which we ride a bicycle or recognize faces. Michael Polanyi introduced the term in 1958, noting that when we ride a bike, we must continually adjust our movements to meet a complex formula that keeps us balanced—a formula that is "followed" but not known to, or even recognized by, successful cyclists.[18] The criteria we use for facial recognition are amazingly complex—as the gradual development of facial recognition software has shown—and yet we are quite expert in applying them. But even when what is known tacitly can be carefully distilled into propositional form—as Polanyi did with the principle of bicycling—it is unlikely that the result will be useful in learning the skill.

The Vagaries of Knowing and Not Knowing

The confusing possibilities of *unknown knowns* suggest a salient point: different explications of what is entailed in knowing something generate hierarchies of stringency. Modern epistemologists, pressed to distinguish genuine knowledge from mere belief, have tended to adopt the most stringent standards. When the standard for possessing sufficient justification for one's belief is set very high, it assures the impossibility of being wrong. In short, it seems that *certainty* is necessary for genuine knowledge.

One assumption of this sort of analysis is that knowing does not admit of degrees or alternate forms. One either possesses it, or one does not. But when we think of knowing as a mental state, that duality is Procrustean. Believing is more psychologically complex than an on-or-off condition: believe it or not. Justification can be strong or weak. Awareness is a spectrum. What does my *knowing X* require of me?

I will take up these issues in the epilogue as part of a claim for revisions in epistemology. The relevant point here, however, is that they imply different meanings of *not knowing*. To be *ignorant of X*, depending on context, may be interpreted as being *unaware of X*, being *unable to articulate X or recognize its articulation*, being *unable to recall X* when given an appropriate prompt, or even being *unable to justify the claims involved in X*. It seems that if multiple factors are necessary for genuine knowledge, the absence of any one or any particular combination of them describes a form of *not-knowing*, of a failure of knowledge. Thus *the formal structure of ignorance becomes multiplex and more complex than that of knowledge*.

What about *false knowledge*—is it covered in this four-fold typology? On the one hand, it is a variety of unknown unknowns because, when I have false knowledge, I don't know that I don't know. I am deluded and unaware, as were Plato's prisoners: they lacked true knowledge and also had false beliefs: that their cavern was the only place, that shadows were "real" objects, and so on. On the other hand, simply having false information (say, having an incorrect phone number) also seems quite different from having unknown unknowns (say, Aristotle's not-knowing that he didn't know about DNA). The difference is that in false knowledge, I have a first-order belief that I (mistakenly) take to be true; I *believe* that I know X, but in fact I don't. Should I apply that mistaken belief in learning or acting or judging, I would likely commit an error. (I believe I know the phone number, and I realize my error when I place the call.) But I can have no beliefs about broader unknown unknowns that would yield mistakes. (Aristotle had no false beliefs related to DNA because he could have no beliefs at all about DNA—and therefore could not have made an error derived from such a belief.) Even the holding of a false belief implies a level of knowledge sufficient for a possible correction.

Because the presence of such a belief is a crucial factor in the explication of the concept of false knowledge and its quality as a mental state, we will do well to treat it as a separate and distinct type of unknown unknowns; it not only entails meta-ignorance, it involves cognitive error.

Introspection and Agnosognosia

Self-knowledge is precious. Self-ignorance can be horrific and may threaten our very selfhood. It has often seemed that self-knowledge is special, privileged, and unmediated. Yet we know that delusions, self-deceptions, and deep repressions are possible; memory can be faulty or false; self-perception is distorted. Nonetheless, we likely believe that we know ourselves better than anyone else knows us, in part because of our unique access to our own mental life. Humans have *introspection*, the ability to monitor or inspect our own mental states and motives directly. But the reliability of introspection has been severely challenged by recent psychological research, and some philosophers have even denied its very existence.[19] Self-insight, it seems, is subject to the same sorts of false knowledge and ignorance as knowledge of others and the world. Thus, all four categories may apply to self-insight, including unknown unknowns.

There are strikingly extreme versions of self-ignorance. *Agnosognosia* (also spelled *anosognosia*) is a pathological defect of self-awareness, a condition in which a person is unaware of an obvious personal disability, debilitation, or injury. Even a patient who is paralyzed may not realize or acknowledge her paralysis; an amputee may not be aware that he has lost a limb. Of course, anyone might, at least temporarily, be unaware of a hidden health problem, but the unknown unknowns in cases of agnosognosia (at least before diagnosis) comprise extreme self-ignorance, since what is denied or ignored is so obvious and indubitable to others. *Amnesia*, the sudden loss of memory, may result from several causes and manifest several forms; but severe cases involve the loss of identity. Amnesia, however, is a matter of known unknowns, since the patient typically is aware of and anxious about the loss.

Plato's troglodytes, among their cognitive privations, certainly lack self-knowledge. They are unaware they are prisoners, oblivious to being manipulated by others, deluded by illusions about the world, and ignorant of their own capacities and possibilities. Where the unknown unknowns are so life-pervasive, and where false knowledge is deeply embedded, a threshold of self-ignorance is crossed, and *dis*illusionment becomes impossible without assistance.

Skepticism

There are those, of course, who doubt that genuine knowledge is a human possibility, who doubt we can find any cognitive touchstone or point of epistemic leverage from which we can truly come to know anything at all. They doubt that anyone has ever escaped the Cave and that such liberation is possible. If we really have no knowledge *and can acquire none*, then our ignorance is irremediable. It is more than a predicament; it is our doom.

The skeptical claim is that even if a belief of ours happens to meet all other conditions of knowledge, we could never really *know that we know it*—and genuine knowing must meet that condition as well. These second-order doubters would back us into the trap of utter ignorance. What could one do in the face of such smothering ignoration? How could one live?

The ancient Skeptics took this position, believing humans incapable of grasping truth or of distinguishing it from falsehood, and claiming that the universe is everywhere incomprehensible to us, a condition named *acatalepsia*. They advocated *epoché*, "a suspension of judgment"—all judgment. How, we might wonder, could one live without judging? Pyrrho of Elis, one of the patriarchs of Skepticism, lived precisely that way, according to Diogenes Laertius: "[Pyrrho] was consistent with this view [Skepticism] in his manner of living, neither avoiding anything nor watching out for anything, taking everything as it came, whether it be wagons or precipices or dogs, and all such things, relying on his senses for nothing. He was kept alive by his acquaintances who followed him around." Diogenes himself seems skeptical of this legend, noting dryly that "Aenesidemus, however, says that he [Pyrrho] only theorized about the suspension of judgment, whereas he did not actually act improvidently. He lived to be ninety years old."[20] We simply could not survive without making judgments (think: *is this edible or not?*). Even the storied Pyrrho survived only by relying on others who made judgments for him—*Wagon approaching! Precipice on your left!*

Skepticism comes in many varieties, of course, some milder than others, with different prescriptions for attitudes and behavior (though in general, skeptics have been long on critique and short on constructive recommendations). The more doctrinaire skeptics make the world a place of utter ignorance.[21] It is not, though, my purpose here to offer a full-scale discussion of skepticism. But I do want to make three salient points, all of which have resonance in later chapters.

First, I believe that epistemological agnostics, radical skeptics, and nihilists self-destructively set the bar for knowledge too high. In the way that perfection can be the enemy of the good, absolute certainty can be made the enemy of knowledge. To be uncertain is to be ignorant, but it is also to know something. Second, to reiterate: claims about ignorance—and about knowledge—can be made only from the perspective of knowledge. To advance the skeptical position—to demonstrate that our senses are fallible, to reveal that our justification is faulty, to assert that we cannot encounter "things-in-themselves"—is to make such claims: to rely on and apply knowledge already possessed and, therefore, to declaim from a perspective of knowledge. To assert our ignoration is to contradict ourselves. Therefore, third, acknowledging the inevitability and immeasurability of our ignorance need not lead to skepticism or nihilism.

4　Innocence and Ignorance

One fatal Tree there stands of Knowledge call'd,
Forbidden them to taste: Knowledge forbidd'n?
Suspicious, reasonless. Why should thir Lord
Envie them that? can it be sin to know,
Can it be death? and do they onely stand
By Ignorance, is that thir happie state,
The proof of thir obedience and thir faith?
—John Milton

Give me the storm and tempest of thought and action, rather than the dead calm of ignorance and faith! Banish me from Eden when you will; but first let me eat of the fruit of the tree of knowledge!
—Robert G. Ingersoll

There is a radically different image of the place of ignorance: a vision of bliss. Were we to deconstruct the various portrayals of such a place, we would reveal two claims about values. The first is that dwelling in this place is good, even the epitome of goodness. The second is that seeking knowledge, perhaps in certain realms, perhaps knowledge about this place, is bad. Knowing things is irreparably destructive of this good place. Learning involves a loss of something precious; it spoils everything. To come to know is to fall from grace.

Whether it signifies our natal state as infants or a golden age of our human past, this image of fortunate ignorance functions as an ideal. But on any interpretation, you and I have already departed that place. And whatever the significance of that loss, it has distanced us from that abode and enabled us to comprehend what was lost. Not exactly outsiders, more like reflective exiles, we may now see that place in perspective and come to understand it as none who dwell there can.

The Garden of Eden

In the account in Genesis, the Lord God, having created the heavens and the earth "in all their vast array," planted a garden in Eden, and in that beautiful and bounteous setting crafted his crowning achievements: man and woman. These creatures, images of God himself, were commissioned to tend and enjoy the garden and to live off its bounty. They were innocent and "felt no shame." To preserve this bliss, they were ordered not to eat the fruit of a special tree, the tree of the knowledge of good and evil. Such knowledge was forbidden to them; should they eat that fruit or even touch that tree, warned God, "you will surely die." And so they remained, in obedience and ignorance ... until, of course, the cunning serpent appeared and said flatly that God had lied: "You will not surely die." And God's motives were not noble: "For God knows that when you eat from it your eyes will be opened, and you will be like God, knowing good and evil."

The moment between the serpent's tempting insinuation and Eve's biting into the fruit is certainly one of the most suspenseful in all literature; the destiny of humanity hangs in the balance. Her hesitation is brief but reflective. She notices the fruit is "good for food and pleasing to the eye, and also desirable for wisdom." She eats it and shares it with Adam. That simple act changes everything.

At once, "the eyes of both of them were opened," with the sudden insight they acquired. They also acquired a sense of shame about their nakedness. The couple seems to dodge responsibility when caught by God, who frames his question, significantly, as a question of place: "Where are you?" Emerging from hiding, Adam reveals that he is ashamed; when challenged, he shifts the blame to Eve, who shifts the blame to the serpent. Their sinful defiance provokes God to curse first the snake, then the woman, and then the man. Wearing clothes God grudgingly makes for them, the couple are banished from paradise and exiled into lives of pain, labor, and death. God is not only angry and dismayed at their disobedience, he is also wary that they will go further: "The man has now become like one of us, knowing good and evil. He must not be allowed to reach out his hand and take also from the tree of life and eat, and live forever." As a precaution, he places "cherubim and a flaming sword flashing back and forth to guard the way to the tree of life."[1]

This familiar story is, of course, the Fall of Man, the Original Sin, Paradise Lost, and the subject of centuries of high art, majestic literature, elaborated theology, and sermonic rebuke. It links our native state—whether we think of the infancy of individuals or the origin of humanity (ontogeny mirrors phylogeny in such myths)—with innocence and grace. The moral seems clear: blissful innocence is despoiled by curiosity, especially regarding forbidden knowledge. Spiritual grace involves obedience and not-knowing, but it is lost forever in *dis*grace as a result of the typically human folly of epistemic defiance and the devastating knowledge it secures.

Like all great myths, however, this one inspires dilation and continual reappraisal. The devout interpretation is that this account portrays how sin brought pain and death into the world. There is so much to notice, however, and its richness may suggest quite different interpretations, especially since there are intriguing puzzles in the story. What might we notice?

A number of details suggest an alternative interpretation, one that is provocatively revisionist. In the first place, the serpent was right: they did not die that day or for a very long time thereafter (930 years later for Adam, according to Genesis). If that's correct, God was deceptive at best. Adam and Eve did not die as a result of their disobedience, for even in their blissful state, they were mortal all along. Remember, it was the chance they might *gain* immortality that prompted God to secure the tree of life. They may have *become aware* of their mortality as a result of their newfound knowledge, but that is a different matter. Moreover, in this (for some, blasphemous) version, their transition can be seen as their maturation and humanization, and the story as a parable that marks the rise of self-consciousness, autonomy, and responsibility—in which case, the eating of the forbidden fruit is an act of self-liberation, a defiant laying of claim for knowing over ignorance. One can, in short, read this story as one of those myths in which heroes defy the gods to purchase their full humanity.

Moreover, God is worried that his creatures will seek to become gods themselves. There seem to be only two steps between humanity and divinity: knowledge of good and evil, and immortality. The serpent also had claimed God's motive for dissembling was a fear that "your eyes will be opened, and you will be like God, knowing good and evil"—which is consistent with God's own expressed worry that the couple had taken the first step: "The man has now become like one of us, knowing good and evil." (I ignore the seeming hint of polytheism as well as God's momentary disregard for the woman's newfound awareness.)[2] Now, it seems that only one step remains for godhood, and it must be denied them: eternal life. God's motives seem more exclusionary than benign.

No doubt, one should be wary of taking ancient creation stories literally or creating fictions of coherence. But what is at stake here is the larger meaning of the story. And this shift away from the devout interpretation seems to pivot less on the question of the couple's motives for their disobedience, and more on the question of God's motives and his goodness—their Lord's "envie," in Milton's term.[3] Why would the Lord God fashion such creatures and put them together—inquisitive humans, clever serpent, and tempting fruit—simply as a test? Why are the prospects of the couple's godhood, and even just their knowledge of good and evil, so worrisome? Was the Fall also a Liberation? However these theologically awkward questions are answered,[4] the response is likely to include this point: the prelapsarian state should be understood primarily as one of *innocence* rather than one of *ignorance*.

What is the difference? To craft an answer, I want first to compare the two storied places—the Cave and the Garden—as places of ignorance. We will then be in a better position to unpack the concept of innocence and its relation to ignorance.

The Cave and the Garden

As a setting, the two places seem quite different: contrast the restraints and claustrophobic barrenness of the dim Cave with the beautiful bounty and dappled sunshine of the wondrous Garden. The Cave is a horrible abode, and, once accustomed to the light, any liberated soul would dread a return. The Garden is a paradise to which any expelled soul would long to return. Nonetheless, there are deep similarities.

Both the Cave and the Garden are presented as native states, the place or circumstance of their inhabitants since their birth (or creation); they originate there. Both places are self-contained and reclusive; there is no breeze from the world outside. Both sets of inhabitants are ignorant of crucial matters. They do not really understand their situation and cannot assess their circumstances: they do not know that they do not know.[5] Both places are places of confinement, enforced by others of greater knowledge and power upon whom they are dependent. They have tasks to busy themselves (Adam and Eve to tend the garden, and the troglodytes to note the passing shadows). Both parties are kept and cared for, though their experience and setting are quite different.

In both myths, the inhabitants are removed from these places and radically transformed as a result; in both cases, the departure is initiated by other agents—the mysterious "someone" who releases a prisoner's chain, and the subtle serpent. The freed prisoner and the banished couple gain understanding (the symbolic "contemplation of the sun as it is" and "knowing good and evil"). They all have their eyes opened; and they look back, regard and assess the irreversible transformation from a new perspective in a world grown much larger. They can finally understand where they were and what they were. They see themselves and the world in a new way. And they have acquired new tasks, new responsibilities that reflect their new stature: Plato's enlightened soul *must* return and attempt to free others—though he can never go back to what he was; Adam and Eve can never return and must labor for their sustenance all their days.

These parallels notwithstanding, the two places are iconic of the bad and the good. What these comparisons miss, one might say (setting aside the theological framework), is the grace and innocence that pervades the Garden of Eden, and the moral coloration that is absent from Plato's Cave. The Garden is a moral ideal, lush with vitality, and home to creatures who are made in God's image; the Cave is a horror, occupied by the living dead. While pain is involved in both transitions, the pain for the prisoner is in the process of learning and the prospect of return; the pain for Adam and Eve is in the irreversible consequences of disgrace. The liberated prisoner experiences the joy of knowing the Good; the fallen couple has the shame and the regret of losing the good, the blessedness of what once was and can be no longer. One has risen from ignorance to enlightenment; the others have fallen from innocence to depravity.

What differentiates the ignorance of the Cave from that of the Garden is the innocence ascribed to Adam and Eve. It is the moral tone of that innocence (which derives from its divine ordination) that renders their ignorance blissful. To pursue this thought further, let us look more closely at the concept of innocence.

The Concept of Innocence

We begin our lives in innocence as well as in ignorance. Infants and children are called "the Innocents," a morally pastel term that suggests a sweet combination of blamelessness and harmlessness. Etymologically, *innocence* from the Latin *in + nocere* (not + to hurt or to injure) is a twin to the term *innocuous*. But even in Latin, the term *innocentia* quickly added "blamelessness" to the fundamental meaning of "harmlessness." The blameless aspect of innocence is explicated as freedom from guilt, sin, or moral wrong (either in general or in regard to a specific matter); to be innocent in this way is to be untainted by evil. Call this facet of innocence the strand of *moral purity*. The harmlessness of innocence refers to the absence of cunning, artifice, or guile; to be innocent in this way is to possess an artless honesty and simple wholeheartedness. This is the strand of *moral simplicity*. Taken together, these strands suggest a third: *moral vulnerability*. The innocent are easily harmed. Innocence is every bit as fragile as ignorance: touch it and its bloom is gone.

These thoughts generate a flurry of questions: What is the relationship between innocence and ignorance? Does "innocence" merely name a way of dwelling in ignorance? Are Plato's Cave dwellers "innocents"? Can innocence be constructed or deliberately maintained, by others or oneself? Is innocence a precious thing to be protected and preserved, a state of grace; or does it carry dangers, moral liabilities? Might we be "blamed for our blamelessness"?

The moral purity aspect of innocence suggests that its opposite is guilt or sinfulness. Taken alone, that seems unrelated to ignorance. The *OED*, in defining this sense of the term, however, includes the phrase, "the state of being untainted with or unacquainted with evil,"[6] which implies a lack of experience of evil, a lack of knowing evil (what I called *being unacquainted with* or *not knowing what it is like* in chapter 2). It might more remotely suggest a lack of knowledge of evil as well (*not knowing that*). Moral purity may involve more than inexperience and ignorance, but it seems tied to both. It is this connotation that led medieval moralists to use *innocence* as a synonym for *chastity*.

We normally find moral purity to be a precious quality when it is a natural quality, as in the biblical tradition that affirms it to have been our primal, paradisiacal condition. That does not mean that its possessor deserves praise. A child does not deserve praise for being "unacquainted with evil," however precious that condition may be, because one's innocence is not an accomplishment for which one is responsible. But protecting such innocence seems morally justified and probably obligatory. It falls to certain others who are *not* innocent to protect the innocence of those who are.

Yet when innocence is prolonged and enforced, moral maturity is kept out of reach. The restriction of experience, the prohibitions and censorship of knowledge that such sustained naiveté would likely require, become a kind of imposed ignorance. The Garden becomes more like the Cave. In normal developmental conditions of freedom, growth, and socialization, we gain experience, we learn and are affected (tainted, if you insist) by what we come to know. But only through such passage do we achieve maturity. An ingénue may be fresh, pure, and ingenuous, as the term indicates; but she has not crossed the threshold of moral maturity. When Adam and Eve lost their archetypal innocence in the knowledge of good and evil, they passed from shamelessness to having a sense of shame. They gained self-awareness, a sense of the possibilities of freedom and the risks of error, the forbidden knowledge of right and wrong, and a foreboding of their mortality—in short, they became full-fledged moral persons, capable of moral maturity and agency.[7]

Similarly, we might take delight in moral simplicity: the open-pored, wholehearted responsiveness of a child. After all, a lack of sophistication and cunning might well be refreshing, even cherished, in a decadent world of deception, guile, and cynicism. But there are cautions here as well. In defining this "guilelessness" sense of the term "innocence," the *OED* adds: "hence want of knowledge or sense, ignorance, silliness."[8] With this nuance, the innocent seem not only to lack a cunning or guileful way of applying knowledge in action,[9] but perhaps also to lack knowledge or good sense at all—to be clueless. In other words, there is a real concern that moral simplicity will morph either into insensitivity and obtuseness, or into silliness. The innocence of children is perilously close to brutishness (a relationship portrayed with horrifying effect in William Golding's *Lord of the Flies*); and feckless simplicity renders one a simpleton. Having a singular will, wearing one's heart on one's sleeve, and acting from uncomplicated motives, are beautiful if sometimes bracing qualities in the young; but they are connected to seeing the world simply, thinking in primary colors, or perhaps judging things only in black and white. In the more experienced person, they are stultifying. They may reflect emotional insensitivity, a dullness of perception or intellect, an obtuseness. As Martha Nussbaum has written, "Obtuseness is a moral failing."[10] Failure to notice particulars is a special form of ignorance, a blindness to subtle but salient information. If moral judgment requires sensitivity to nuance and detail, a high-resolution perception of particulars, an understanding of subtleties, then such obtuseness or ignorance impedes the moral life. Living morally requires more of us than innocence; it may require that we shed our moral simplicity.

The third strand—moral vulnerability—alerts us to the risks involved in innocence. The innocent are susceptible to exploitation, betrayal, and defilement. A corollary of moral vulnerability is that innocence requires protection by a guardian. It is, in that way, a state of moral dependence. Thus, *a place of innocence is a place of perpetual dependence.* Moreover, it is an uncomprehended dependence, because the innocent, by definition, do not understand what they are being protected from. They may confuse protection with imprisonment. As with the attribution of ignorance, the attribution of innocence in this primal sense can be delivered only from an outside and privileged perspective. Only the noninnocent (the no-longer-innocent, if you prefer) are in a position to ascribe, understand, and protect another's innocence.

How are we to mark the difference between "protecting" and "prolonging" innocence? The story of Adam and Eve implies a sudden transition, an immediate eye-opening recognition that is triggered by a single rebellious act. It is true that innocence can be lost or taken in that way, by dramatic acts that defile or disillusion or reveal, despite the most alert efforts to protect. But the loss of innocence is for most a more gradual process, coinciding with human development and normal encounters with a wider world. Prolonging innocence involves the retarding of such development and the restriction of otherwise normal encounters. It is a paternalistic infantilization that anticipates perpetual dependence and ignorance, not a preparation for independence and awareness.

To sum up: the moral purity, simplicity, and vulnerability of innocence entail an immature moral goodness and a lack of awareness, experience, and knowledge. To be innocent is indeed to dwell in ignorance, especially of moral matters (and by extension, to other worldly matters). One can certainly be ignorant without being innocent, but the reverse is not possible. Innocence has liabilities: purity prolonged may become immaturity;

simplicity may slide into obtuseness or silliness; vulnerability requires dependency. Attempting to sustain innocence beyond its natural span imposes a distorting ignorance—a Peter Pan flight from the responsibilities of awareness and agency. Innocence prolonged is artificial, a constructed condition of ignorance maintained by those who are more experienced. *Dwelling in protected or prolonged innocence, taken in context, cannot therefore be wholly innocent.* The place of innocence is not really an innocent place at all.

Might one act purposefully to protect one's own innocence? Would it not be virtuous to shield oneself intentionally from mental corruption, degradation, and vice? Suppose Marlene wants to prevent troubling images from entering her consciousness and so seeks to avoid images that are horrific, pornographic, and disgusting. To that end, she shuns many films and newscasts. And Juan, who wants to evade all moral fault and "dirty hands," habitually rejects positions of responsibility and action. These actions are autonomous, rationally proactive, and not imposed by others. In all such cases, however, the desire for innocence feeds an area of ignorance. And both Marlene and Juan are calculating in their attempt to secure a compartmentalized innocence; their innocence is not thorough. But is their motive laudable: is it morally good or acceptable to dwell in innocence?

I believe the answer is: it depends. One can remove the wretchedness of the world from sight and mind for short periods—it is difficult to live a rich life *without* doing that on occasion—or reject an area of knowledge or type of experience. But yearning to dwell in innocence throughout one's life is morally hazardous, as is shielding oneself from troubling but significant aspects of one's lifeworld. To attempt to secure one's virtues by avoiding any situation that would test or exercise them is moral evasion, a vice. To act always with the primary concern of protecting one's virtues is not virtuous. Moral maturity requires taking on the risks of agency.

Learning and Loss

This analysis, though it acknowledges the preciousness of "natural" (not artificially prolonged) innocence, presumes that awareness, experience, and knowledge are good things. Yet it seems we value innocence, at least in part, because we fear the corruption that learning of the world will bring. Is there some knowledge it is better not to possess? Is not ignorance, if not bliss, at least sometimes preferable? As John Milton queried, "Can it be sin to know, /Can it be death?"[11]

Approaching these questions is easier when we think in terms of experience (*knowing what it is like*) rather than propositional knowledge (*knowing that*). Certainly there are terrible experiences—intense suffering, horrifying sights, humiliations, unendurable losses—that anyone would prefer not to have, no matter what insight or benefit might result. Not all experiences are to be desired or welcomed, despite occasional Faustian urgings or Nietzschean dithyrambic passions. Enduring, surviving, even triumphing over may bring beatific transformations; but that does not always make having the experiences preferable to avoiding them. Being alert to particulars may be an important quality, but certain particulars may provoke disgust or horror, not edification; and others, such as heeding my neighbor's dog barking, may merely be annoying, not illuminating. Control, selectivity, and the intrinsic value of experiences count for something.

When we think about these questions in terms of *knowing that*, they become more difficult to answer. Certainly I may come to know things I wish I didn't—though often this simply means that I wish the *truth* were different, not that I wish I didn't *know* the truth. But it is concern with the knowing itself that is at issue, and it is the case that knowing some things can be psychologically damaging, causing shock, chagrin, disillusionment, envy, rage, or other negative emotions. A barrage of such knowledge can make one jaded and world-weary. Sometimes, knowing can be dangerous—as is made vivid in the need for witness protection, for example. Not just bits of information, but whole domains of knowledge are considered unsafe, and so prohibited; some are deemed sinful and so are forbidden. All these judgments have provided the standard justification for prolonging innocence and for imposing ignorance.

Places and types of ignorance may be constructed intentionally. It matters whether this construction is self-commissioned or erected by one party for imposition on another. In the latter case, it also matters how this imposition of ignorance is carried out: does it involve concealment, deception, disinformation, or mutual agreement? The asymmetry of privilege and power that is embedded in the relationship of the knower to the ignorant also applies to the relation of the guardian to the innocent: *cognoscenti* over *ignoscenti*, the judge over the judged, expert over layperson, master over novice, the informed over the uninformed, the one who knows over those in the dark who have not a clue. That power may be purely self-absorbed, relishing superiority over the ignorant; it may be self-interested, alert to exploiting the advantages of the epistemic inequality; or it may be paternalistic, expressed through the benevolent intent to save the ignorant or innocent from harmful experiences or knowledge.

In any case, however benign the original intent, the effect is to create and maintain secrets and lies, censored learning, dire taboos, esoterica, "the classified universe" of government documents, and places of ignorance. The same is true with places of prolonged innocence. Because of the differential in power, they easily become places of dependence and oppression. Ignorance, like innocence, has a strand of vulnerability, especially with regard to the watchful ones who know.[12]

Epistemic Community

In chapter 2, I noted that first-, second-, and third-person ascriptions of ignorance function differently: *whose* ignorance one asserts matters epistemically. Adding metalevel discourse—first- and second-order claims—produces a dizzying, mix-and-match array of epistemic possibilities. Just to cite random examples of these metacognitive claims: there are things I know you know, and things I know you don't know; there are things you don't know I know; things we know that others don't know we know; there are things others know that we don't know that they know; and so on. Such different forms have correspondingly different epistemic warrants and implications.

These are not mere logical possibilities conjured as pedantic niceties. There are practical contexts in which it is crucial, for example, for us both to know X and for us each to *know* that the other knows X—and to know that we share that knowledge. Many common transactions, such as paying something by check, depend on such shared or communal knowledge. The game of poker, on the other hand, relies on the players' shared knowledge of their shared ignorance: players need to know that no one at the table knows the cards being held by others or the next card to be drawn, and need to know that all other players are aware of that fact. When the recently enlightened prisoner returned to the Cave, he knew the others did not know things that he knew—indeed they might have killed him, had he pressed his point to tell them.

These tortuous shifts in perspectives and metalevels remind us that we are not solo knowers; we are members of an *epistemic community*. An epistemic community is a network of interactive, cognizing communicators; that is, of individuals who may seek, possess, forget, communicate, share, and conceal or protect information, knowledge, and ignorance. To do these things, they must either share a language or develop reliable translation processes. Their activities, though interactive, may be pursued individually or cooperatively. More formal communities have shared procedures for inquiry, standards for warranting beliefs, and domains of confidentiality. Such a community contains many epistemic roles, including: learner, instructor, researcher, discoverer, witness, testifier, expert, judge, critic, confidante, liar, whistle-blower, and so on.[13]

Epistemic communities overlap and nest within each other, and all of us are active in many, from the largest and most general to small and narrowly specialized ones. Science constitutes such a community, as do families, neighborhoods, belief-based religious groups, professions, corporations, legislative bodies, individual professionals and their clients/customers, academic disciplines, and so many others. Those engaged in a game of poker form a short-lived community.

Interestingly, the prisoners in Plato's Cave also comprise an epistemic community, not because they are in the same circumstance, but because they share a common language in which they name things (the shadows) and possess beliefs about them; they make predictions, hold competitions, and honor those who are cognitively adept. And they would be hostile to any outsider who challenges the framework of their shared beliefs. We can, however, delineate a larger community that includes both the prisoners and their "keepers" who tend the fire and carry objects; or even larger ones that include the unnamed liberator, Plato, and readers of Plato. The Garden of Eden is also such a community, including Adam, Eve, the serpent, and the Lord God. (Or again, we could expand the focus to include even biblical scholars and readers.)

But unlike those in progressive epistemic communities, the cave dwellers and the first humans seem to have no awareness of the possibility of meta-ignorance. Unknown unknowns drive the narrative of both myths, because they are so significant, and because they are known knowns to us readers. But no matter how encompassing the epistemic community—even to include all those who can know—we are all haunted by unknown unknowns.

Places of Ignorance as Thought Experiments

Imagined places of ignorance have long been used to stimulate thought and test ideas—from quite simple scenarios, such as the proverbial "fork in the road" at which one must make a fateful choice without knowing where either path leads; to stories about the advantages of imposing ignorance, such as Plato's tale of the Ring of Gyges,[14] which questions the effect on behavior of possessing a ring that makes one invisible to others at will; to more elaborated situations of ignorance like the Cave and the Garden of Eden. Especially in recent years, philosophers have developed purpose-designed places of ignorance as thought experiments: settings contrived so as to support an argument or explore a problem through the interplay of what is known and not known. We might think of these as fanciful vignettes of ignorance drawn within an implied epistemic community.

The most widely known of such places, like the Cave, involves prisoners—specifically, interrogation rooms in which two prisoners are each offered a deal. Developed by Merrill Flood and Melvin Dresher at the RAND Corporation in 1950 (and later formalized by Albert W. Tucker), the "prisoner's dilemma" has become a stock example in decision theory, generating innumerable variations and elaborations. The situation is familiar to anyone who watches crime shows: it portrays the prosecutorial strategy of divide-and-conquer. I offer a brief version:

Police arrest two partners in crime. They separate the prisoners and offer each a deal: Confess and testify against your partner, and you will receive immunity (no jail time) and he will get five years in jail. Know that your partner is getting the same deal—and if you both confess, you will each receive a three-year prison sentence. If neither of you confesses, you will each get one year in jail. Each prisoner must choose either to confess and betray or remain silent. They are ignorant of the each other's decision, yet the best choice depends on what the other will decide. What should they do?

In this form, the self-interested and rational prisoner will choose betrayal, other things being equal. That is why it is a good game for prosecutors. Yet mutual silence would result in the lower total years in prison. Varying the conditions and sentences may generate different lines of reasoning, but the basic structure of this place is clear: the best decision for oneself depends on someone else's decision, but both are made simultaneously and without knowledge or coordination. The predicament is a stark example of what the German social theorist Niklas Luhmann called situations of "double contingency."[15]

In his magisterial treatise, *A Theory of Justice*, John Rawls created a place of ignorance that is structured with exquisite care. He called this place "the Original Position."[16] We are asked to imagine individuals who are to formulate the social contract. More specifically, they are to choose the principles that will govern the basic institutions of the society in which they will live. These are rational individuals, not given to gambling with important matters, and though they are self-interested, there is a catch: they must do their choosing behind "a veil of ignorance." It is as though they have severe amnesia: they do not know their own identity; and, although they know that they do have interests and value certain things, they do not know what those are. They undoubtedly have talents and liabilities, gender and an age, genetic propensities, a position in the social scale—all the particulars of a human life—but the individuals are ignorant of what they are. Rawls uses such ignorance to construct a situation of fairness, and he deems as just whatever principles would be chosen in such a situation.

Those two imagined places exemplify effects of ignorance on decision making. But other thought experiments are designed to address different issues. Take, for example, "the Chinese Room," devised by John Searle:

Imagine that someone who understands no Chinese is locked in a room with a lot of Chinese symbols and a computer program for answering questions in Chinese. The input consists in Chinese symbols in the form of questions; the output of the system consists in Chinese symbols in answer to the questions. We might suppose that the program is so good that the answers to the questions are indistinguishable from those of a native Chinese speaker. But all the same, neither the person inside nor any other part of the system literally understands Chinese.[17]

Searle's interest in this place is analogical: he uses it to deny the possibility of "strong artificial intelligence," concluding that no computer program, however sophisticated in functional output, creates thought or understanding. Though the messages flow in and out of the Chinese Room in a smoothly functional way, the intelligence is simulated and conceals a particular form of ignorance, a lack of understanding.

Introduced by Frank Jackson, the imagined place known as "Mary's Room" also involves a specific form of ignorance.[18] Mary has been forced to live in a black-and-white room and to learn about the world through a black-and-white monitor. Never has she seen a color (except black or white). Despite these constraints, she has become a brilliant scientist, studying the neurophysiology of vision. She acquires all the information about the physical processes involved when we see objects like ripe tomatoes, or use color terms like *red* and *blue*. She can specify which wavelength combinations from sunlight stimulate our retinas, and she understands how this affects our nervous system; she even knows the neural connections that lead to the physiological changes when we utter the sentence, "The sky is blue." What will happen, Jackson asks, when Mary is released from the room? If she encounters a red rose, would she learn anything new? Jackson intended this thought experiment to argue that Mary would learn something, that seeing a shade of red or tasting a pineapple (mental phenomena called *qualia*) constitutes a genuine form of knowledge, and that therefore the world is not reducible to the physical. Mary's situation portrays an interesting form of *being unacquainted with*. Jackson would argue that Mary in her room lacks understanding because she lacks experience; she lacks *knowing what it is like* actually to see red, despite her brilliance and sophisticated knowledge.[19] The existence of qualia is vigorously debated in philosophy; it is also contested just what, if anything, Mary would gain from this experience. But in sensory deprivation and the later immediacy of her experience we find an echo of Plato's Cave as a place of ignorance.

Yet another example is a place first imagined by John Locke and later elaborated by Harry Frankfurt.[20] A person sits in a room with two doors, A and B. He considers which one to use, but is unaware that A is locked. As it happens, he chooses B and therefore remains ignorant of the fact that, had he chosen A, he couldn't have opened it. Frankfurt argues that the person is responsible for the choice he made even though he, in fact, had no other possibility. Frankfurt's ultimate purpose is to separate the ascription of voluntary, responsible choice from the existence of alternate possibilities—thus permitting us to hold people accountable even in a deterministic world.

I offer these necessarily truncated distillations of philosophical thought experiments as a sampler of constructed places of ignorance. Each has given rise to robust debate and a responsive literature. But though these samples by no means exhaust the genre, their recital shows how illuminating it can be to examine a structured interplay of what is known and what is not. We are provoked by these epistemic thought experiments, imposing ignorance on our imaginary subjects, observing that place from our privileged perspective, and drawing on our metalevel knowledge to interpret what we learn and display.

Numerous cognitive psychologists and experimental economists have designed research projects in which ignorance is imposed on real human subjects. I am not referring to "double-blind" research or "hidden purpose" experiments—though they too are research techniques that impose ignorance. What I mean is research on human decision making under conditions of uncertainty or ignorance. Typically, subjects are asked to make a decision based on information that is inadequate, conflicting, or ambiguous, so researchers may observe the resultant reasoning, response, or behavior. Usually, these experiments are conducted to reveal our cognitive biases, the ways in which—deprived of adequate information—we tilt our judgments. As this research accumulates, we are learning how we behave in situations of structured ignorance.

In part 2, we have explored ignorance as a place within which one might dwell. Places are defined by their boundaries, so in part 3 we turn to ignorance as boundary. The boundary of a place of ignorance is both a reclusion and a threshold to knowledge. When we dwell within knowledge, however, we confront ignorance at the boundary of what is known. Mapping the geography of ignorance is the goal, and so I now turn to the epistemic landscape and its boundaries.

III   Ignorance as Boundary

By charting uncertainty, we reveal possibility.
—Lawrence Tribe and Joshua Matz

5 Mapping Our Ignorance

Ignorance is not just a blank space on a person's mental map. It has contours and coherence, and for all I know rules of operation as well.
—Thomas Pynchon

Hanging in my office is an ornately framed map of the world, inked and painted in Florence in 1472, as part of the luxury edition of the *Cosmographia*. Rather, it is a reproduction; the original is in the Vatican Library. Despite its date, its publication by Jacopo d'Angiolo, and the fact that the map was drawn by Pietro del Massaio with miniatures painted by Ugo de Comminelli, it is known as the Map of the World by Claudius Ptolemy (Klaudios Ptolemaios)—a geographer who lived thirteen centuries earlier. For me, it is not only a lovely, historical artifact; it is a wondrous image of the interplay of knowledge and ignorance.

In the second century CE, Ptolemy produced a remarkably advanced map of the world, using a coordinate system that reflected the spherical form of the Earth. But his text and his map were, for all practical purposes, lost to Europe with the fall of Rome. The rediscovery of his work, and its publication in Latin as *Geographia Claudii Ptolemaei* in 1406–1407, caused a sensation. New maps of the world could be prepared using his coordinates and incorporating his earlier topographical knowledge along with contemporary understanding. As a result, many maps that followed, including this ambitious map of 1472, were named in his honor.

This one is a map of *Oikumene*, the inhabited world—more accurately, the world of the pre-Columbian fifteenth century as known to Europeans. In remarkable detail and annotations, it presents geographical information that was hard won over the centuries, and I marvel at the confident delineation it displays in detailing such areas as the headwaters of the Nile River and the interior of Asia. But, at its edges, on three sides, are inked the words *Terra Incognita*: "Unknown Territory."

Boundaries, Borders, and Maps

The first and fundamental act of reason, the primal action of the *Logos*, is the drawing of a line. The setting of a boundary is the drawing of a line, the marking of a distinction between *this* and *that*. It is the basis of order, and order is the primary effect of the force of reason. A *boundary* both distinguishes two domains and simultaneously conjoins them in their adjacency. It is its boundary that identifies a place and defines its shape. The boundary of something also marks the beginning of something else, some other place, the edge of what-is-not-the-defined-place. It may serve as a barrier, protecting the integrity of what it defines; but it may also be a threshold, a limen, channeling and filtering exits and entrances from one place to another. Such boundary crossings, depending on context, may be described as passages, transformations, journeys, filtrations, or violations. The drawing of a boundary creates a *border*, a liminal area immediately on both sides of the boundary. Where the boundary is in doubt or thought to be moveable, or where the border is a transitional zone, it becomes a *frontier*. The term suggests the need for exploration or defense and the possibility of alteration or advancement of the boundary. Frontiers are areas where spatial claims are made.[1]

Maps are visual representations of the relationships of places; they locate places in relation to each other and orient the viewer. Places on a map are "nested": there are places within places—cities within provinces within countries, for example. Some are only points (such as the North Pole); others are larger and contain many points. Larger-than-a-point places on a map have boundaries; they are domains, places that contain places. The whole territory mapped is the largest place shown. Which places are of which type depends on the scale of the map—whether it is map of Venice, of Europe, or of the world, for example. Cartographers employ criteria of salience to select which features of a territory should be included; these features are *re*presented in symbols, arrayed so as to show spatial relationships. We map many types of terrain today: our maps are geographical, astronomical, political, historical, demographic, architectural, conceptual, curricular, and of many other varieties.

The 1472 Ptolemaic map aspired to map the world. But tracing the boundary of the known or inhabited world, *Oikumene*, is pointing simultaneously to the unknown world, to that which is beyond. Though it displays geographical knowledge, it also points to ignorance. (Indeed, Ptolemy's *Geographia* is believed to be the first to use the term *terra incognita*.) As an epistemic map, its cartographic message is that, although we do not dwell *in* ignorance, we dwell *with* ignorance: our knowledge is bounded by ignorance.

The ideas shift smoothly, subtly, and deceptively in meaning: a map of the world displays our knowledge; our knowledge maps the world; we may map our knowledge; and what is known comprises a domain. It is true that spatial or geographical metaphors for knowledge may be misleading or pernicious—as, for example, in encouraging the territorial attitudes of experts over some domain. They are, nevertheless, suggestive, and what they suggest here is not only the image of ignorance as the boundary of our knowledge, but also the interesting possibility of mapping our knowledge— and our ignorance.

We not only speak of "areas of specialization," "fields of study," and "domains of inquiry," we also refer to the "frontiers of knowledge." Although our knowledge is bounded by ignorance, the border is transitional; the boundary is permeable and may be advanced by research and learning. Ignorance is the domain where learning has not yet penetrated. Not just the exterior, but the interior of a territory may also be unexplored. Ignorance is not only located at the outer rim of our knowledge; it is also found in pockets within the known, impervious and isolated like locked rooms or "eyes" in a game of Go.

We each have personal maps with our own boundaries of terra incognita, of course; we might imagine that these individual maps combine or overlap to form a collective, "human race" map—the universe of the known. My personal terra incognita is vast—*incomprehensibly* vast, of course—which is to say that even the domain of things I know I do not know is beyond measure. And so, if I may presume, are yours and everyone else's.

Maps of knowledge change significantly over time, just as the maps of the known world have altered. Antique maps are more often historical artifacts or aesthetic objects than useful representations of their domains today; but when studied in sequence, they show the progress of learning. They also reveal that maps may contain mistakes. My 1472 map is rife with errors. There are significant omissions: much of the Southern hemisphere and of course all of the Western hemisphere are missing. There are displacements and distortions of proportionality and shape. There are fabricated features, even in some areas that are replete with detail: the headwaters of the Nile, the coast of China ("the Silk Land"), and Africa as a broadly extended southern land. These examples are manifestations of false knowledge, that form of ignorance that is obscured by embedded belief. As with other unknown unknowns, the veiled nature of such errors makes them more dangerous in practice than declared areas of ignorance. We expect the unexpected when we enter terra incognita, but not in a tidily mapped domain. Yet sinkholes of ignorance can appear in what were long thought to be cleared, well-plowed fields of knowledge.

Mapping Professional Ignorance

Suppose we were to focus on mapping our ignorance instead of our knowledge—at least for a specific domain. It is an interesting proposal, a type of figure–ground reversal, a switch from photographic print to negative. We might well see our situation in a different way. The process of mapping would bring to consciousness the outstanding questions in a topic and prompt us to articulate what we know we do not know. It would require more than locating the boundary, though that is the first step; it would entail the delineation of the contours and structure of our known unknowns. We might indulge this exercise with the hope that the resulting map would deepen understanding, guide practice, and direct research. Though we can map only from the survey of our current knowledge (which may be disrupted), the process of mapping ignorance may incidentally expand what we know.

One field in which this idea has gained some traction is medicine. Medical ignorance is particularly dangerous, whether it involves an attending physician's not knowing relevant information about a patient, or the lack of knowledge within the medical science community about the proper diagnosis or the effective treatments of a disease. For the practitioner, having a vivid sense of one's own medical ignorance may produce a prudent outlook and alter therapeutic procedures. For the researcher, carefully specifying what is not known may establish an agenda. Mapping medical ignorance is a more structured task than simply assembling a list or compendium of what is not known in a given field (such as the *Encyclopedia of Medical Ignorance*);[2] while both are useful, the map yields insights that are directed toward a specific problem at hand, and it also marks relationships between what is known and what is not.

At the University of Arizona, Marlys Witte has developed this idea into a signature program. She was inspired by a remark made by her mentor, the celebrated science writer Lewis Thomas: "I wish there was some medical school in this country that taught a class on medical ignorance."[3] Not everyone appreciated the original proposal for a class on medical ignorance: one foundation official even vowed to resign before funding a class focused on ignorance.[4] No matter: Arizona's College of Medicine today offers the "Curriculum of Medical Ignorance" (CMI), a "Medical Student Research Program" (MSRP), and the "Summer Institute on Medical Ignorance" (SIMI) for high school students. The learning goals of CMI are clearly defined: (1) to "gain understanding of the shifting domains of ignorance, uncertainty, and the unknown"; (2) to "improve skills to recognize and deal productively" with those domains; and (3) to "reinforce positive attitudes and values of curiosity, optimism, humility, self-confidence, and skepticism."[5] To achieve these goals, the university deploys the usual array of educational techniques: seminars, clinics, workshops, lectures, logs, conferences, even field trips—all devoted to medical ignorance.

Yes, these programs display both the hype of marketing and the desire to make room for irony and fun within medical education,[6] but they do present a serious route to learning. There are important cognitive benefits: articulating what we do not know leads to the framing of cogent questions. The framing of a question is like the launching of a grappling hook from what is known into what is not; when it gains purchase in the zone of ignorance, it can be a line for further research and ultimately a stimulus for advances in knowledge.

Moreover, mapping one's ignorance has affective benefits as well. Wherever mastery of knowledge and skills creates professional status, especially in practices that give professionals power over clients, there arises a natural pride that rests on what one knows, and a regrettable tendency for authority to develop arrogance. We know the effects: failure to listen, premature dismissal of relevant information, overreaching and overbearing professional conduct, mistakes and the denial of them, and so on. An explicit acknowledgment of ignorance may generate a corrective humility, a desire to seek rather than presume understanding, alertness to unforeseen consequences, and openness to alternative approaches. Building such a focus into the training of professionals is a means to developing the reflectiveness of what Donald Schoen has called "the reflective practitioner."[7]

Mapping one's ignorance is a valuable approach for all fields—not just for medicine and not just for practitioners; it is also a stimulating heuristic exercise for all researchers. It is easy to see how it might benefit scientists, historians, biographers, and genealogists, but also detectives, investigative journalists, debaters, lawyers, teachers, and students. The pursuit of scholarship, scientific research, investigations, or strategic planning can all be advanced by mapping what one does not know about the topic. In a broader view, constructing a map of ignorance is but one of many techniques for *managing* our ignorance (the topic of chapter 10).

Natural and Constructed Boundaries

Boundaries on maps often follow the natural terrain—where the land meets the sea, along a river, or astride a mountain pass. But boundaries may be political constructs as well—the products of treaties, agreements, decrees, or enforced claims. Maps of knowledge are no exception. Some boundaries of knowledge seem "natural": our personal knowledge reflects where and when and to whom we were born; our genetically enabled sensory systems and cognitive capacities provide natural boundaries in the terrain of our knowledge. The boundaries may mark personal frontiers of inquiry and learning. Scientific knowledge seeks to "carve nature at its joints," coordinating concepts and domains of knowledge with natural phenomena. These boundaries are not arbitrary, constructed, or imposed by any agency. They are best understood by contrast with epistemic boundaries that are intentionally drawn. When epistemic boundaries are "artificial," when they are deliberately drawn or constructed, they are intended as barriers to knowledge; they establish areas of ignorance.

On a map of ignorance, one may locate known unknowns, both matters of "natural" ignorance and zones of constructed ignorance. Unknown unknowns can be acknowledged only at the outer border—"Here there be monsters"—or left outside the frame; there is no way to locate them in relation to what is known. The domain and scale determine what elements of recognized ignorance may be identified and placed on the map.

The whole of what we know we don't know—individually and collectively—is so vast and so amorphous as to defy listing or counting. We may, however, catalog some object types. We may not know (but seek to learn or discover): (a) facts; (b) data, such as numerical values, dates, correlations, and other quantifications; (c) entities, such as substances, objects, creatures, or places; (d) persons, names, roles, or relationships; (e) causes, origins, motives, or reasons; (f) effects, outcomes, or implications; (g) concepts, principles, laws, or theories; (h) errors or discrepancies; and (i) clusters or systems of all these, including subjects, fields, and disciplines.

When we identify any known unknown, our specification reflects our cognitive frame—that is, the concepts, knowledge, theoretical assumptions, and the like, with which we specify what is unknown. In this way, our recognized ignorance is given structure by our knowledge: it is re*cognized* and ac*knowledged*. Just as on my Ptolemaic map, terra incognita has its coordinates.

In the remainder of this chapter, I will be concerned with boundaries of ignorance that are of the natural or unconstructed type, which I will call *simple ignorance*; the next chapter will examine created or constructed ignorance.

Locating the Boundary of the Known

The proposal to map one's ignorance relies on the possibility of drawing accurate and reasonably precise borders. In chapter 3, however, I raised the question of whether knowing is an on-or-off state or whether it might be a continuum or spectrum of epistemic states, a matter of gradation. As shorthand, let us call these two views the *disjunctive* and *spectral*, respectively. It is obviously more difficult to limn the boundary if knowledge and ignorance are spectral and not disjunctive (as is implied in mainstream epistemology); rather than a precise boundary, we might well have a transitional zone. And that may indeed be the correct view, as the following considerations suggest.

The disjunctive approach suggests that the boundary may be drawn firmly and with a fine line. Anything beyond that line, any cognitive state that fails to meet the standard of certified knowledge is generic *not-knowledge*. But there are distinct varieties of *not-knowledge*; it is not generic. Among the various forms are: *conjecture, hunch, estimate, prediction, unwarranted belief, false knowledge, the forgotten, the unknowable*, and *simple ignorance*. All these and related forms are varieties of ignorance in a larger sense, since they are forms of not-knowing. But notice that lumping them together discounts germane differences in cognitive content and in their prospective paths to completion as genuine knowledge.

Moreover, there are common experiences of "borderline" knowing that challenge the disjunctive view. Consider how one might set the boundary in this array of cases—is it knowing or not-knowing? Do I know:

• my password to an account if I cannot immediately recall it but succeed on my fifth trial?
• the product of $1,738 \times 1,567$ now if I cannot specify it without calculation?
• what wine my host served if I can't remember the vintner, but would recognize it if I saw the label?
• what a polygon is if I can identify examples but am unable to define it?
• why I bought my car if there were also subconscious factors in play?
• how to tune a piano if I cannot explain it; or if I can explain it accurately, but have never done it?

Some of these conundrums might be resolved by more precisely specifying the object of knowledge, formulating more precisely the facts I do or do not know. But that would not resolve all the cases. A relevant issue is the expectation of memory and recall in ascribing knowledge: does asserting "Bob knows that p" entail that Bob has immediate recall of p when asked, or that Bob must (simply) be able to remember eventually, to calculate, or to recognize p? Another issue is the role of verbalization: whether one who knows p must be able to articulate, define, or explain p. Conventionally, knowledge of a fact entails belief in that fact; yet, in some of the examples, it is not at all clear how belief is involved: in the examples above, what is it I believe about the wine or polygons or the numerical product?

Yet another issue concerns the role of awareness or consciousness: must Bob's knowing be focally conscious; must Bob *consciously* believe p in order to know that p? The traditional disjunctive schema for knowledge is not equipped to accommodate levels of consciousness, though decades of research have shown that consciousness represents only a small portion of our cognition. We continually process perceptions and ideas without attentive awareness of them. Such subliminal cognition can be epistemically effective, affecting decisions, evaluations, and behavior. But it seems, in the disjunctive approach, that only when we bring such cognitions to attentive consciousness—as beliefs expressible in propositional form—can they be *known*. Beyond that, possessing adequate justification for a belief seems to require being fully aware of the justifying conditions. Only then is the knowledge securely "possessed."[8] Thus, the disjunctive model presumes implicit standards of recall and verbalization, direct awareness of one's factual belief and its justification, and the formulation of beliefs in propositional form.

Finally, there is the issue of forgotten knowledge. Though it is rarely examined by philosophers, there is an epistemic difference between that which we have not yet learned and that which we once knew but have now forgotten. We are ignorant of both, of course, because we know neither. Yet they are different: something I once knew—perhaps the contents of a book—may have influenced my thinking, altered my conceptual network, and yet I cannot recall it. Knowledge leaves traces, even when it fades.

These considerations suggest that the setting of a boundary will depend on conceptual decisions, and that a disjunctive approach will make those decisions provocatively arbitrary. The spectral approach focuses more on borderlands than boundaries. But where the boundary can be drawn precisely, such as within certain domains of science, relatively specific agendas for research can be formulated; success results in discovery that may expand or realign the boundary. We may fill gaps in our knowledge; occasionally, however, discoveries reveal whole new domains of ignorance that alter and expand our map significantly.

When Antonie van Leeuwenhoek peered into his handmade microscope in 1676 and saw single-celled organisms, he discovered a whole domain of microbiology populated by amazing creatures of which everyone else was ignorant—including the Royal Society, whose members doubted, even ridiculed, reports of his discovery. Or, to take a humbler example, one who becomes curious about stamp collecting may be startled to discover the huge, specialized, philatelic literature that provides a scholarly context for the hobby—a domain well known to aficionados, but astonishing to novices. Moreover, learning can be subversive as well as expansive, both in terms of human discovery and personal knowledge. The borderland in which inquiry and research occur has an unstable dynamic.

Maps are snapshots of the state of our knowledge and ignorance. The boundaries of our knowledge, however we locate them, not only expand over time; they are redrawn as the terrain of our knowledge changes, and not just at the borders. Indeed, the period of "obsolescence" for our knowledge is rapidly shortening. (Or, if you prefer the more stringent interpretation: much of what we believe we know turns out to be false knowledge—it never was real knowledge.) Even the most accurate map of our knowledge and ignorance is soon outdated. As sociologist Sheldon Ungar has stated, "Clearly, ignorance is inextricably tethered to knowledge, and in so far as the latter is uncertain, contested and possibly permeated with ignorance, no sharp divide can be drawn between knowledge and ignorance."[9]

Borderlands and Public Ignorance

All maps, including maps of ignorance, are drawn with a purpose. Frankly, much of our ignorance is of no matter to us; it is therefore inconsequential for our mapping purposes, and we rightly ignore it. A physician who attempted a map of medical ignorance for a specific case would exclude trivial and irrelevant unknowns. If she does not know the number of hairs on the patient's head, the make of automobile the patient drives, or the patient's high school grades, it is in all probability irrelevant to her purposes. There is no need to mark such distracting ignorance. When dealing with the unknown, however, it is not always an easy matter to know what might be relevant and what is not. Symptoms are not always conclusive, nor are other forms of evidence. The hunches, guesses, and intuitions that generate hypotheses certainly help determine salience. In the end, however, only coming to know will settle the matter.

The borderlands between knowledge and ignorance, like all borderlands, are dynamic places. The buzz of cognitive activity reflects our attitudes: for the inquisitive, these are frontiers of learning, gateways to new knowledge; for the defensive, these are militarized zones, blockades of willful ignorance against the forbidden or the undesired. Gazing at the Grand Canyon of our ignorance, we might be simply in awe at how much is not yet known. Or we might be anxious at the prospect of learning or depressed at the impossibility of learning it all.

An immense subset of our recognized ignorance comprises things it is *possible* to learn. Of course, the specific set varies by individual, since we already have different bases of knowledge from which to learn. But for each of us, there are additional practical constraints: some unknowns would be immediately comprehensible; some could be learned given proper instruction; other things (like fluency in an exotic language) might take a lifetime. Some learning requires concentration and long practice, and we differ dramatically in our aptitudes. Learning some things is dependent on elaborate technology or special access: it was, for instance, impossible to know the major features of the dark side of the moon until our space technology permitted its imaging. Yet another practical constraint is that our attempt to know may be hindered or prevented by other agents or social systems that occlude relevant information or forbid our learning. It is helpful, therefore, as we map our unknowns to distinguish those that are *knowable in principle* from those that are *knowable in practice (for a particular person at a particular time)*.

Nonetheless, although we have different individual epistemic profiles, and although each of us is subject to a gradient of practicality for learning, we all have a huge territory of known unknowns that it is quite possible to know. Regarding these things, taking time to learn is an option. Of course, merely having the *option* to know X does not imply any particular attitude toward learning or knowing X. It does not even imply that learning X is a "live option," in the sense that learning X is retained in consciousness as a plausible activity. One may be quite indifferent toward X; having the option to learn X means one also has the option *not* to learn it.

Given the profusion of public ignorance (chapter 1), it appears that many citizens are exercising their options not to know. Ungar has called public ignorance "an under-identified social problem." Indeed, he believes the situation has become so extreme that it is "pockets of observed public knowledge—rather than ignorance—[that] are exceptional and require specific explanation."[10] The worry is that this "undertow of ignorance" diminishes public life and discourse, debilitates private life and social interactions, and introduces dangers for one and all in public policy.

Such extensive personal ignorance—whether political, historical, mathematical, scientific, or whatever—is judged to be reprehensible, I believe, because of a combination of factors: (1) any citizen has many occasions for acquiring the knowledge; (2) it is not difficult to learn; (3) the knowledge is functionally important in our daily lives and basic to our culture; and therefore, (4) others will rightly expect and rely on what should be "common knowledge." What excuse is there for public ignorance? And what causes it?

"Incompetent teaching" is a handy explanation, and when that is challenged, "intellectual laziness" is a cheap alternative. Though there is certainly a worrying amount of each, it seems misguided to blame individuals when the phenomenon is so widespread. A more likely explanation would be found in large-scale cultural forces or aspects of our social system.

A defensive response is that surveys of public ignorance cover information that is of less interest in today's society, especially to students, who are frequently the target of these surveys and reports. Today's students, one might claim, may be ignorant of the information asked in a survey, but they now cultivate a sophisticated knowledge of other things. Perhaps, but the concern is about *functional knowledge deficits*, and its inescapable implication that some knowledge is just more important than other knowledge. So, when we see a viral video taken at a public university,[11] in which most interviewees do not know who won the Civil War (some cannot even name the two combatants), and yet know details about reality TV celebrities, the claim that public ignorance is no more than "old knowledge" giving way to new seems weak—more an accusation than a defense.

There is a more thoughtful response to public ignorance that focuses on effects of the explosion of knowledge and our access to it. Ignorance is increasing—for all of us. Because of the overwhelming cascade of information and the expansion of knowledge, the ratio of what any one individual knows to the total sum of available knowledge is shrinking rapidly. Knowledge is not only exploding; it is evolving into highly specialized forms. As we go our separate, specialist ways, our personal maps of knowledge have less and less overlap. Professional, academic, and technical occupations require specialized knowledge. These domains of discourse are not easily entered by the nonspecialist public. In fact, great effort is required of experts to stay current in their fields, a pressure that leads to the adoption of even narrower subspecialties that comprise a more manageable domain. Technical terminology proliferates. Interspecialty communication becomes more difficult as language actually becomes an obstacle to discourse; the public, baffled by jargon, becomes disinterested. In addition, our more complex world demands more in terms of functional knowledge. To cope, we increasingly rely on what Ungar calls "pre-digested knowledge packets"—summaries, abstracts, blurbs, cut lines, headlines, and articles that promise "the five things you need to know about X." In addition, preference-based information delivery serves to diminish common knowledge as well (a topic for the next chapter).

Beyond specialization, there is the impact of technology, which has given us immediate access to enormous banks of information; one consequence is valuing the access to knowledge over the assimilation of knowledge. Why learn the names of your political representatives when you can easily locate them if needed? Why memorize the provisions of the Constitution when you can look up any passage? The logical extension is: why learn anything except the skills of "finding out"? Ungar's observation is on point: "Information is no longer a scarce resource: attention and interest are."[12]

But accessing is not learning. The genuine assimilation of information into knowledge, which requires attention and interest, affects the knower. It creates within the mind of the learner informational networks, conceptual connections, cognitive frameworks, and expanded moral, intellectual, and artistic imagination. These aspects of the life of the mind alter our ways of speaking, acting, and responding to the world—and influence what other knowledge we might choose to "look up." In the end, access to information is only as valuable as the intelligence that selects and applies it.

The democratic ideal of the well-informed citizen is premised on the concept of "common knowledge." But today it seems impossible in practice to secure a consensus on what content basic public knowledge must include. Well-intentioned essentialist proposals for a list of "what every American needs to know" have been widely and rightly criticized as conservative, biased, idiosyncratic, and hegemonic. Yet where there is no shared agreement regarding expectations for public knowledge, there will be no agreement as to which aspects of public ignorance are reprehensible.

Even if exponential increases in human ignorance are an inevitable by-product of the advance of knowledge, we need not resign ourselves to a parallel growth in reprehensible public ignorance. But we cannot simply look to enlightened media or more education to solve the problem—at least not advanced, commodified, specialized education. Liberal arts education is designed to address this issue, and I have elsewhere argued for its many merits;[13] but it is unfortunate that liberal arts programs are now subject to the same social pressures I have described here: increasingly specialized majors, reduced breadth of study, short-term utilitarian approaches to valuing knowledge and skills, and a lack of consensus regarding expected knowledge. Ungar argues that the issue of public ignorance is, regrettably, not a "marketable issue."[14] Among his reasons: there is no clearly discernible class of victims who can organize and drive for reform. I would add that when the problem is identified, the all-too-common knee-jerk response is to blame schooling and ascribe stupidity.

Much of the ignorance we can map is removable both in principle and in practice. In this chapter, I focused on the open borders of simple ignorance, where the only hindrances are those involved in the tasks of learning. Attitudes and aptitudes, as I noted, determine our interest in learning, and I'll later consider other factors, such as our desires, needs, rights, and obligations regarding knowledge (chapter 7). Simple ignorance, however, is not constructed, not intended, and not deliberately preserved; it is natural in that it is "found" and usually vincible. We may recognize it as a known unknown, but simply acquiesce: we neither decide to maintain our ignorance nor to remove it, and it pales in our consciousness. Let us turn now to artificial ignorance, to the ways in which we actively choose, even construct, our ignorance.

6 Constructed Ignorance

There are two ways to be fooled. One is to believe what isn't true; the other is to refuse to believe what is true.
—Søren Kierkegaard

Aristotle famously opened his treatise on First Philosophy with the claim, "All men by nature desire to know."[1] For Aristotle, this desire is rooted in our very biology, in our delight in our sensory systems and our cognitive faculties. It is a useful desire: knowledge is advantageous. From an evolutionary perspective, we would say that knowledge has survival value. It seems obvious that there is advantage in coupling a capacity for knowledge with a keen desire to learn: understanding means that right responses need not depend on luck. Conversely, ignorance and resistance to knowledge are maladaptive traits; each is a serious liability in general, and in some circumstances, a fatal one.

It is both natural and desirable, therefore, to attempt to enlarge the boundaries of our knowledge. The idea that our ignorance might be intentional, that we might choose to construct our ignorance, seems odd at the least, and at most a perversion of our natural cognitive desire and joy. As I observed earlier, however, boundaries may be natural to the terrain, or they may be artificial; and that is true of boundaries between the knowledge and ignorance. And, just as a wall marking the boundary of my property may be erected by me or by my neighbor, so my ignorance may be shielded through my own deliberate construction or through the works of others.

My general term for intentional ignorance is *nescience*. Different from what we do not yet know, different from what we can never know, nescience designates what we or others have *determined* we are not to know. I will identify five major forms of nescience, which are distinguished by factors that motivate a decision to barricade the boundary. They are: *rational igno-rance, strategic ignorance, willful ignorance, secrecy,* and *forbidden knowledge.*[2] We will examine each in turn. Finally, we will consider how ignorance may be constructed inadvertently.

Rational Nescience

Rational ignorance is perhaps the easiest to describe. There are occasions when I make the more-or-less conscious decision that something is not worth knowing—at least for me, at least not now. I browse the shelves in a bookstore, select a thick volume, ponder reading it, and then put it back. You see the long, fine-print, legal statement of policy you must agree to before installing the software and you decide, without reading it, to click "agree." An eager student, finding it difficult to choose among available courses, first rules out certain subjects. To put the point in economic terms (which is the field in which the concept of rational ignorance originated): there are times when we believe that the investment in learning X would outweigh the benefit of knowing X. In such circumstances, the reasonable decision is to forgo learning, to decide not to know. The ignorance that we choose to retain is called "rational" ignorance.[3] The judgment is often comparative: it is better to learn Y than X. The key element is that the indi-vidual makes a judgment about learning based on the perceived costs of learning in relation to the perceived benefits of knowing.

This narrowly utilitarian formulation ignores the possibility of learning for its own sake, leaving unaccounted the intrinsic value of knowledge. It appears to commodify knowledge, as though learning is a simple exchange in the marketplace. But the human condition makes epistemic choices inevitable: equipped with different aptitudes, we pursue our interests, pur-poses, and plans within an unyielding finitude. When we do not feel the press of time, it may seem that we purely choose what to know; but when time weighs on us, we realize that choosing what to know is choosing what not to know by default. A young person might happily look forward to a lifetime of reading in which possibilities seem endless; but demanding responsibilities or the weight of years might cause even an avid reader to triage reading selections. I once calculated that if one read and assimilated a book every day for eighty years—which seems an outer limit—one would have absorbed 29,220 books. Impressive, yet it would represent a small fraction (currently about one-tenth) of the books published in the United States *in one year*—to say nothing of other countries or all the journals, newspapers, magazines, blogs, reports, and other forms of knowable publications in many languages. Where to begin?

As available knowledge burgeons around us, choices of rational ignorance loom larger for individuals and for our society. In a "knowledge-based" society, both the pressure to know and the difficulty of deciding what is worth knowing increase. Though we may soften this dilemma by thinking we can always "pick up" the knowledge at a later point, in most situations, we are not deciding merely what we will learn now or sometime later or whenever we have time. We are deciding what we will *never* learn. We have chosen rational ignorance.

Knowing how to make such decisions wisely is, therefore, an increasingly valuable personal skill.[4] It requires judgment, because such choices are not clear-cut. Often one cannot really understand what one is rejecting, what it would mean to know it, or what will be the liabilities of one's ignorance of it. Perhaps the book I chose not to read would have been transformative. Perhaps you will one day regret not reading the user agreement for your software. Just as with the choices of other activities, these choices are never made in isolation; they are made in comparison with other uses of our time, with other potential knowledge.

Usually, the choice is autonomous and made by individuals only for themselves: I may think it would be interesting to know the Latin names of all the plants in my garden, but I soon decide it is not worth the time and effort to learn the information. I am invited to attend a workshop to learn all the features of my office voicemail system—and I quickly think, "I have better things to do." These are personal choices. Sometimes, however, the decision for rational ignorance is made by one party for another (individual or group). Consider this example: school district officials decide their students no longer need to learn cursive writing. Again, judgment is required, and unintended consequences may arise for rational ignorance: perhaps students who never learn cursive writing will be unable to read certain historical documents without remedial training.[5]

The term "rational" is seldom purely descriptive; it usually carries normative force. That ambiguity is present in "rational ignorance" as well. The descriptive sense includes the possibility that we may mistakenly or imprudently choose ignorance; the normative implies that we have a plausible justification. We need both senses of the concept. Though we may reject the narrow cost–benefit interpretations of knowledge, it is inescapable that we must choose to bypass some opportunities to learn. Such choices should be made wisely. Simple found ignorance, when learning is recognized as a live option, becomes intentional, rational ignorance.

Strategic Ignorance

Strategic ignorance is also calculated, but in this case the intent is to use ignorance as an advantage. (It would be more accurate to call it *tactical ignorance*, since it is usually a tactic to advance a larger objective or purpose—but the term is now embedded in the literature.) There are situations in which one's not-knowing something is advantageous, making ignorance an asset rather than a liability. For example, an official who remains ignorant of a questionable internal office matter has "deniability" regarding it and may prefer that state to being implicated. The criminal attorney who tells her client, "I don't want to know whether you did it or not," is trying to preserve the greatest latitude for the defense (and perhaps also to avoid subornation of perjury). These are strategic uses for a barrier to knowledge.

What drives the reaction in such situations is avoidance of the responsibility of knowing; it is the preservation of a future excuse, like pocketing a "Get Out of Jail Free" card. In chapter 4, I questioned whether it is virtuous to attempt to protect one's innocence; the same moral question applies regarding the tactic of seeking to avoid situations of moral liability. So, one might wonder whether the deliberate cultivation of exculpability is itself morally culpable. But in many systems of law and policy it is not illegal or violative; professionally, it may be savvy and even wise. Strategic ignorance is not a trait of character or an epistemic phobia; it is episodic and anticipatory, directed toward problems of knowing something in a particular context. Nonetheless, even when looking at the case level, typical cases do seem to involve "gaming the system," in that the individual who chooses ignorance for strategic reasons often has more than an inkling of the content of the information being refused.[6]

There are, however, other kinds of cases of strategic ignorance that are morally comfortable. Suppose I am up for a promotion and my colleagues must, in my absence, consider my qualifications; afterward, one gossipy friend offers to fill me in. Realizing that in any event these people will remain my coworkers, I might prefer not to know who said what, believing it might affect our interactions; and so I might rebuff my friend's offer of juicy revelations in order to protect collegial relations with strategic ignorance. Or, to take a less convoluted situation: I do not want to read any previews of a mystery thriller, even the teaser on its back cover; I prefer to begin in total ignorance of the plot, guarding my lack of foreknowledge for maximal impact later. Both these examples see ignorance as an asset, a tactical advantage to achieve or protect a larger goal. The motives here are not avoiding responsibility, but preserving a comfortable collegiality and preventing ruinous spoilers, respectively.

In the iconic image, Justice is blindfolded, not blind. It suggests that her ignorance is not a liability, but a strategy. From ancient times, strategic ignorance has been used to promote fairness and a just outcome. The judge and jury are screened from the knowledge of particulars that may otherwise bias judgment. John Rawls's "veil of ignorance" (chapter 4) was employed strategically for precisely this purpose in selecting social principles that are just. We might set this notion against its equally venerable opposite: does fairness require strategic ignorance or full knowledge? The biblical God of judgment is omniscient: "Even before there is a word on my tongue, Behold, O Lord, you know it all."[7] Various philosophers, seeking a nontheistic morality, have developed such God-substitutes as an "Impartial Spectator" or "Ideal Observer," who possess all relevant knowledge, a condition that is deemed necessary for objective, wise judgments.[8]

These opposing conceptions may reflect the gap between human realities and ideal projections. As the Psalmist says, "Such knowledge is too wonderful for me; it is too high, I cannot attain to it."[9] Since no human can be omniscient, or even be assured of possessing all knowledge relevant to a case, a strategy is required: the removal of prejudice and the prevention of bias are essential—and assuring the ignorance of particulars is an effective tactic.[10] This is not a straightforward matter: what information should be kept from a jury to assure a fair trial is hotly contested; in order to impose punishment wisely, judges may seek to know particulars through a presentence investigation; and many investigative panels want to determine for themselves the relevance of information. Errors and injustice can easily result from the withholding of salient facts.

Maintaining ignorance is, then, a strategy for preserving deniability and innocence, for keeping options open, for avoiding responsibility, but also for assuring fairness and just decisions. What unites all these cases and distinguishes them from rational ignorance and other forms is the tactical use of ignorance to gain a benefit, the decision to act with what we might call "ignorance aforethought."

Willful Ignorance

Willful ignorance is a more complex matter. Although all five types of nescience are intentional and therefore "willful" in one sense, this variety typically stresses the role of the will in maintaining one's ignorance of a specific subject, rather than calculative reason. This is not a matter of laziness or distaste for learning in general. A person is commonly called willfully ignorant about a matter when he persistently ignores the topic despite its likely salience and even resists learning about it or assimilating facts that bear on it. The concept is variable along two dimensions: (1) the degree of awareness or decisiveness one has about one's will to remain ignorant, and (2) the vigor of one's negative response to the subject and learning about it, ranging from complacent avoidance to rejection and hostility. As these factors increase, maintaining ignorance requires a stronger will, takes greater mental effort or psychological energy, and generates acrimony. Cases in which both decisiveness and resistance are strong usually involve fear of the truth. Learning the truth can be difficult; embracing it can be even more difficult.[11] Better not to know.

A tidy example of willful ignorance is the wife who ignores indications and rumors suggesting her spouse's infidelity. But there are many significantly nuanced possibilities in such a scenario. The wife, for a variety of reasons, may have chosen in full self-awareness to ignore her spouse's waywardness. Or, the wife may not be aware of either the supposed indications or her resultant attitude. Perhaps they are repressed or subconscious, though still operative. Furthermore, the wife may be well aware of the possible infidelity but choose to avoid investigating the situation; or she may be vigorously resistant to learning anything about her spouse's infidelities and hostile to would-be informants because knowing the truth might "ruin everything." In all these psychological nuances, the wife displays a willful ignorance.

These subtleties point to another aspect of the complexity of the concept: in many cases, willful ignorance involves *self-deception*. The wife may be deceiving herself—about what she knows, about what she wills, or about how she is responding. Alone among types of ignorance, willful ignorance connects *being ignorant of something* with *ignoring that thing*. As I noted earlier, *ignoring X* seems paradoxical because it implies that one is sufficiently aware of X to engage in *ignoring* it. Ignoring involves a refusal of attention.[12] Self-deception notoriously involves, *prima facie*, a bifurcation of the self: there is the self who is aware (the self who deceives), and the self who is unaware (the self who is deceived). We cannot stop to examine these issues—they have generated a fascinating literature—but we can observe that self-deception and denial also require mental energy. Even in the central cases of willful ignorance in which the lack of knowledge is quite genuine, if the will is exercised at all, it is directed toward a specific subject or epistemic object—and that requires at least a minimum level of awareness, else why would the will not-to-know be directed toward the topic that it is?

Not only individuals, but large groups as well can be willfully ignorant, and their resistance often reflects bias, prejudice, privilege, or ideological commitment. Racism and xenophobia, for example, may be characterized and sustained by willful ignorance about members of the targeted group. Philosopher Charles Mills has examined the source of racial ignorance, arguing, "White ignorance has been able to flourish all these years because a white epistemology of ignorance has safeguarded it against the dangers of an illuminating blackness or redness, protecting those who for 'racial' reasons have needed not to know."[13] Similarly, fundamentalists in several major religions resist acquiring accurate portrayals of gays, lesbians, and transsexuals. A self-reliant individual might persist in disparaging homeless people with crude stereotypes, but ignore articles that give an informed picture. Students who see themselves as mathematically incompetent may resist quantitative learning that is in fact well within their reach. Technophobes may refuse even to try to learn how to operate common devices. Willful ignorance is, of course, a serious problem for teachers, who encounter it in classrooms as active resistance to learning. Philosopher Jennifer Logue has written, "Re-evaluating ignorance as neither a simple nor innocent lack of knowledge but as an active force of both psychic and social consequence might help us to engage the resistance with which we are often met when dealing with 'difficult' subjects like racism, sexism, or heterosexism in educational settings."[14]

The willfully ignorant may prefer to repeat false knowledge, even to wear their ignorance like a badge, rather than to entertain unsettling truths. They may resist information that contradicts their prejudices, frantically discredit evidence, and reject attempts to inform—even if, at some level, they may suspect they are wrong. They are, we say, "closed-minded."

Fear seems to me the deeper motivator than bias or prejudice; it is active even when the other factors are missing. Consider a mother who is so upset about her son's military service that she refuses to discuss it while he remains on active duty, rejecting all information about his assignments and experiences. Except for wanting to know that he is alive, she remains willfully ignorant. This is not bias or prejudice at work, but it is fear. Or, imagine a father with a headstrong, teenage daughter; regarding her activities, her friends, and even her whereabouts, he is willfully ignorant. Again, this is not a matter of prejudice or false knowledge, but it is still not benign: it may be motivated by fear as well, though it is surely an abdication of parental responsibility. "Putting one's head in the sand" is a cliché for the attitude of willful ignorance.

Willful ignorance has become quite topical among writers because it appears to be in fashion in society. Perhaps the startling accessibility of information makes ignorance of important matters seem more likely willful: *How could he not know?* But there is little doubt that we are witnessing a wave of reprehensible, willful ignorance among political leaders as well as citizens. All the marks are there: fervent commitment to an ideology, the mantric rehearsal of false knowledge and slogans, resistance to evidence that challenges beliefs, absence of open-minded curiosity, and outright hostility to those who offer different claims, often tending to personal abuse. There are alarming signs that a more radical epistemology is developing in which data, facts, knowledge, and truth itself are discounted in favor of ardent assertion, conformity to a comfortable ideology, and the right to believe whatever one chooses. The masterful and blunt Harry Frankfurt called the effluvium of this rhetorical disinterest in truth "bullshit."[15] Those who take the view that repeatedly broadcasting any strong claim is as good as uttering the truth are even more difficult to reach than the willfully ignorant or the closed-minded, who still at least espouse a claim to truth. The cognitive irritation of genuine contradictions occurs only in those who have a regard for truth. The others openly do not worry about contradiction; they are free, for example, to dismiss scientific knowledge while embracing the technology on which it is based.

The concept of willful ignorance seems to be loaded negatively in not being motivated by "rational" or strategic considerations; in its complacency or hostility to knowledge; and in the analysis of its sources in bias, prejudice, and fear. And if one judges from its use in contemporary discourse and in scholarly accounts, it is a cognitive dereliction with ethical import, a personal and public epistemic vice. I will discuss some of the ethical implications in the next two chapters, but first we should consider whether there are any examples of justifiable willful ignorance. I think the answer is yes. One sort of case would be maintaining willful ignorance about the particulars of a traumatic event in order to avoid deepening the trauma and to permit healing. Suppose a terrible tragedy occurs that costs a loved one her life—and the event was filmed. Willful ignorance—refusing to watch the film, to hear the details of damage to her body, to follow the specifics of the investigation into precise causes of the event—might be justifiable. A grief therapist might recommend it as therapeutic, even as necessary, to cope with such tragedy.

I want to be cautious on this point, though. Recommending the adoption of willful ignorance creates a very slippery slope. The current debate over "triggers" for students—advanced notice of potentially disturbing content, themes, or experiences in their assignments—began with defensible cases: someone who had been raped might need the protection of a warning that a particularly vivid and horrendous rape scene is included in the required reading or viewing, and thus be excused from that assignment or given an alternative; or moral vegetarians and those with queasy stomachs might deserve to be forewarned about the slaughterhouse scenes included in a film for a class on animal rights. But if a system of rights to such triggers is established, the slope becomes slippery because: (1) the student must judge in ignorance the impact of course content; (2) the instructor must judge in ignorance the potential for students' latent traumas and likelihood of distress; and (3) the range of trauma that is relevant is undefinable (does once being bitten by a dog count?). Moreover, the benefits of willful ignorance tend to be overestimated by those who exhibit it. The grief therapist in the above example might well caution that, while dwelling on the details of the accident, repeatedly viewing the film, and so on, would not be healthy, at some point, the process of acceptance and healing may involve letting go of the psychological barriers to discussion of the tragic event. Even when willful ignorance is justifiable as therapeutic, its value is often temporary.

Privacy and Secrecy

Cultures recognize spheres of *privacy*; many elevate it to the status of a right. We need a safe space in which our thoughts, plans, and actions may be formed and reviewed without the immediate scrutiny and judgment of others. Privacy may be claimed by individuals, families, corporations, and other entities. It is required for the development of intimacy, and so sought by couples in love. I define *intimacy* as mutual and replete self-disclosure over time. Such an unfolding of the self would not be possible if it were fully public as it proceeded. Indeed, a sphere of privacy may be required for the formation of identity.[16]

A domain of privacy erects an epistemic boundary that others should not seek to cross. To assert a sphere of privacy is thus to leave those outside the sphere in ignorance. Strictly speaking, privacy is not always nescience because it need not be intended or pursued, but it becomes such when it is affirmed or actively safeguarded. The same is true for *confidentiality*, which derives from privacy. Private matters, when shared with certain professionals or other confidants, are given a confidentiality that is assured, affirmed, and protected similarly to privacy. Those outside the sphere "have no business" seeking to know private or confidential information and are forbidden from taking direct actions to reveal it; they should rest content in their proper ignorance. Normally, only the subject to whom the protected information pertains has the right to disclose it. Should someone else within the sphere divulge such matters, it would be a violation, a betrayal of epistemic trust.

Of course, there may be issues of public interest that justify such a violation. *Whistle-blowing* and various forms of reporting to authorities are examples, and many such acts of disclosure are not optional: they are legally if not morally required. Courts may subpoena private or confidential documents and compel testimony (though professional confidentiality is recognized for specific relationships). Thus the boundary crossing may be a choice for the individual whose privacy is at stake, but not for others with whom the information was shared. Nonetheless, under legitimate authority, the normally forbidden disclosure may become obligatory.

Secrecy differs from privacy. It involves purposeful acts to keep others from knowing, and it imposes ignorance without the presumption that what is kept secret is justifiably private and outside public interest. One could conduct secret treaty negotiations, for instance, or secretly stash money from a bank robbery. While privacy has a quite general target of ignorance (namely, all other individuals), secrecy tends to have a more specific target: a boy might keep something secret from his mother, though he tells his friends; an employee may keep a health problem secret from her employer, though it is known to family and friends. Of course, the target may be as broad as the general public, as in the case of secret treaty negotiations. One can share a secret, but the epistemic bonds that are created differ subtly from those created within a sphere of privacy, intimacy, or confidentiality; a primary difference is that those kept ignorant in secrecy may, in fact, have legitimate interest in knowing the secret.[17] Disagreement over the right to know tinges many arguments between teenagers and their parents, and between politicians and journalists: the debates often turn on whether the matter is one of privacy, confidentiality, or secrecy.

When an individual makes unusually strenuous efforts to protect his privacy, especially about rather insignificant aspects of his life, others do indeed construe it as a form of secrecy. Someone who erects high walls around his property, who rejects normal public interactions, who deflects all talk of home life and background, is bound to arouse the sense of secrecy in others.

The simplest technique of secrecy is withholding information: an employee simply keeps to herself the information that she has interest in leaving the firm; she talks openly of her attendance at the convention, but fails to mention the contact she made there. But because withholding information by itself is not foolproof, she feels the need to take specific steps to assure secrecy; she may engage in *concealment*—hiding the letter offering her a job elsewhere or shredding evidence of her recent interviews. Methods and means of concealment may become quite elaborate (think of stealth bombers), but the effect is simply to hide information from others. Another technique, even more implicative of cunning, is *deception*. The intent to mislead can be done verbally (by *lying*), quantitatively (through statistical or graphic misrepresentation), visually (through image manipulation), and in still other ways. Not all secrecy or concealment involves deception, but all deception entails a secret.

The techniques of secrecy exploit the power differential between those who know and those who are ignorant—in this case, those who are intentionally denied knowledge. Repressive governments exploit this power by establishing expansive zones of secrecy that employ the protective measures of withholding, concealing, and deceiving. About a decade ago, I visited the University of Tartu, in Tartu, Estonia. I was told that during the forty years in which Estonia was part of the USSR, no maps of the city were published, and any stray foreign guest was forbidden from staying overnight in the city. The reason for these measures was the presence of a strategic Soviet air-base nearby. The University of Tartu has a quite distinguished history as one of the oldest universities of Northern Europe, and holds an amazingly large, rich, and rare library collection with strong holdings in the seventeenth through the nineteenth centuries. (Its librarians twice heroically preserved the collection against Kremlin edicts.) But since an entire generation of outsiders never had free access to the library, few outside scholars are now aware of the startling treasures the library contains: rare incunabula, first editions from the Age of Discovery, early scientific journals, Immanuel Kant's death mask, and even a handwritten dinner invitation from Thomas Jefferson. It is but one remarkable case of a constructed boundary, a zone of secrecy that kept the rest of the world in ignorance.[18]

Even whole industries may suppress research, create doubt or uncertainty, and impose public ignorance. For decades, the tobacco industry notoriously bolstered such a zone of public ignorance regarding the effects of smoking. When that barrier began to crack, the industry combined the suppression of knowledge with a campaign to spread misinformation. Confusion about the truth, it was hoped, would prevent knowledge of the hidden.[19] The soft-drink industry now stands accused of the same tactics.[20]

Epistemic communities operate on presumptions of trust, which reflect the fundamental assumption of human communication: that what is said is truthful, or at least sincerely believed. Trust is gradually eroded in environments that are rife with secrecy. Wherever ignorance is imposed, freedom is effectively diminished; an uninformed or misinformed agent cannot think or act in full awareness. Spreading bullshit or misinformation, inciting doubt, not only disrespects and misleads; it induces cynicism in the public. The continual poisoning of the well of public knowledge—in political discourse, Internet postings, advertising—is surely a factor in our contemporary culture of ignorance.

This is not to condemn all secrets: a benign secrecy is needed for happy surprises, for the play of various games, and for protection of things of value. But I reassert the advice of Sissela Bok that we should be alert to the hazards of relying on secrecy, wary of employing it for paternalistic motives, and should seek to expand transparency in our words, deeds, and policies.[21]

Forbidden Knowledge

Forbidden knowledge is our final and most dramatic form of nescience. It is the construction of a barrier at the boundary of ignorance, sealing a zone marked "Verboten!" To cross this boundary would be a sin, a violation, a danger, a shameful or hubristic knowing. Paradigmatic is the Lord God of Genesis drawing such a boundary in the Garden—actually twice, counting the tree of life, where the warning signal was an angel with a flaming sword. But the creation of forbidden zones is widespread in all cultures and recurrent in history. Taboos, censorship, systematic suppression of research, the Vatican's *Index Librorum Prohibitorum*—all establish forms of forbidden knowledge, or (which is the same thing) *required ignorance*.

The concept of the forbidden implies an authority or power that draws, sanctions, and probably enforces the boundary. Religious and governmental authorities are certainly the most common sources of the commands, edicts, and laws that set such boundaries. Their pronouncements redound in the culture, and educators may be enjoined to assure that prohibited matters are absent from the curriculum. The justification—in cases where one is offered—is that what is forbidden is disgusting, defiling, dangerous, or immediately harmful.

Sexuality is an obvious and important example in Western culture. The view that sex is shameful resulted in centuries of imposed ignorance. Knowledge of sexual response, even of sexual anatomy and physiology—especially female sexuality—was long forbidden. Medical texts that discussed masturbation or described female genitalia, for example, were shockingly, often hilariously, and sadly in error until well into the twentieth century.[22] Since homosexuality was condemned as a perversion, even studying it was forbidden and thus risky for the few who dared; references to it needed to be oblique and euphemistic. A topic like pederasty has been even more peril-ous. In 1873, John Addington Symonds, wrote his courageous, pioneering study of homosexuality and pederasty in the Classical era under the deli-cate title *On a Problem in Greek Ethics*. He is at pains to reinforce respectabil-ity in his subtitle: *Being an Inquiry into the Phenomenon of Sexual Inversion, Addressed Especially to Medical Psychologists and Jurists.*[23] He wants to remove any whiff of prurience. Moreover, he waited a decade before printing only ten copies that he circulated privately; it was published without attribution three years later. Similarly courageous, if mincing, treatment was required for studies of prostitution and pornography.

Many scientists and scholars who have attempted to study sexuality and other forbidden topics have faced the problem of negotiating safe passage across the border into the forbidden. Classic works in the history of science display their author's tactics: gratitude for and dedication to a prominent patron; pious profession of religious faith and commendation of the work *soli Deo Gloria* ("to the glory of God alone"); the use of fig leaves and euphe-misms; and elaborate efforts to evince an exaggerated professionalism. When even these techniques seemed risky, authors might use pseudonyms, esoteric writing, or publish secretly (using secrecy defensively against the authorities).[24] Researchers today may still require special scholarly protec-tions to study certain topics, such as sexual response, sex workers, child pornography, or psychedelic drugs.

All such practices construct and regulate ignorance. These forms of for-bidden knowledge are established with a variety of motives that range from paternalistically benevolent to viciously self-aggrandizing. Censors, for example may be motivated by heartfelt concern for those who are denied access, or by manipulative self-protection. Censorship shows the asym-metry of knowledge (the censor presumes to know better than the pub-lic, and may know the content determined to be unfit for others) and of power (assuming the secrecy or prohibition is effective). If one accepts the authority of the agent that forbids knowledge, the judgment may become internalized as one's own. Sometimes the result is that a zone of ignorance is ignored for years, even centuries; but, at other times, the very act of des-ignating it "forbidden" piques curiosity and spurs stealthy forays across the border to snatch knowledge or experience of what has been disallowed. Banning a book is notoriously good for sales.

There are cases of forbidden knowledge in which it is difficult to pinpoint the authority that imposed the barrier. A forbidden zone may simply evolve as part of the ethos of a culture, enforced only by social habits, as though by some implicit agreement—more neglected than explicitly forbidden. In the West, for example, knowledge of alternative medical practices, research in certain lines of technological innovation, recipes for the meat of many nondomesticated animals—these are not formally forbidden, but they have been discouraged and neglected through social habit and corporate practice.

Consider a benign example: most people in the United States know little or nothing about the cherimoya. Also known as the "custard apple" or "the ice cream fruit," it is the fruit of the large shrub or tree, *Annona cherimola*. Mark Twain supposedly expressed the view of many authorities when he described the cherimoya as "the most delicious fruit known to men."[25] Though this fruit, which has long flourished in the Andes and Central America, is now widely grown around the world—even in Southern California—widespread ignorance continues. It remains an unknown; were local grocers to stock it, few consumers would know how to select one or how to serve it. The cherimoya awaits the sort of corporate welcome and marketing that introduced the pineapple, banana, and other "exotic fruits" to the populace of the continental United States.

There are also cases, much rarer, in which a group declares a zone of forbidden knowledge with application to itself; these are prohibitions against inquiry. We might call these cases of *contractual ignorance*. The sort of case I have in mind has occurred in biological research: at the Asilomar Conference of June 1975, an influential agreement was reached by biological scientists and others that imposed restrictions on recombinant DNA research. The example is noteworthy because it is a rare case of the community of scientists declaring for themselves a *no-inquiry zone* and establishing protocols for acceptable research. The danger they foresaw was the possibility of creating and letting loose—whether by accident or malevolence—a virus or other organism that would be lethal and uncontrollable.[26] The prospect of genetic engineering raises similar concerns with the public and even within the research community. Recently, the development and distribution of CRISPR—an inexpensive, convenient method for manipulating the germline of any organism, including humans—has raised calls for "another Asilomar."[27]

The same concern has been raised regarding developments in artificial intelligence and virtual reality technologies—though no Asilomar-type, clear-cut, influential agreements have been reached. In 2000, Bill Joy, an inventor and founder of Sun Microsystems, called "the Edison of the Internet," published an article in *Wired Magazine* titled "Why the Future Doesn't Need Us,"[28] in which he expressed profound reservations about the future implications of our technological developments, especially in robotics, artificial intelligence, and the dramatic extension of the human lifespan. He even quoted Thoreau, saying that we will be "rich in proportion to the number of things which we can afford to let alone."[29] He concluded that "we must now choose between the pursuit of unrestricted and undirected growth through science and technology and the clear accompanying dangers."[30] Thus far, his call for a *no-inquiry zone*, a consensual restraint on technological development, has been unsuccessful—although no less a scientist than Stephen Hawking among others has warned of the dangers to the human race posed by increasingly intelligent androids.

When unrestrained, knowledge naturally tends to application. The temptation to create—even just to confirm one's knowledge—may render that knowledge dangerous. As with the recombinant DNA concerns at Asilomar, the condition that triggers a call for a contractual ignorance in the scientific community is not only the worry of deleterious effects; it is the concern that *a self-replicating cycle* of deleterious effects beyond human control can be created. No wonder everyone cites the myth of the forbidden and the tragedy of revelation: Pandora's Box.

Forbiddance can be used to maintain secrecy, not just to protect from sin and danger; but not all forbidden knowledge involves secrecy. The Asilomar declaration was quite public, and it forbade certain forms of research. (Anyone who would defy the agreement and conduct forbidden research, however, would likely keep it secret.) In cases of secrecy, someone (or some group) possesses the knowledge already; but sometimes the forbidden has contents not even known by those who forbid it.

Constructing Ignorance Inadvertently

Nescience requires the intentional construction of ignorance, but it is also possible to construct ignorance unintentionally, or with dim awareness, or with awareness only after the fact. That can happen when the ignorance is produced as an unintended by-product of an intentional activity. Pursuing our own preferences may today become such a process, and it is the source of considerable public ignorance.

If you live in a fortunate environment that is open and rich with options, it is natural to express your preferences across a wide range of choices, depending on your resources. You can buy the products you like, hear your favorite music, pursue the activities you enjoy, associate with groups you like, and watch your preferred programs. Your habits of choice form a "lifestyle." This pattern of human social action is nothing new. What has changed, however, are two factors: (1) the range of live options has increased enormously—there are many more products, programs, and other possibilities for consumption, investment, and enjoyment; and (2) we have developed technology that identifies and delivers preference-based options—determining and presenting whatever fits your pattern of choices and screening out options that do not. Together, these developments allow us to live a "preferred" life, experiencing *only* what we prefer, ignoring all else. Without direct intention, we erect epistemic barriers. We become prisoners in a *self-reinforcing* cave of ignorance—an ignorance we comfortably share with like-minded peers.

Today, online retailers promote "suggested" items based on our past purchases. We conveniently use preset buttons and "Favorites" bars to find our "personal places." Individuals may habituate themselves to news outlets that reflect their personal viewpoint on the world—Fox or MSNBC, the *New York Times* or the *Wall Street Journal*. When we add these technological assists to physical controls like gated communities, exclusive clubs, professional associations, and so on, we may come to have thorough control over our epistemic input. We screen out and remain ignorant of whatever we do not learn through those selected experiences. We banish the Other.

Preference-driven technology creates a cognitive comfort zone, but from an epistemic perspective it is a system structured to serve *confirmation bias*, our tendency to seek and privilege information that confirms our preconceptions, and to skew interpretations toward those preconceptions. Our natural default pattern is to hunt for confirmation of our beliefs, rather than to test them and to seek the truth. In chapter 5, I mentioned that increased specialization creates epistemic communities that cannot easily communicate and contributes to public ignorance. Preference-based information also creates affinity communities that structure public ignorance. It fuels the growth of ideologies and their "true believers," who can interpret and judge the world only through the lens of unassailable beliefs. As this process grows, confirmation bias becomes more extreme: any contrary evidence is considered threatening and denied out of hand. The reinforcement provided by nodding, like-minded believers causes beliefs to become more extreme, more firmly held, and "hardened." For the most closed-minded and cynical, it ultimately does not matter if the truth is contrary to one's cherished ideology: one has the right to believe whatever, in much the same way that one can stoutly affirm, "Chocolate ice cream is best."

This self-imprisoning effect may happen without intent or awareness, although self-deception seems to be involved at some stage. Indisputably, the practice of restricting one's experience to the reinforcement of prior beliefs protects and increases ignorance.

There are many significant practical problems that result from this process, but it is the ethical dimension that is my concern here. The blinkered true believers, the ideologues, are no longer persuadable, and persuadability—openness to rethinking beliefs in light of evidence and argument—is a central norm of epistemic communities, and (as we shall in the next chapter), a key epistemic virtue of individuals. To lose persuadability is, to use Lee McIntyre's phrase, to "disrespect truth."[31]

7   The Ethics of Ignorance

Where attainable knowledge could have changed the issue, ignorance has the guilt of vice.

—Alfred North Whitehead

We make moral judgments about a wide range of things—motives, acts, practices, emotions, relationships, character traits, and so on—and among them are moral judgments about beliefs, knowledge, and ignorance. "She should not have known about the merger." "He should have known where his child was." These judgments go beyond prudence to imply an epistemic ethic in which we may be morally responsible for what we do and do not know. Indeed, in the examples given, one may be legally responsible as well: insider trading and parental negligence are crimes.

Four factors affect our moral assessment of knowledge and ignorance: *process, content, purpose,* and *context.*[1] Each can be morally scrutinized; together they color our overall assessment. *Process* refers to the means by which one pursues and acquires knowledge, or to the causes of ignorance. The way in which one comes to know may be reprehensible: ethical violations may occur in research procedures, in violations of confidentiality or privacy, in the theft of proprietary information, and in other aspects. The negative judgment about one's ignorance will be more severe if the ignorance was calculated or willful.

Cognitive *content* may be ethically significant independent of the methods used to acquire it. The knowledge may be forbidden or restricted or hazardous in itself; it may be worthless, trivial, or disgusting; or it may be knowledge that, however acquired, is embarrassing because it violates someone's privacy. Ignorance may be ethically significant when one should have known specific information that is salient to a decision or action.

One's *purpose* in seeking the knowledge is also significant. One's ultimate purpose for knowing various ways to make a bomb or how to clone a human being may taint the moral worth of knowing; prurient interest taints clinical knowledge. Similarly, since nescience is purposeful, one's purpose—self-protection, fear, privilege, manipulation of others, and so on—is ethically relevant. The strategic ignorance of a leader who seeks deniability while directing subordinates to act may be ethically questionable.

Context includes many subtleties, including, among other factors, our relationships and roles; the rights of privacy and confidentiality of others; the nature of the immediate social context; and the standards and expectations of the relevant epistemic community. A professional is responsible for knowing specialized information that the public is not; a father should know things about his children that his neighbor need not know, perhaps should not know. Our moral judgment of their ignorance will likely vary depending on their roles and relationships and other such contextual aspects. Context also affects the appropriateness of delivering information or expressing one's knowledge. "Telling tales out of school," divulging classified information, and similar acts of knowledge dissemination are judged inappropriate or unethical based on context—however truthful they may be.

Keeping these four factors in mind, let us turn to a hierarchy of claims one can make regarding knowledge or ignorance, and to the ethical considerations that arise. Our concern is not with the epistemology of morality, but with moral epistemology; and that concern begins with belief.

The Ethics of Belief

Beliefs are factive; they aspire to truth. It would be absurd, as the British philosopher G. E. Moore observed, to say "It is raining, but I don't believe it is raining."[2] To believe is to take to be true. Beliefs may be false, however, and they may be false without being morally wrong. Yet there are beliefs we judge to be morally wrong. Among likely candidates: beliefs that are sexist, racist, or homophobic; the belief that proper upbringing of a child requires "breaking the will" and severe corporal punishment; the belief that the elderly should routinely be euthanized; the belief that "ethnic cleansing" is a political solution, and so on. Note that we condemn not only the potential acts that spring from such beliefs, but the content of the belief itself, the act of believing it, and thus the believer.

Making these moral assessments and holding individuals responsible for their beliefs imply that believing is a voluntary act. Or so it seems. It requires special circumstances to consider someone responsible for an act that was *not* voluntary—negligence, for example, or complicity through the foreknowledge of an act, or action from ignorance that is itself reprehensible. But some beliefs, like some personal values, seem not to have been chosen; they are "inherited" from parents and "caught" from peers, acquired inadvertently, inculcated by institutions and authorities, or assumed from hearsay. For this reason, I think, it is not always the coming-to-hold-this-belief that is the problem; it is the reflective maintaining of such beliefs along with the refusal to disbelieve or discard them that may be voluntary and ethically wrong.

If the content of a belief is judged morally wrong, it is also thought to be false. The belief that one race is clearly inferior or not fully human is not only a morally repugnant, racist tenet; it is also thought to be a false claim—though not by the believer. The falsity of a belief is a necessary but not sufficient condition for a belief to be morally wrong. Neither is the ugliness of the content sufficient for a belief to be morally wrong. There are morally repugnant truths, but believing them does not make them so. Their moral ugliness is embedded in the world, not in one's belief about the world.

There are irresponsible beliefs; more precisely, there are beliefs that are acquired and retained in an epistemically irresponsible way. One may disregard evidence; accept gossip, rumor, or testimony from dubious sources; ignore incoherence with more embedded beliefs; or display cognitive bias—these are examples of what might be called *doxastic dereliction.*[3] I do not mean to revert to the evidentialism of the mathematical philosopher William K. Clifford, who claimed, "It is wrong, always, everywhere, and for anyone, to believe anything upon insufficient evidence."[4] Clifford was trying to prevent irresponsible "overbelief," in which faith, wishful thinking, or sentiment (rather than evidence) stimulate or justify belief. But as William James showed, some of our most important beliefs about our world and the human prospect must be formed without the possibility of *sufficient* evidence. In such circumstances—which are sometimes defined narrowly, sometimes more broadly in James's writings—one's "will to believe" entitles us to choose to believe the alternative that projects a better life.[5]

Unfortunately, in today's culture of ignorance, many people seem to have taken great license with the right to believe, flouting epistemic responsibility. The willful ignorance and false knowledge that are defended by the assertion, "I have a right to my belief," do not meet James's requirements. Rather, the right to believe is proclaimed as a negative right; that is, its intent is to fend off epistemic challenges, to enjoin others from interfering with the formation and holding of the believer's beliefs. But, as Clifford also remarked, "No one man's belief is in any case a private matter which concerns him alone."[6] Beliefs guide motives, choices, and actions. Usually, the public-sphere claimant is arrogating more than belief-rights, and also wants the freedom to act on those beliefs. The "right to believe" is used as a shield against the normal interactions of an epistemic community; it is meant to obstruct or shut down discourse.

From Possibility to Moral Necessity

The ethical issues that arise for ignorance concern vincible ignorance, the sort that prefigures knowledge that might be gained. The moral issues of not-knowing are correlated with, but not exhausted by, the implications of knowing. For vincible ignorance, the possibility of knowing permits an array of claims and judgments that form a hierarchy or progression.[7] Let's look at this progression in simple schematic form, then quickly move to examples. (You may ignore the parenthetical designations in this discussion without loss of meaning, if you choose.)

For any individual or group (S) and any knowable thing (X), one may claim that:

A. S has the *option* to know X.
B. S has the *desire* to know X.
C. S has the *need* to know X.
D. S has the *right* to know X.
E. S has the *obligation* to know X.

One may deny any of these claims, of course, claiming that "S does *not* have (the option, desire, need, or right) to know X." (Label these ~A to ~E, respectively.) Logically different and more interesting for our purposes, however, are these affirmations of ignorance:

A*n*. *S* has the *option not* to know *X*.
B*n*. *S* has the *desire not* to know *X*.
C*n*. *S* has the *need not* to know *X*.
D*n*. *S* has the *right not* to know *X*.
E*n*. *S* has the *obligation not* to know *X*.

These affirmations of ignorance serve to protect the border of our knowledge, even to defend the barricades, thereby constructing or maintaining ignorance.[8] It will require patience to parse these differences, but we need a simple scenario, a nonschematic description that illustrates the progression clearly. So let us imagine Tom, who is exploring an unfamiliar cuisine and has selected a soup with an exotic name, which he is now sipping. At least in principle, Tom has the *option* of knowing the ingredients of the soup. This implies, of course, that Tom also has the option of *not* knowing. (Statements A and A*n* are practical equivalents; that is the nature of options.) In practice, Tom may also be denied the option of learning the ingredients (~A): if, for example, the recipe is kept secret or if the soup was the culinary improvisation of a forgetful chef.

If Tom has an interest in cooking, he may *desire* to know the ingredients (B). Of course, if he is preoccupied or indifferent to his food, he may have no such desire. But *not desiring to know* (~B) is different from *desiring not to know* (B*n*). Though both seem directed toward ignorance, there is no desire present in the former; there is a specific desire in the latter. Tom may be enjoying the taste of his soup, but—being squeamish in general and suspicious about what he is now ingesting—Tom desires *not to know* what is in the soup (B*n*). The presence of desire is motivational: in B, it is directed toward learning; in B*n*, it is directed toward deliberate ignorance. (Statement ~B, *not desiring to know*, suggests a neutral affect and carries no epistemic motivation.)

Suppose now that Tom *needs* to know the soup's ingredients (C). We commonly distinguish between a *desire* or *want* and a *need*—a distinction familiar to any parent who has taken a small child shopping—though we may conflate them when our desire is intense. ("I really *need* those wild shoes!") A genuine need, however, is tied to one's *interests*. One's needs and desires can be quite divergent. Tom may *need* to know the ingredients of the soup if has a severe food allergy—whether he particularly wants to know or not. He may also need to know them if his job is to review the restaurant, or if he is tracking the use of salmonella-infected produce, or if he is preparing a pot of the soup as substitute chef. These latter examples show that not only one's interests but also one's *purposes* may give rise to needs, especially those purposes that are related to roles and obligations and secure the means to a sanctioned end. Our needs also vary in their scope (how much it would take to satisfy the need) and in the value of their fulfillment (how important it is to meet that need). We could imagine an intense need devolving from a project that is not really important. Needs form hierarchies that range from basic survival needs to more elaborated and contextual needs; they are arrayed in hierarchies of value and sequence.

The health authorities responsible for emergency medicine and public health need to know what was in Tom's soup if everyone who ate it became ill. It is essential information to enable them to function competently and fulfill the purpose of their roles. Note that asserting a need always carries an implicit conditional: one needs to know what was in the soup *if one is to determine the cause and treatment of the resulting illness*; or, at the most fundamental level, one needs oxygen *if one is to survive*. Thus, although the assertion of a need seems to be a descriptive report, it is value laden: the need is asserted and evaluated in reference to the importance of the conditional. The need for oxygen carries great weight only because we value life so highly, and life is basic to the fulfillment of other needs. If Tom claims that he needs to know the ingredients in the soup in order to replicate it at home, his need carries little moral weight: his intended project is not vital; his cardinal interests are not at stake.

The concept of need serves both as a solicitation and a restraint. While one "in need" may seek its satisfaction or even have thereby a moral claim on resources, one's need may require certification. "Demonstrated need" is often a requirement for various forms of assistance, and the burden is on the needy. Corporate, military, and intelligence organizations may share information only on a "need to know" basis, and justification of such a need will be required of anyone seeking to know. A *desire* may require explanation, but when one elevates it to a *need*, justification may become necessary.

Can we imagine that Tom *needs not to know* what went into the soup (C*n*)? Yes: for example, he may be attempting a blind taste test to determine whether a more expensive ingredient makes a difference in taste. Research in medicine, psychology, and the social sciences often relies on double-blind experiments and trials in which there is methodological need for subjects *not* to know key elements of the experiments—whether they fall in the placebo group or not, for example; or if the experiment actually tests something different from what they are told, because the research design requires their ignorance as a precondition for valid data.

Claims about having options, desires, or needs to know or not to know are descriptive assertions—though "need" may, as I say, gain normative force from its implied conditional. But standing alone, they do not imply that it is good or bad for one to learn X. A burglar may truly need to know the combination to the safe if he is to steal the jewels.

Epistemic Rights

When we move to claim a right, however, the assertion has more normative force—and how much force depends on the nature of the right. Different sorts of rights are established in different contexts: contractual rights, parliamentary rights, legal rights, parental rights, moral rights, and human rights differ in their grounding and in the sort of normative weight they carry. In any event, having a *need* to know does not lay a claim on others in the way that having a *right* to know does (D). Asserting a right declares an entitlement and enjoins others to divulge the relevant information or to refrain from interfering in one's inquiry. And having a right *not* to know (Dn) serves to enjoin others not to reveal the information, at least not to the rights-holder.

Let's get back to Tom. Tom may indeed have the *right to know* what is in the soup (D), but we would need to imagine a context that creates that entitlement. Perhaps the soup made Tom ill, and he suspects that, despite denials, the chef added monosodium glutamate, a flavor enhancer to which he allergic. So far, we have only Tom's need to know. But if Tom gains a court order requiring the chef to specify all the ingredients, he would have the (legal) right to know. Farfetched as this example may be, there are many cases in which courts determine whether an individual or group has a right to know something. Does an adult who was adopted as an infant have the right to know the identity of her birth parents? Does a divorcée have the right to know the full value of her ex-husband's assets? Do police who stop a speeding car have a right to know what is stored in the trunk? Courts create and enforce legal rights; moral rights are "recognized," either for a specific context or as a concomitant of human life.

Sometimes we speak broadly of a universal human right to know. It is essentially an affirmation of freedom of inquiry, our freedom to learn and to choose what we will seek to know. This, in turn, obligates others not to prevent the pursuit or acquisition of knowledge, not to restrict education and inquiry. Within the catalog of human rights, the right to know seems to be fundamental. But its scope is surely not universal: everyone does not have the right to know everything. In the first place, no individual can learn "everything." We cannot be entitled to something that is impossible. That is why the general right to know devolves to a right to free inquiry. More importantly, an individual's seeking to know may be trumped by certain rights or obligations of others, such as the right to privacy and the obligation to confidentiality. In some cases, I may have a *prima facie* right to know that is overridden by other considerations: for example, although Sheila has a *prima facie* right to know the identity of her biological father, a priest may refuse to divulge the information, under the obligation of confidentiality. But in many cases, it seems more appropriate to say that the *right to know* did not exist, even *prima facie*. Do I really have a right to know whether my neighbor plans to install a swimming pool or what my friend paid for her new car? Surely not. In these sorts of cases—matters that are relatively inconsequential for me—the urge to know is hardly a right, not likely a need, and more like a nosy desire.

What are the factors that create one's right to know a particular X? The relevance of the knowledge to one's self-interest or well-being seems an obvious condition, though it is less obvious how one is always to determine the relevance of information before actually obtaining it. It is difficult to predict what known unknowns, let alone unknown unknowns, will be salient to my self-interest; however, information in certain spheres of personal importance, such as health, personal finance, family relationships, and conditions of employment, is clearly pertinent. Relevance to personal well-being is the rationale for the "Right to Know" movement that was inspired by Rachel Carson's environmental classic, *Silent Spring*.[9] Indeed, the legal principle that an individual has the right to know the chemicals to which she may be exposed in her job or in daily living *because some are dangerous to well-being* has been used to frame federal workplace law and community environmental law.[10]

Rights are also created by speech acts and their written elaborations: promises, agreements, contracts, treaties, by-laws, constitutions, and so on.

In addition, as intimated earlier, they may be attached to social or official roles: parents, doctors, teachers, counselors, judges, jurors, buyers, government officials, club officers—all these have special rights, including epistemic rights that devolve from their respective roles.

Do we also have a *right not to know*? It may seem that this is implicit in the *right to know*: after all, just because one has the *right* to know *X* doesn't mean one has the *obligation* to know *X*. But, to be logically precise, that inference conflates *not having the right to know X* (~D) with *having the right not to know X* (D*n*). Notice that the former (~D) denies a right, while the latter (D*n*) affirms a right. The *right not to know* may require special affirmation, since it would enjoin others not to inform or to divulge specific information. In such cases, informing me would violate my right.

The right *not* to know (D*n*) is articulated and defended today largely in bioethical contexts. A patient may assert her *right not to know* whether she has a degenerative genetic condition such as Huntington's chorea, arguing that, if she were to learn of a positive diagnosis, the knowledge would create extreme stress and hamper her remaining life. The rationale for a right to ignorance is thus tied to protecting one's autonomy, not just in the choice of not-knowing, but also in regard to the self-determination that would be altered afterward by the knowing. Knowledge affects us, and some knowledge about ourselves can be debilitating; it can sap our confidence and hope, diminish our motivation, and drain the joy and fullness of our experience. Once known, it cannot be unlearned. Especially if there is nothing we can do about it anyway, we might well assert our right not to know the truth, our right to ignorance. Like other rights claims, the entitlement not to know is subject to the rights and obligations of others—a circumstance that has made it a contested claim in bioethics. Some genetic information is relevant not only to the patient, but also to the patient's children, spouse, or other family members. *Their* right to know, which does not depend on their explicitly claiming it, may trump the patient's right not to know.

Consider this case:

Barbara, a 35 year old woman and mother of two children, has a family history of breast cancer. Urged by her relatives, she decided to undergo the BCRA1/2 testing. If Barbara has the mutation, she has 80% risk of developing breast cancer. Three days later, depressed by the difficult decisions she would have to make in case the mutation was found, she asked the doctor not to inform her about the test results.[11]

Several epistemic claims are implicit in this case. Barbara asserts her right not to know; moreover, she assumes that right overrides her doctor's duty to inform. The relatives who urged Barbara's screening have a stake in the results, so a case might be made for their right to know the results. They would be affected by a cancer diagnosis and its prognosis, especially so her spouse and children. If Barbara does have cancer, her nescience will likely have dire consequences—which might have been prevented or ameliorated. Her test results may bear on the medical prospects of her female relatives. If so, Barbara may have the obligation to inform them, which entails her obligation to know. Whatever the results, they will otherwise remain in anxious ignorance. From this perspective, Barbara is "in denial," avoiding the truth out of fear, and violating her epistemic responsibilities.[12] In most medical situations (but not all), the decision to inform others is left to the patient; the doctor's obligation to inform is directed only to the patient (though the doctor may urge a patient to tell affected others). Clearly, such situations, which are quite common, are ethically complex.

In recent years, there has been formal, even legal, recognition of the right not to know. In 1995, the World Medical Association, in its amended "Declaration on the Rights of the Patient" declared that "the patient has the right not to be informed on his/her explicit request, unless required for the protection of another person's life." Two years later, the European *Convention on Human Rights and Biomedicine* stated: "Everyone is entitled to know any information collected about his or her health. However, the wishes of individuals not to be so informed shall be observed." And the UNESCO *Universal Declaration on the Human Genome and Human Rights* proclaimed: "The right of every individual to decide whether or not to be informed of the results of genetic examination and the resulting consequences should be respected."[13]

These declarations are similar, though not congruent. The shared assertions are: (1) that there is a right not to know; and (2) that it applies to patients in regard to their own medical information (though the UNESCO assertion is restricted to genetic information). The rationale, more or less explicit, is that the patient's right to self-determination underlies these assertions. It also seems that, while the right to know does not require an explicit claim, the right *not* to know does: the patient must explicitly request the doctor to withhold the information.

In some situations, however, the patient cannot make the request in advance. Suppose a child needs a kidney replacement and family members are tested as possible donors; the tests disclose incidentally that the father is not the child's biological parent. If the father anticipated this possibility beforehand, he might choose not to know; if he did not imagine this result, he has no opportunity to claim his right. There is no way now for the doctor to place the choice before the patient without implying that the information is significant; and the doctor may wonder whether the father or the mother has the greater stake in the information.

While I accept the recognition of a right not to know in specific circumstances, I think one's claim to such a right is deflated when one decides to undergo medical testing. So, it is not an inalienable right; it can be undone by one's own actions. Moreover, I am wary of the extension of the right not to know into other contexts. It easily becomes a justification for epistemic irresponsibility, for willful ignorance and epistemic injustice.

Are there spheres other than the medical in which the right not to know might apply? Might a student claim a right not to know his grades during a course on the grounds that knowing them would affect his performance? Unlikely, perhaps; but it's possible. Might a bride claim a right not to know the appraised value of her rings, not wanting the knowledge of their monetary value to affect her sentiments? In adopting a child, might prospective parents claim a right not to be told anything about the child's history or biological parents—whether the information offered is genetic, medical, or socioeconomic—on the grounds that it would bias their parenting? What is apparent in such cases is how easily a *desire* not to know something may be elevated to a *need* and asserted as a *right* that obligates others.

Epistemic Obligations

My wariness about the right to ignorance turns our attention to the epistemic claims of the greatest weight: the *obligations* to know and not to know (E and En). Asserting the *obligation* to know (E) denies the right *not* to know X (Dn). Having the obligation to know X means that one is responsible for knowing X and would be in violation or at fault for not possessing that knowledge. The parent who doesn't check the label of a cleaning product and therefore takes no precautions to prevent a toddler's poisoning is negligent. Whitehead's principle applies: "Where attainable knowledge could have changed the issue, ignorance has the guilt of vice."[14] Imagine the worst scenario in the case of Barbara's medical tests: the suppressed information is that she indeed has breast cancer, and her ignoring it results in her death. If receiving the results would have led to treatment that "changed the issue" and saved her life, her ignorance is reprehensible.

Obligations are created within the same contexts as rights; they may be attendant to agreements and promises (implicit or explicit, formal or informal), endemic to various roles and positions, established in law, or incurred as a moral agent. As we have seen, normal interaction among adults in an epistemic community presupposes that members know certain things. Ignorance of this common knowledge may be merely embarrassing to oneself and surprising to others, but—especially if the ignorance has the potential to harm oneself or others—it becomes a more serious lapse, a failure to know what one should have learned. We may, in short, have both an obligation to know X and the responsibility that comes with knowing it. One might argue that Barbara has an obligation to know the test results *and* to inform others. And remember our Tom? One might argue that Tom is *obligated* to know the ingredients of the soup if he is serving it to a group known to include ethical vegetarians and individuals with food allergies.

There are times when we hold persons morally and/or legally responsible for their ignorance. The "ignorance of the law is no excuse" principle applies broadly across many jurisdictions. The same applies morally: obliviousness to the harmful impact of one's actions on others does not deflect blame—it may intensify it. In many cases, ignorance is reprehensible because one could reasonably be expected to have known: "Any normal person would have known" that remark was insulting, that vehicle was not safe, or that tactic would produce civilian casualties. In other situations, however, the ignorance is a violation of a clear obligation to know: the physician should have known the drugs were incompatible; the teacher should have known the child showed signs of abuse. There is also a large domain in which we are not obligated to know, we could not easily have known, and yet we are responsible. For example, unbeknownst to the owner, there is a buried fuel tank on her property; it leaks and contaminates a neighbor's well. Though the cause was an unknown unknown, the owner may still be held responsible.[15]

Conversely, the same sources, contexts, and derivative responsibilities apply to the obligation *not* to know (E*n*). There is one exception: there is no natural, universal obligation not to know. One might argue, for example, that all moral agents have the obligation to know the reasonably expectable consequences of their actions, but there is no parallel argument for content that they must not know. The obligation not to know is specially created; it arises only in constructed contexts. Acting as a blind referee or judge, waiving one's right to access letters of reference, promising not to read a diary—such situations carry the obligation *not* to know certain things. Jurors routinely have such a special obligation: they are enjoined not to learn certain information; they may be sequestered to protect and ensure their ignorance.

As an obligation, this negative epistemic imperative is quite odd. In usual cases of obligation, if *S* has an obligation, its force is directed toward *S*; it enjoins *S* to do certain things (and in a minority of cases, *not* to do certain things). But *S*'s obligation not to know *X* not only directs *S*'s conduct, it also serves to enjoin all others *not to inform S* about *X*, directly or indirectly. One who deliberately gives a juror illicit information may be held responsible, even charged with a crime; and whether the juror comes to know by design or by accident, the obligation is violated and juror must disclose that fact to the judge. A breach of this negative epistemic obligation usually disqualifies a juror. My obligation not to know may lead me to refrain from seeking information, to deflect willing informants, and even to take protective steps to avoid accidentally receiving forbidden information. Fortunately, obligatory ignorance is typically directed toward an explicit and rather narrow slice of knowledge.

I referred earlier to a doctor's obligation to inform a patient of diagnoses and other findings regarding the patient's health. It is a familiar example of another epistemic obligation: *the obligation to report or to inform.* Many such disclosure obligations are recognized in professional codes of conduct or institutionalized in laws, and those who keep silent may be prosecuted; but sometimes the moral obligation falls on anyone who knows. Who is responsible for reporting suspected child or domestic abuse or sexual assault? Laws may identify specific persons in certain roles who must report or face penalties; the moral responsibility, however, belongs to anyone who has a reasonable suspicion. A responsibility to report may apply even when the victim pleads to keep the matter secret. The rationale for overriding the victim's right of privacy seems to involve the judgment that the individual's autonomy is already compromised by victimhood. Thus, regardless of the victim's expressed desires, the self-interest of the victim and the public good require the information to be known by authorities.

In some situations, there is no specific person or agency one is obligated to inform, but one nonetheless has a responsibility to reveal, to make public disclosure. That is the obligation felt by whistle-blowers. When these epistemic obligations are distributed across a group, and when the obligation is simply to reveal rather than to inform someone in particular—"someone needs to expose this"—it seems easier to avoid responding. Just as individuals are less likely to help someone if they are among a group of bystanders than if they are the only spectator, so a collective responsibility that falls on everyone who knows seems to fall on no one in particular, not on each one.

One might also be obligated *not* to inform. Everyone knows there are times when it is wise to keep silent even though it may be difficult. But silence may be legally or morally obligatory. The case of Edward Snowden is seen by many, apparently including President Obama, not as a courageous case of whistle-blowing in which putatively unconstitutional practices of government surveillance are made public, but as a treasonous violation of Snowden's obligation not to disclose classified information. (It seems now that he did not actually take an oath, but signed a standard form that made nondisclosure a condition of employment.)[16] In any event, oaths and pledges, confidentiality and nondisclosure agreements, and gag orders may be used to create obligations not to inform or reveal.

Divulging personal information about a friend may be disloyal; spilling a shared secret may be a betrayal. Breaking a client's confidences may violate a professional code of ethics. But how much weight one gives to those obligations, legally and morally, may depend on other factors. Acknowledging an obligation does not imply that it may never be overridden by more serious obligations, though clearly the intent of these restrictive instruments is to constrain one's actions and to exact a penalty if they are breached. A *prima facie* obligation is real and its violation is not to be taken lightly. Granted, the obligation to keep confidences is voluntary if it derives from a contract. But in practice, the signing of such agreements is often coercive: parties to a suit are told they will receive settlement only if they sign a nondisclosure agreement. In many cases, there is not even coerced agreement—as when a judge issues a gag order that no parties to a case before the court may speak with the media, for example.

All these practices bear a burden of ethical defense because: (1) they restrain freedom of expression; (2) they are frequently motivated by secrecy rather than privacy; and (3) they are instituted without regard for the interests of the greater public and its possible right to know. For example, nondisclosure agreements are used appropriately by corporations to protect proprietary information from being used by competitors. But they are used to protect not only information about products and plans, but also corporate practices and communications that may violate public interest. Their restraining effect is displayed clearly when these agreements intersect with a more open epistemic context. Consider this conflict: an able undergraduate science student pursued a research internship for academic credit, a condition of which was to present the results of the research at a campus colloquium. His internship, however, was with a chemical company that required him to sign a nondisclosure agreement under which he could not discuss the nature of his work with anyone outside the company. Or, to take a more general case: boards of trustees and university presidents have imposed gag orders on employees who are party to information about personnel matters that have become controversial on campus or newsworthy. Apart from the fact that such orders have no legal standing, they conflict with the transparent-and-free-flow-of-information ethos of colleges and universities. In short, it is too easy to use such practices to protect shabby, embarrassing, dangerous, or unethical practices.

Ignorance, Action, and Responsibility

Aristotle set the framework for analyzing the relation of ignorance to voluntary action—and hence to moral responsibility.[17] He observes that actions that are coerced or produced by external forces are not voluntary. Aristotle also asserts that actions are not voluntary if they are done because of ignorance. Speaking broadly, for an action to be considered voluntary, the agent must know what she is doing. But this claim requires further distinctions, for which I will use a more contemporary situation.

Imagine passengers on a train that is equipped with an emergency cord that will stop the train precipitously. There are three ways to pull the cord. (1) Sarah pulls the cord deliberately, knowing what she is doing. This is a voluntary act for which we might praise or blame her depending on the reason for her act. (2) Philip pulls the cord thinking it is used to call the conductor. Philip acts from ignorance; in a sense, he does not know what he is doing. The action is not voluntary. (3) Michelle is very drunk and pulls the cord; in a different sense, she too does not know what she is doing. She pulls the cord *in* ignorance, not *from* ignorance. Oddly, Aristotle gives some classificatory weight to the agent's feelings *post factum*: if Michelle regrets her drunken act when she is sober, it was a "nonvoluntary" action (neither voluntary nor involuntary).

From our perspective, the responsibility we bear for our ignorance forms a continuum. Recall Tom and his soup? If a chef unknowingly were to serve Tom soup that contained a poison, he would be acting from ignorance, not voluntarily. In Aristotle's terms, he was ignorant of the particulars of the case: he did not know there was poison in the soup. We do not blame or condemn the chef. (The chef might feel that he was in some sense responsible, that the action was piacular if not immoral.) But suppose the chef knew there was arsenic in the soup but was ignorant of the commonly known fact that arsenic is poisonous: his ignorance is more culpable, though the act of poisoning is not intentional. But, if the chef was, as Aristotle would say, ignorant of universals and somehow did not know that poisoning was wrong, we are likely either to show little tolerance for his ignorance and hold him fully responsible, or—if he is unable to tell right from wrong in general—treat him as sociopathic or mentally incompetent and in need of therapy.

As I noted earlier, we may rightly be held responsible for our ignorance based on a wide range of factors, but ignorance may also serve as an excuse. Professions of ignorance are often used to deny responsibility. Genuinely exculpatory ignorance that has resulted in a tragic or harmful outcome involves the agent's unknown unknowns, or things the agent could not have known or had no occasion or obligation to know.[18]

Epistemic Injustice and Ignorance as Privilege

First, the general statement: the quality of relations in an epistemic community may raise moral concerns. Now more specifically: systematic epistemic bias, disregard for legitimate epistemic authority, patterns of willful ignorance, practices of withholding or distorting vital information—all raise questions of justice. British philosopher Miranda Fricker has offered an incisive critique of two forms of epistemic injustice: "testimonial injustice, in which someone is wronged in their capacity as a giver of knowledge; and hermeneutical injustice, in which someone is wronged in their capacity as a subject of social understanding."[19] The first occurs when a source is routinely given more or less credibility than is deserved. The second occurs when actions or practices are denied the meaning and import they "deserve" epistemically, perhaps because relevant concepts are inchoate or suppressed. If women's testimony about sexual harassment is regularly discounted, it is epistemic injustice. It required the development of the concept of sexual harassment to bring into focus the import of many kinds of interpersonal actions; it placed a pattern of behavior under a concept carrying ethical weight. If the concept is inchoate, resisted, contested, or suppressed, those interpersonal interactions are not understood. The victim is not understood as victim, rights are not seen as rights, and the harasser is not seen as harasser. As Fricker argues, those who are marginalized experience both forms of injustice; indeed these tendencies contribute to their marginalization.

Ignorance is often the privilege of the powerful. One in power has the luxury of not needing to know. If, for instance, Samuel has no desire to know about the homeless, or perhaps desires *not* to know about "those people," he will remain ignorant because he has no need to know. He can ignore them. And insofar as Samuel does cognize homeless people, he is cognitively free to use distorted stereotypes and false knowledge. Whether such ignorance is constructed willfully or inadvertently, it is endemic, and yet complicity in it will likely be denied. It is natural to seek innocence, reject guilt, and deny implication in subordination. Such blasé ignorance serves to protect one's self-image of goodness, or at least one's moral luck. In our society of economic inequality, privilege becomes another contributing factor in the culture of ignorance.

According to philosopher José Medina, such privileged ignorance is a form of epistemic injustice that sustains gender and racial oppression. However deeply embedded, it is vincible ignorance, and Medina advocates a "resistant imagination," a "kaleidoscopic" consciousness of epistemic pluralism and dissonance, as tools for breaking down the barriers.[20] Another philosopher, Barbara Applebaum, has argued that an additional technique is required: instead of teaching only the conception of language as communication, we must teach language as discourse, a mode in which language acts, transmits power, and "constitutes subjects as certain types of beings."[21] These analyses suggest a different type of epistemic obligation: not simply to inform, but to disrupt privileged ignorance and the conceptual framework that creates it.

In a survey of moral claims on knowledge and ignorance, we frequently find references to the dispositions of knowers and to the qualities of epistemic communities. Medina speaks commandingly of a "resistant imagination" and a consciousness that is "kaleidoscopic"; Fricker advocates "critical openness"; I have mentioned "epistemic laziness" and "hostility" to the truth. Such dispositions, individual or collective, affect both individual learning and the dynamics of epistemic communities. So, I turn next to a discussion of epistemic virtues and vices, and to the possibility of virtuous ignorance.

8 Virtues and Vices of Ignorance

There are many things of which a wise man might wish to be ignorant.
—Ralph Waldo Emerson

When I was a child, my elementary school sent home report cards that were bluish-green bifolds in a brown envelope. The inner left-hand page listed the various academic subjects and my grades for each six-week period. The right-hand page listed various aspects of "citizenship," including my attendance record, "times tardy," and a list of traits or behavior patterns that the teacher evaluated with an "S" or "U" (for "satisfactory" or "unsatisfactory") or even a gold star. They were the virtues of a good school citizen. Some of them were designed to encourage the sort of docility and deportment conducive to an orderly class: "controls talking," "works well with others," and "follows instructions." (Versions of these same traits, I later learned, were also quite popular on report cards in countries with totalitarian regimes.) But there were other traits that seem more directly relevant to learning: "pays attention," "works up to ability," and "practices self-control." These were my introduction to epistemic virtues. Oh, it would have seemed better, in a democratic epistemic community, if the school authorities had also elevated such traits as "thinks independently" or "reasons logically," but their list is nonetheless important and perhaps more basic.

This bifolded view of learning is reflected in traditional epistemology, in which the focus is on knowledge as a cognitive structure (the left-hand page), not on the process of coming to know (the right-hand page). To use Hans Reichenbach's well-known distinction, epistemology is usually directed toward the "context of justification," and has no interest in the "context of discovery."[1] How one learns is left to psychologists and educators. Technically, analytic epistemology views knowledge as a set of propositions: justified, true beliefs.[2] This is compatible with common conceptions of knowledge as something one may possess, a cognitive fund from which one may draw.

Nevertheless, it is also illuminating to regard knowledge as an epistemic achievement, as success in the effort to learn. Taking this "right-hand page" viewpoint directs our attention to the labor, the skills, the mental faculties, and relevant dispositions that facilitate such an accomplishment—the epistemic virtues—along with the obstacles and vices that inhibit it.

The Moral Assessment of Learning

Let us take a *virtue* to be a trait that is conducive to success in a purposeful activity; vices are traits that tend to inhibit such success. Traits are virtuous or vicious in relation to that activity and to the larger practice or enterprise encompassing such activity. Having a heavy body weight is a virtue for the actions of a sumo wrestler, but likely a vice for a baseball shortstop. In playing poker, it is irrelevant. If we then take our purposeful activity to be the pursuit of knowledge, it is not difficult to develop at least a preliminary list of epistemic virtues. The researcher, the inquirer, the detective, the investigator—all knowledge-seekers—might find virtue in being open-minded but judiciously skeptical, in having intellectual courage and imagination, in attending to evidence and to the credibility of sources, in remaining exact and considered in judgment—and, as my report cards suggested, in paying attention, persevering, and displaying self-control. The list of epistemic vices that inhibit the search for knowledge begins with similar ease: rigidity of thought, obtuseness, prejudice, disregard for evidence, gullibility, and so on (the reverse of the traits listed above).

This approach is known as "virtue epistemology." Its roots are traceable to Aristotle, who first distinguished intellectual virtues from moral virtues (though he then interrelated them);[3] but it emerged in its contemporary form in a set of essays in the 1980s by Ernest Sosa,[4] and has since been elaborated and refined by many others. It has opened new lines of inquiry, sometimes with the hope that it might benefit traditional problems of epistemology, but increasingly with the conviction that it is a valuable approach in its own right, offering novel and important insights. One group of thinkers, including Sosa, attends primarily to the normative functioning of those faculties that are engaged in achieving knowledge, such as sensation, memory, introspection, intuition, and the like. Another group, including Linda Zagzebski, Robert C. Roberts, W. Jay Wood, and others, focuses on particular epistemic virtues and vices.[5] They have produced intriguing analyses of such epistemic traits as curiosity, humility, open-mindedness, intellectual courage and caution, persistence, and respect for evidence; and of intellectual vices, such as gullibility, cognitive inertia, and intellectual dishonesty. Both groups agree that the epistemic virtues are dependent in some way on cognitive faculties.

This approach allows us to reconnect process with product, learning to knowing, and education to epistemology. It serves to bridge Reichenbach's two contexts, though there is less preoccupation and patience with the thorny issues of justification. The normative concern remains, of course: that is, the result is regulative in the sense that it aims to guide practice. But the normative spotlight is now on the individual who seeks to know.

While this is an exciting and long-overdue development, I want to advocate three supplementary elaborations of what I take to be the now-standard view of virtue epistemologists. The natural focus of this approach is *acquisitionist*; that is, a focus on traits related to the *pursuit or acquisition* of knowledge. It is also expedient, in the context of virtues and vices, to think in terms of an individual searcher who displays them. My first point is that epistemic virtues and vices may be displayed not only in the *pursuit*, but also in the *possession*, the *protection*, the *transmission*, and the *application* of knowledge. Second, these aspects remind us that we are individuals in epistemic communities; we are not just autodidacts and solo knowers. Many virtues and vices are manifested in epistemic interactions with other people: they are related to ways in which we withhold and share information and to our regard for other informants.

The virtue approach shares with traditional epistemology the assumption that knowledge (which rests on truth) is not just the premier epistemic value; it is the *sole* and *unqualified* epistemic value (though it is, of course, dependent on truth). Knowledge is the goal; it is good, and the more the better. And the more widely it is possessed, the better: the greatest knowledge for the greatest number, one might say. My third point is that we have just discussed circumstances in which *not knowing* is right and sometimes good (chapter 7). Taking account of such ignorance is quite possible with a virtues epistemology framework, but only if we introduce the possibility that judicious ignorance has value within a community too. Once we do that, we can include such candidates for epistemic virtue as discretion, caution, and keeping one's counsel, along with vices such as blabbing, nosiness, and the propensity to offer (in Internet parlance) TMI—"too much information."

Adding these three dimensions expands the promise of virtue epistemology. In this chapter, I propose to extend this discussion by examining received claims for various virtues and vices of ignorance. To begin, let us turn to a contested attribute (and incidentally, another trait that never appeared on my report cards): curiosity.

Curiosity

Curiosity may refer to an ephemeral, occurrent attitude or emotion, or it may denote a stable quality of character. It is the difference between, say, a passing curiosity about the price of a luxury car and the trait of being naturally curious about the world. A suitable definition for the ephemeral usage of *curiosity* is "having a focused or eager desire to know *X*." The trait of curiosity could be interpreted simply as the *tendency* to display occurrent curiosity, but it is more informative to define it as "a general inquisitiveness or interest in knowledge, explanation, and understanding." To put it in our reverse language, both senses of the term refer to *the desire to remove ignorance*. So, is curiosity an epistemic virtue or a vice?

In Classical Greece and Rome, curiosity (*periergia* in Greek; *curiositas* in Latin) was generally considered a vice,[6] though we might identify three separate conceptions. In the first, curiosity is a vulgar character flaw, identified with snooping, eavesdropping, peeping, and pursuing useless inquiries (what we might call *idle curiosity*), and usually accompanied by gossiping, blabbing, and voyeurism. The second interpretation exploits the etymological entanglement between the Greek word for curiosity, *periergia*, and *perierga*, which means *strange*. It highlights the strangeness that arouses our curiosity and the accompanying danger it portends, often through myths and morality tales: Pandora's curiosity releases all life's evils; Psyche's obsessive curiosity results in successive, dire plights; and the metamorphosed Lucius's picaresque sojourn as a donkey is precipitated by his curiosity about magic spells.[7] Especially when directed to the dark arts or to forbidden knowledge, curiosity can kill.

The third conception regards curiosity as a sin. This seems to begin with the Stoics, but once adopted by early Christians like Tertullian, it greatly influenced Christian theology for centuries. The core idea is that the only knowledge that is worthwhile is knowledge that pertains to the Divine, including one's own conduct in relation to God. All other knowledge is useless; to pursue it is vanity; and curiosity about it is sinful. It is difficult to find a Christian theologian from this long period who doesn't condemn curiosity, though Augustine and Thomas Aquinas seek to distinguish *intellectual* curiosity from its more vulgar forms. Thomists, more Aristotelian in spirit than Stoic, usually attempt to identify subject matter that is worthy of learning—studies of nature, practical studies, studies useful for governance, and so on. To pursue literary studies, liberal arts, theoretical studies without practical import, was for many theologians a form of misdirected, perhaps sinful, curiosity.

Modernists, however, tilt toward judging curiosity a virtue, indeed the key epistemic virtue. Proto-modernist Thomas Hobbes thought that curiosity—"the desire to know why and how"—was found "in no living creature but Man," and therefore humankind was "distinguished not only by his Reason, but also by this singular Passion."[8] And curiosity is valuable: for the Enlightenment, curiosity is the motive force of scientific inquiry and its patiently systematic advancement of our knowledge of the world. In wresting secrets from Nature, we will not find unless we are moved to seek. Not only "natural philosophers," but also progressive educators prize intellectual curiosity and work to arouse it in those who seem uninterested in learning.[9]

The deepest etymological roots of *curiosity* lead to the Latin word *cura* (care).[10] To be curious is to care about what lies beyond the boundary of our knowing. As *eros* is the yearning for beauty, so *curiosity* is the yearning for truth. But like erotic love, epistemic love can include the vulgar, the dangerous, and the wrongful. Moreover, the urge to tell can overcome discretion.

There is wonderful moment in Berthold Brecht's play, *Galileo*, a garden scene in which a "Little Priest," despite his training in physics, urges Galileo to repress his desire to know and to publish things that will only disturb long-held beliefs and rile the peaceful order. Galileo, serpent in the Garden, tempts the priest with his manuscript on the tides: "Here is writ what draws the ocean when it ebbs and flows. Let it lie there. Thou shalt not read."[11] But of course the priest can't resist and picks up the text. Galileo gloats, "Already! An apple of the tree of knowledge, he can't wait, he wolfs it down. He will rot in Hell for all eternity." But then, in words that echo Plato's cave, he offers poignant self-recognition: "Sometimes I think I would let them imprison me in a place a thousand feet beneath the earth, where no light could reach me, if in exchange I could find out what stuff that is: 'Light.' The bad thing is that, when I find something, I have to boast about it like a lover or a drunkard or a traitor. That is a hopeless vice, and leads to the abyss."

Epistemic Restraint

It is not surprising that an epistemic disposition like curiosity is subject to moral concerns. The intense desire to discover (and to tell) can become obsessive, and its persistence is tainted when it is directed toward subjects that are forbidden, dangerous, worthless, or that should be occluded by the privacy of others. And if its satisfaction, the truth gained and told, is likely to be deeply disruptive of the established order, curiosity is discouraged by those in power and a curtain of willful ignorance may fall—as Galileo witnessed in his trial and subsequent prohibition against publication. But skepticism regarding establishmentarian censorship is wise. We know that moral currency is widely counterfeited, and a halo of pious rhetoric often hides the real motive and value of the claims. There is no substitute for practical wisdom in these matters. Traits of character form an ecology: the value of curiosity, like other traits, is shaped by its relationship to other traits and circumstances.

The philosopher Neil Manson identified the four factors I applied in discussing epistemic ethics: *process*, *content*, *purpose*, and *context*. I used them in the evaluation of knowledge, but Manson introduced them as factors that affect the virtuousness or viciousness of curiosity.[12] Recall that *process* refers to the means of pursuit and acquisition of knowledge. No doubt, curiosity may be dangerous because of the methods employed, the authorities disrupted, the activities involved (such as intrusive prying), or because of collateral, damaging revelations that come with success. One might imagine a journalist's investigation, for example, that involves all of these elements. But the process of curious inquiry may also display intellectual courage, brilliant research technique, dogged effort, and a judiciousness that avoids jumping to conclusions.[13]

The *content* of the knowledge sought may be ethically significant independent of the methods used to acquire it: it may be forbidden or restricted or hazardous in itself; it may worthless, trivial, or disgusting; or it may be knowledge that, however acquired, is awkward because it violates privacy or confidentiality. There are also opportunity costs in the acquisition of knowledge, and the quality of one's judgment about what knowledge is worth pursuing can reveal epistemic virtues and vices. There is epistemic virtue in the astute selection of promising lines of research over blind alleys. We might imagine a virtue—in my old report card's language, "uses time wisely"—which polarizes an opposing vice: the unwise use of learning time, such as spending hours to acquire information about the affairs of the cast of a reality show instead of, oh, learning about the Civil War or pursuing research on cancer. Curiosity, in short, is tainted when it is directed at unworthy content.

The *purpose* one has in seeking knowledge is also significant. Thomas Aquinas observed that "those who study to learn something in order to sin are engaged in a sinful study."[14] This is a case of the ends infecting the means. If we replace "sinful" with "morally wrong," we can surely find cases that fit Aquinas's category. Manson gives us the case of two researchers who are studying whether ingesting a certain substance will cause pain. One has the vicious purpose of finding a more effective means of torturing captives for his brutal state's regime; the other is seeking a cure for bowel cancer and wants to minimize side effects—a virtuous purpose.[15]

Context includes the many aspects I listed earlier (chapter 7), including our relationships and roles; the epistemic rights and responsibilities of others; the immediate social context and the protocols of the relevant epistemic community. Manson gives several excellent examples of how these facts can poison even an otherwise pure desire to know, but I will summarize only one here: A man who is curious about the value of a porcelain figurine he owns proceeds to ask detailed questions of an expert (so far, a reasonable desire to know), but he does this while the expert is grieving at the funeral for his young daughter (an inappropriate social context for the pursuit of this information).[16] His lack of sensitivity and judgment taints his curiosity.

As Manson notes, even a thoroughgoing analysis of curiosity as vice and virtue still focuses on the desire to gain knowledge. He champions an alternative virtue directed toward ignorance, which he calls *epistemic restraint.* This is not a virtue in how we form beliefs (like open-mindedly weighing evidence and noting its reach, assuring consistency with known truths, or judging the credibility of testimony); it is rather a virtue that values *not desiring to know* (*not pursuing knowledge, not knowing*) and seeks to protect ignorance when it is appropriate. To celebrate epistemic restraint is not to endorse anti-intellectualism or to reject scientific inquiry. But it does challenge the simplistic view that the desire to know is always and everywhere a good and proper motive, and the assumption that acquiring knowledge is to be valued without reference to methods or content or context. In short, Manson builds into the conception of epistemic restraint proper sensitivity to the ethical issues of process, content, purpose, and context—issues that are left open in the neutral concept of curiosity.

Discretion

Discretion is a virtue that primarily concerns the protection and sharing of knowledge and ignorance, rather than the pursuit of knowledge or the formation of belief. With etymological roots in the ability to separate or distinguish, *discretion* refers to a moral discernment, the power to make salient distinctions in social contexts. Thus a discreet person is one who avoids speaking or behaving in such a way as to violate privacy or confidentiality or to cause offense, except for due cause; she has sensitivity to and sound judgment regarding the ethical issues that arise in the relationships of an epistemic community.

One who is discreet appreciates the occasional value of ignorance, or at least the value of keeping one's counsel and of certain people *not knowing* particular things at a specific time. The intent is not to manipulate people, but to serve ethical as well as the epistemic guidelines. Discretion will occasionally require resistance to requests for information, to the prying efforts of busybodies, and to the sharing of dangerous knowledge with inappropriate individuals. It will reject not only improper divulgence of information, but also the attempt to gain social status through what one knows and will or will not tell. The heart of this virtue is good judgment in epistemic interactions.

Looking even so briefly at discretion reminds us yet again that epistemic virtues and vices are manifested by individuals in an epistemic community. The value of discretion or epistemic restraint, for example, will not appear when one attends only to the solo search for knowledge. And both epistemic restraint and discretion show that ignorance may be valued in epistemic interactions.

Trust

Sissela Bok has written, "*Whatever* matters to human beings, trust is the atmosphere in which it thrives."[17] Her wise observation includes what matters to us epistemically as well. Our epistemic interactions thrive when we can trust our sources and informants, and they us; when we can rely on the discretion of others, and they on ours; when we trust each other to carry out our epistemic obligations—and when such trust is justified.

"Trust" can be a noun or a verb; that is, *trust* can be a state or an action. Trust and doubt both arise within ignorance. To trust is to extend credibility and forgo continual verification or justification;[18] to doubt is to deny credibility absent compelling independent evidence or proof. Trust not only arises in ignorance (if I know certain information myself, I do not need to trust another's testimony regarding it); trust extends both confident credence and ignorance: if one partner trusts another, he does not continually ascertain his partner's whereabouts, corroborate claims, or search possessions. To trust is to be willingly vulnerable. If my trust is misplaced, I have opened myself to exploitation, hurt, and loss. It is the willingness of trust that makes poignant the vulnerability of ignorance.

Most of our knowledge comes from others. Yet "testimony," as epistemologists call information received from others, is somewhat devalued in traditional theory because it is second-hand. (Recall the emphasis on the solo, autonomous knower.) In an epistemic community, however, we rely— indeed we must rely—on the testimony of others. Skeptics refuse. But no one has the time or energy or will to track down and personally verify all the information one must use in a day. My calendar this morning claims it is Lincoln's birthday. Just imagine what it would take to verify just that one claim first-hand. Instead, I rely on what my fourth grade teacher told me, what my calendar reports, what the Internet sources or textbooks state, or what a Lincoln scholar says. But all of these sources provide mediated knowledge. Even scientists who seek first-hand information must rely on the knowledge provided by other scientists, including those in other disciplines, and on the engineers who designed their instruments. For the epistemic good, we work on trust, extending at least initial credence to those who teach and tell us. Knowledge thrives in a trustworthy environment, which involves the acceptance, even the affirmation, of ignorance.

Unfortunately, this also means that epistemic communities are vulnerable, and indeed they are—to fraud, misinformation, rumor, outright lies and subtler deceptions, exaggeration, secrecy, incompetence, and violations of privacy and confidentiality. Political discourse has been poisoned by all of these sins and, as a result, trust in political discourse has withered. It is now very difficult for even truthful political claims to be believed. The integrity of science is threatened by premature publication, fraudulent data, biased research, sensational claims, and retracted conclusions. Those who reject inconvenient scientific conclusions, such as evolution or climate change, engage in doubt-mongering, which undermines the trust in science generally and fosters ignorance. A once-trusted friend caught in an important lie will not be trusted again. Sadly, restoring trust is more difficult than earning trust in the first place.

It is prudent, of course, to extend trust cautiously based on knowledge; but, in the end, trust (like faith) is a commitment one makes, a risk one decides to take; it creates a sphere in which epistemic standards are relaxed and sharing knowledge becomes more efficient. But being trustful is always perilously close to being gullible. Being trustworthy, however, requires epistemic competence and a set of epistemic virtues. The prudent person reduces the risk that comes with ignorance, one element of which is to trust only the trustworthy. As we shall see (chapter 10), we have developed numerous instruments and techniques to reduce the risk associated with trust, either by certifying trustworthiness or bypassing the need for trust.

One might perhaps confuse trust with willful ignorance, since both involve the voluntary acceptance of ignorance. But willful ignorance involves a resistance to knowing; it arises from fear; it often entails self-deception or false knowledge; and it discounts contrary evidence. Epistemic trust is not resistant to knowledge; it requires a minor form of courage; it involves a commitment not to seek evidence; and it can be broken by contrary evidence. Both are painful when broken.

Intellectual Humility

To this point, we have not focused on the arena of the *application* of knowledge for epistemic virtues and vices. To that end, I want to look at another recent work on ignorance: *The Virtues of Ignorance: Complexity, Sustainability, and the Limits of Knowledge*, a collection of essays edited by Bill Vitek and Wes Jackson.[19] Because it summarizes the message of this unified anthology nicely, I will quote from the dustjacket for the book:

> The contributors argue that uncritical faith in scientific knowledge has created many of the problems now threatening the planet and that our wholesale reliance on scientific progress is both untenable and myopic. ... [They] offer profound arguments for the advantage of an ignorance-based worldview. ... All conclude that we must simply accept the proposition that our ignorance far exceeds our knowledge and always will. Rejecting the belief that science and technology are benignly at the service of society, the authors argue that recognizing ignorance might be the only path to reliable knowledge.

The summary is accurate and informative, and I wish to mark several points:

(1) The book is primarily concerned with the *application* of knowledge in determining public policy, especially regarding practices and decisions that affect the natural environment and shape the built environment. It is also true, however, that they argue that "recognizing ignorance might be the only path to reliable knowledge," which is a claim about inquiry. (2) The authors are concerned with an epistemic vice: the overconfidence in what we know, especially as seen in our undue reliance on science and technology. They charge that this has resulted in policies and practices that are ineffective, and—often because of unintended consequences— self-defeating, and disastrous for the environment and human society. (3) Reliable knowledge, as distinguished from false knowledge and belief, remains their ultimate goal. (4) The authors advocate an "ignorance-based" worldview, but this seems to amount to recognizing our ignorance.[20] In practice, this means developing and implementing policies with caution and alertness to side effects, long-term implications, unintended consequences, opportunity costs, sustainability, and so on. Although they do not provide detailed strategies for mapping relevant ignorance (and recall the difficulty of determining "relevant" ignorance), they do argue that "those who hold an ignorance-based view" actually learn more. (5) It is

the recognition of ignorance that is virtuous in this presentation, not the ignorance itself; despite its provocative title, the real virtue lauded here is *intellectual humility*. And for that, the authors collectively make a compelling case.

It seems clear that the intellectual humility that follows from recognition of our own ignorance is an epistemic virtue. It is unwise in pursuing knowledge on one's own or in one's epistemic interactions to be arrogant, overconfident, judgmental, or resistant to new information and correction—and the same is true when we apply our knowledge.

Modesty as a Virtue of Ignorance

A traditional virtue with a subtle connection to humility is *modesty*. In this case, the etymological roots trace back to the Latin, *modus*, which means "measure or manner" and its derivative, *modestia*, which means "moderation or prudent conduct." But it is with Christianity that *modesty* becomes a self-regarding, self-effacing virtue distinct from moderation. Perhaps because Aristotle saw all virtues as forms of moderation that avoided excesses and insufficiencies, or because of the lingering influence of the warrior hero image, he had not regarded personal modesty as a virtue.

In a paper published in 1989, Julia Driver argued that modesty is, as her title termed it, one of "The Virtues of Ignorance."[21] What she means by this, and the argument she makes for it, is worth our attention here, and it has generated several lively rebuttals. She claims that modesty is a virtue that depends on, indeed requires, ignorance. Her argument proceeds as follows:

1. Virtues require practical wisdom (*phronesis*), a blend of sensitivity to context, self-reflection, and sound judgment that enables one, in Aristotle's formulation, to do the right thing, at the right time, for the right reason, and in the right way. It is through practical wisdom that the courageous or generous or honorable act is determined.

2. Modesty is a virtue. (This is certainly a mainstream view today, even if there are dissenters. Presumably—though Driver does not say so— modesty is like all other virtues in appearing within an ecology of virtues and being subject to moral constraints. There also may be noxious forms—just as nosiness is a noxious form of curiosity.)

3. But modesty is a *disposition to underestimate one's self-worth*. (This characterization of modesty opens the door for Driver's main point.)

4. Therefore, *modesty requires ignorance*, specifically, the ignorance of one's own worth; along with systematic error, namely, the continual underestimation of one's worth. Modesty must be based on a genuine (not feigned) ignorance of one's worth, Driver claims, because otherwise it would be hypocrisy—a deliberately false projection of one's worth, and a vice, not a virtue.

5. We hear the utterance "I am modest" as oddly self-contradictory. That is because the statement asserts my self-awareness (knowledge) that I consistently err about my self-worth, which requires a lack of awareness (ignorance). It conceals a paradox.

6. Practical wisdom would, in fact, undermine modesty, because it would achieve a *sound* assessment of one's own worth. Therefore, Driver claims, if modesty is a virtue, we must reject the first proposition above: *phronesis* is not, in fact, necessary for all virtues; and for a certain type—the "virtues of ignorance"—it is detrimental. (The only alternative would be to deny that modesty is a virtue.)

7. She claims the class of "virtues of ignorance" also includes *blind charity*, a "virtue of thought" in which one sees only the good in people, not the bad. It is a disposition not to see flaws or defects, but to focus on the virtues of persons. For blind charity, ignorance of the negative aspects of persons is an essential element. (To me, it seems more like a virtue of *ignoring* than a virtue of ignorance—if indeed it is a virtue at all.)

Driver thus has laid out a provocative position that bristles with points of controversy. I join several philosophical critics in wondering: *why, under her account, is modesty a virtue*? How is it different from error, self-deception, or illusion? Why is it not simply a recurring epistemic mistake?

Most readers agree with her observation (5) that there is something odd about asserting "I am modest"; but most respondents have disagreed with her characterization (4) of modesty as the systematic underestimation of self-worth. And some have noted that her account of blind charity is also troublesome and might even describe a vice more than a virtue.

Owen Flanagan responded quickly.[22] He argues that Driver makes an important but false claim when she says there is a class of virtues such that "If the agent knows that she has the virtue, she does not." He claims that the oddness of "I am modest" is a performative oddity, not one of direct self-contradiction. In fact, he argues, a person can be genuinely modest and know it, but the occasions and circumstances under which it would be appropriate to assert it are rather limited. Bragging that one is modest *would* be self-contradictory. Although Flanagan accepts Driver's analytical framework of modesty as related to evaluation of self-worth, he takes the position that it is a disposition *not to overestimate* one's self-worth. Therefore, error and ignorance are not entailed. Just the opposite: modesty requires epistemic restraint (to impose Manson's term) and practical wisdom; it arises from the desire not to overreach, not to exaggerate or overstate one's worth or accomplishments.

George Frederick Schueler had an interesting exchange with Driver in the late 1990s.[23] Schueler also found her account of modesty to be problematic. He counters with the case of the third-best physicist in the world who thought he was the fifth-best physicist and regularly bragged about it: on Driver's account, he would be a modest man, consistently underestimating his accomplishments. Schueler, however, rejected estimation-of-self-worth theories—both Driver's and Flanagan's—arguing that modesty is the *lack of desire to be evaluated for one's accomplishments*. Thus, it is not tied to error and ignorance.

Nicolas Bommarito offered a different interpretation: modesty is "a virtue of attention" that directs one's attention away from one's own accomplishments and toward other matters.[24] It is, therefore, a matter not of self-knowledge or ignorance, but of where one places one's attention and concern.

My quick sketch of these positions cannot do justice to the richness of this dialogue (nor to other participants),[25] but suffice it to say that Driver has generally reaffirmed her arguments in rebuttals to her respondents. Nonetheless, I do not find her account of modesty satisfactory. Modesty is not a virtue of ignorance. I too reject the interpretation of modesty as a systematic estimation error based on ignorance of one's self-worth, and the notion that such a trait could be a virtue. While there are virtues that require *recognition* of one's ignorance, such as humility, I do not believe there are virtues that *rest on* ignorance, or virtues that exist only if one is ignorant that one possesses them.

Precisely the same issues arise with the cardinal virtue, wisdom. It seems a kind of contradiction or performative oddity to say "I am wise." But that is because it would not be wise to assert one's wisdom. It does not require that the wise person make the systematic error of underestimating her own understanding. And it does not mean that one is not wise unless one is ignorant of one's wisdom. Wisdom surely requires knowing what one understands and what one does not—and acknowledging the factor of unknown unknowns.

The Virtuously Ignorant Schoolmaster

An unusual and bold claim for the virtue of ignorance is made by the French postmodernist philosopher Jacques Rancière, in a fascinating work titled, *The Ignorant Schoolmaster: Five Lessons in Intellectual Emancipation*.[26] As he later commented, his book takes "a most unreasonable position: That the most important quality of a schoolmaster is the virtue of ignorance."[27]

Rancière recounts the story of Joseph Jacotot, a teacher who created "quite a scandal in the Holland and France of the 1830s." Jacotot was assigned to teach French to students who spoke only Flemish—a language he himself did not know. He found a bilingual text and, with the help of an interpreter, told the students to read the first half of the text, using the translation, and to rehearse repeatedly what they had learned; then they should read the second half of the book briskly, ending by writing *in French* what they had learned. He was amazed at the result: without directly imparting any knowledge to his students, they had learned to express themselves in French remarkably well. Jacotot proceeded to "teach" other subjects of which he was ignorant in the same way—and claimed to achieve similar success. He reached the provocative conclusion that one who is ignorant might enable another who is ignorant to come to know something previously unknown to both. He declared and promoted this approach as an emancipatory method of "universal education." A good teacher is virtuously ignorant.

Set aside the empirical questions of whether such a method works for all students and all subjects (for these are outside our concern), and turn instead to the claim that it is an "emancipatory" pedagogy. Traditionally, teaching is viewed as the attempt to transmit knowledge (possessed by the teacher) to the ignorant (the pupils); the acquisition of this knowledge is liberating for the students. Thus, knowing facilitates explanations that convey understanding, which is then emancipating—or so the standard view claims, according to Jacotot and Rancière. In actuality, they say, this transmission of knowledge is an imperialism of intellect, a coercion of the pupils' minds into established patterns of thought to obtain the "correct" answers and proficiency as judged by the teacher. They point out (a now familiar point) that those who know have power over those who are ignorant, exhibited even in the ascription of their ignorance; and teaching-as-transmission-of-knowledge is an official imposition of that power. The result of knowledge-based teaching is, in fact, stultifying, not liberating.

This is not to be understood as a rediscovery of the Socratic method, according to Rancière, which he regards as questioning based on a *feigned* ignorance that is designed to elicit a response already known to the master. Jacotot's pedagogy, by contrast, relies on the *genuine* ignorance of the "master." There is a disconnection between what the schoolmaster knows and the knowledge he facilitates—and indeed the teacher may not certify the "correctness" of the outcome, says Rancière. (One may wonder how Jacotot knew that his innovative method succeeded.) Both men laud this pedagogy as proceeding under the assumption of human equality, the postulate that teacher and student are equal in their ability to learn and to understand, rather than the traditional model of the teacher's epistemic authority and superiority. It is thus a truly emancipatory education.

For Rancière, the implications are larger than pedagogical strategy: his analysis is a key part of a larger postmodernist political critique and a "new logic of emancipation."[28] The freedom that democracy promises is not something one person can give another; all genuine emancipation is ultimately self-emancipation. Those who would attempt to emancipate us through knowledge—like the unnamed liberator of the prisoner in Plato's Cave and perhaps the serpent in the Garden—do the opposite. They exercise the epistemic power of master over disciple, and they proffer cognitive enslavement by leading us to adopt their own truth.

The American philosopher Richard Rorty famously contrasted the right and left views of education, saying that those on the right begin with truth, saying "Know the Truth, and the truth shall set you free," while those on the left put freedom first, saying "Assure freedom, and the truth will take care of itself."[29] For Rancière, however, it is equality, especially the equality of human intelligence, which must be presumed, though we can never know it to be true. Freedom cannot be assured anyway; it must be earned. His is undoubtedly a utopian vision: "We can thus dream of a society of the emancipated that would be a society of artists. Such a society would repudiate the division between those who know and those who don't, between those who possess or don't possess the property of intelligence."[30]

A related theme seems to inform Alejandro González Iñárritu's film, *Birdman: Or (The Unexpected Virtue of Ignorance)*. In its multilayered plot, the protagonist, Riggan Thomson, is a wasted actor whose signature movie role was a superhero, Birdman. Riggan is delusional, hallucinatory, and tormented by the mocking, inner voice of Birdman; he is unable to find love. To resuscitate his career, he pursues the wild idea of writing, acting, and directing a Broadway production. Lacking relevant experience—his lead actor says Riggan doesn't even know what his own play is about—he perseveres: in defiance of critics and despite numerous disasters, fights, and a suicide attempt, the play goes forward. Amazingly, from ignorance, Riggan has created a masterpiece. Its creativity and superrealistic power could not have come from those who are knowledgeable, experienced, and expert in the realities of Broadway production.[31]

But let us return to Rancière's schoolmaster and zoom in on the "virtue of ignorance." I understand Rancière's central claims to be: (a) paradoxically, a teacher's state of ignorance about the subject matter is conducive to student learning—provided the right method is used; (b) the effect of ignorance-based teaching is genuinely "emancipatory," whereas knowledge-based teaching is cognitively enslaving; and (c) ignorance is therefore a virtue in teaching.

In evaluating these claims, I want to be cautious and not let the conclusion drawn outstrip the evidence (to apply another epistemic virtue). Let us assume that Jacotot's account of his pedagogical success is factual, and (this is more of a stretch) that the method is universally effective with students. The method he advocates involves the teacher's genuine ignorance of the subject matter (not ignorance in general); the provision of modest resources for self-teaching (in his original case, a bilingual text); and students' engagement in independent and self-directed learning activities.

What triggered Jacotot's discovery of this method was his complete ignorance of the language his students spoke—he did, of course, know French, the targeted language. He shifted in later experiments to his ignorance of the targeted subject matter. One might wonder: would not the method work just as well if the teacher were to *feign* ignorance, hypocrisy aside? If the method has a distinctive genius, would it not lie in the teacher's activities, the nature of the assignments given the students, and the forms of acceptable learning outcomes—not in the teacher's lack of knowledge? Rancière rejects this, claiming that a teacher who feigns ignorance will not be able to restrain the impulse to correct and explain, to subtly direct the students to preestablished learning goals. But even genuine ignorance alone seems insufficient to accomplish emancipatory learning as Rancière describes it; one needs the rest of the pedagogy Jacotot describes. Suppose one argues as follows, which I believe Rancière does: because ignorance of the subject can contribute to emancipatory teaching, the way to achieve that is to assure the teacher's ignorance of the subject. This is a variety of the *post hoc ergo propter hoc* fallacy, assuming causality from sequence. Just as although a truck always sounds a beeping warning before it reverses, we cannot deduce that the beeping causes the truck to reverse, so we cannot conclude the students learned *because* the teacher was ignorant of the subject matter.

Then there is that shift in Jacotot's examples. In the original case of teaching French to Flemish-speaking students, Jacotot was surprised at his success; but he knew he was successful *precisely because he knew French himself.* It was Flemish he did not know. He was not, in other words, ignorant of the target subject; in fact, he applied his knowledge in selecting the bilingual textbook and in evaluating students' written work. But he then began to target subjects of which he was ignorant, and it is then that the issue of determining what *success* might mean becomes complicated. What are the self-evident markers of genuine learning that the ignorant schoolmaster discerned in his students? Did he rely on student self-assessment? Must one invoke experts to assess the outcome? How does one know that genuine learning has occurred? Rancière wants to avoid prescribing learning goals in advance, allowing for multiple valid outcomes. But the question remains: on what basis can one affirm the success of this method? And if these questions still seem tainted with a colonialism of thought, is it even possible, under Rancière's account, to retain a goal of gaining any genuine knowledge; or is the very concept of knowledge antithetical to the emancipation of thought he seeks? If we give up the concept of knowledge, we lose the concept of ignorance as well.

The radical pedagogy Rancière prescribes requires the presumption of equal intelligence. There is, as a result, no individualized teaching, no reason to address any student's special needs or skills, no chance to harness personal interests. All instructional feedback is viewed as didactic correction. The energy that can emanate from a teacher's enthusiasm for a subject is banned. Beyond providing a prompt, the method thereafter is reduced to independent study.[32]

Nevertheless, so much seems perceptive and important in Rancière's text: his critique of didacticism as the model of teaching; his framing of explication as an exercise of the power of knowledge over ignorance; his insistence on the epistemic potential of the teacher and every pupil; his demand for emancipation through learning coupled with an alertness to the stultifying effects of teaching for "correctness"; and his insight into the relationship of education and political life. Implicitly, he has revealed the ways in which knowledge defines ignorance. Though he and Jacotot have shown how ignorance may sometimes be liberating for a teacher (and students), that does not elevate it to a virtue for teachers. It is rather that the state of ignorance may sometimes release the virtues and suppress the vices of teaching.

Epistemic Achievement

Given the discussions of this and the previous chapter, an adequate regulative epistemology should guide us not only in the acquisition of knowledge, but in the construction, imposition, and protection of ignorance. It should guide our epistemic interactions within communities, not just in our solo pursuit of knowledge. Gaining knowledge is often an achievement that requires skillful use of our cognitive faculties and epistemic virtues; it usually relies on others. But, although I am reluctant to call ignorance an achievement, its wise recognition, construction, protection, imposition, and divulgence may require skillful use of our faculties and epistemic virtues. Indeed, some virtues, like intellectual humility, discretion, and trust, are possible only *in relation to* ignorance. Some of these are possible only in epistemic interactions with others. Ignorance has its uses, but wisdom and virtue lie in our actions regarding it. Being ignorant per se is not a virtue.[33]

IV   Ignorance as Limit

Bounds ... always presuppose a space existing outside a definite place and inclosing it; limits do not require this, but are mere negations which affect a quantity so far as it is not absolutely complete.

—Immanuel Kant

9   The Limits of the Knowable

Human reason has this peculiar fate that in one species of its knowledge it is burdened by questions which, as prescribed by the very nature of reason itself, it is not able to ignore, but which, as transcending all its powers, it is also not able to answer.
—Immanuel Kant

Immanuel Kant distinguished between a boundary (*Grenze*) and a limit (*Schranke*): "Bounds (in extended beings) always presuppose a space existing outside a certain definite place and inclosing it; limits do not require this, but are mere negations which affect a quantity so far as it is not absolutely complete."[1] It is his distinction I have in mind in thinking of ignorance as the limit of knowledge. A boundary encloses and incorporates a place; it implies that which it excludes, that which lies outside, on the other side of the border. We can map our ignorance when we know the location of the boundary, which also means we mark what is beyond the border. But when something has a limit, there is no intimation of what lies beyond except as a negativity. There is only a sense of something having run its course, finish and exhaustion, the end, whether in completion or incompleteness.

There is such a limit to what we can know. In that respect, ignorance is the negativity of the knowable. What is knowable in practice and what is knowable in principle: both have their limits. These limits apply to us as individuals, both at any given moment and over any interval, including our lifetime; they apply to all humankind, at any historical moment and in our span as a species. Knowing about limits to our knowledge, to the extent we can, is a form of metaknowledge. It involves knowing, in a general sense, what sorts of things are knowable and what sorts are unknowable; and it aspires to know when everything *is* known regarding a particular domain.

Completion is one way to reach a limit. It is a form of perfection. The collector strives for completion of her collection, the full set that represents its elusive limit. Omniscience would be the outermost limit of the knowable: everything would be known that could be known. Omniscience is, of course, one of the traditional perfections of God: the comprehension of the totality of truth.

There was a time when scientific minds spoke of the ideal of a "completed science," a science that would explain all phenomena. One interpretation of this ideal was cartographic: scientific investigation maps reality, and that map would be complete when it mapped everything—presumably including the map itself. But, of course, an ideal atlas of this sort is a myth, an impossibility. A map that included everything exactly would be isomorphic with reality, a duplicate of reality itself. A more plausible interpretation is explanatory completeness, yet that too would require more than we can deliver: knowledge of all the laws of nature, all the entities, individuals, and states of the world. Nonetheless, if we could achieve this ideal, we would have reached the limits of knowledge—we would have explained all that is explainable.

A second way to reach a limit is simply to come to an end of resources or options, to finish what is available, to exhaust capacity. This has no implication of completeness or perfection; indeed, it suggests incompleteness. It implies an actualization constrained to a subset, not a full set. For instance, there is a maximum number of miles I can drive my car on a full tank of gas; I have reached the limit when the tank is empty. The genealogical reconstruction of my family tree has a limit: it is the earliest relevant surviving document. (Note that I haven't driven *all* the miles possible or identified *all* my ancestors.) In chapter 6, I proposed an estimated limit to the maximum number of books one could read in a lifetime. (If my goal were to read all of Trollope's novels, however, I could *complete* the task—and reach a limit in the first sense.)

Both these senses are applicable to knowledge. My concern here will not be to list the specifics of our limits to the knowable—an impossible task that would only exemplify my point. It is rather to identify the types of limits and their sources, to identify the ways in which the knowledge acquirable by individuals, and even by the grandest of epistemic communities, is forever limited and incomplete.

Temporality

When we speak of knowledge, it seems a possession, an object that persists (though an abstract entity). When we think of knowing, however, it seems to be a private mental state. It is a gerund, more than a participle: if I'm asked, "What are you doing?" it would be odd to reply, "I'm knowing X." Knowing is obscured from our inspection, so we detect it through other cognitive processes, such as recalling, identifying, expressing, applying, and so on. Knowledge presupposes knowing, and knowing is a state that occurs in time. The temporality of our knowing limits what we can know. There is a time before and after we live, and a time before and after we know. Whenever we live, whenever we know, much of the past and future are unknown and unknowable to us.

For thousands of years, humans have encoded their experience and recorded it in durable objects. These texts, images, recordings, and objects preserve past experience for transmission to the future. Over time, we developed institutions that collect, store, catalog, and share this precious cultural legacy, from physical libraries and museums to their digitized analogues.

We have not, unfortunately, been able to preserve all aspects of experience equally well. Language, and especially written language, permitted the encoding of all sorts of experience; but any language is limited by its syntax and its vocabulary. "*The limits of my language* means the limits of my world," said Ludwig Wittgenstein.[2] And rendering experience into language involves transformation: we can develop a rich vocabulary to designate smells, for example, but rendering them in language does not preserve the smells.[3] Similarly, forms of notation were developed to record salient aspects of music, but notation has no sound; it took many centuries before we could capture sounds. Some smells, sounds, and sights are gone forever. And motion is only suggested by static drawings. Preserved "moving pictures" and recorded musical performances have been available to us only for little more than a century. The sense of touch still lacks a technology of preservation; and holding on to tastes requires reassembling from preserved recipes and ingredients.

Since I live when I do, I fortunately can know many things about the past; my knowing the past includes not only *knowing that* but also cases of *knowing what it is like*. I can see images of my grandfather from before I was born; I can enjoy musical performances recorded decades before I lived. But there are limits. Though I may know important facts about my great-great-grandfather, I will never see his face. None of us will never hear Chopin or Mozart or Bach at the keyboard; never inhale the "Great Stink" of London or the fragrance of extinct flowers; never watch the debut of Euripides's plays or see Nijinsky dance. Barring time travel, the unrecorded past will remain but a dim conjecture.

History must be reconstructed from ruins because what survives is often incomplete. We must interpret Aristotle's thought from the one-third or so of his works that have, by chance, survived. Unrecorded facts, records that have perished, facts kept secret—all lie beyond the reach of our knowing. The destruction of nearly all the 1890 United States Census records by fire is an unfortunate and permanent loss of information. Luck is a determinant of what can be known about the past (despite the strictures of epistemology, which deny that genuine knowledge can derive from luck). Our knowledge of the past and therefore our ignorance of it—even more than we might know—are matters of luck. Knowable facts about the past, not just sensations, are therefore limited. We will never know, for example, the identity of the last female gladiator to die in Rome's Colosseum.

Sometimes human actions are responsible for the loss. As I write these words, the self-declared Islamic State (ISIS) is determinedly destroying archaeological treasures, tombstones, and local historical records. We may have recorded images, but the objects are destroyed. The Nazis notoriously destroyed many works by artists they considered "decadent." And, of course, beyond such perishing, there is all of "prehuman history," a time from which we can have no human artifacts, a time we can imagine only from grand inferences and extrapolations based mostly on geological and paleontological studies.

But hold on! Doesn't it seem brash to declare anything permanently unknowable? Who can say that new evidence won't appear? Think of the recent discovery of Richard III's remains and how much was learned from what was previously thought to be lost forever. Recall the impact of the discovery of one of Aristotle's lost works, *The Constitution of the Athenians*, on papyri in the late 1800s. How can one confidently assert that any facts are lost forever?

There is certainly some truth in this point. Innovations in technology can open up new lines of inquiry and confirmation—DNA analysis is a prime example. We are, of course, becoming more sophisticated in our methods of detection, recovery, reconstruction, and preservation, and also in our techniques of inference from disparate data and simulation. But we cannot recover all the facts of the past, create records that were never made, or capture works that were obliterated. An enormous number of facts about the past, including many of great significance, will surely lie beyond our reach forever.

The epistemic loss produced by the flow of time derives from ontological loss: knowledge has limits because worlds disappear. Some contemporary physicists propose that our universe is a hologram, in which no information is lost. This is a vision that sees the unity of the universe in the prehension of events, the past and future embedded in each other. But even if the conservation of information is true, information is not knowledge.

All loss, especially loss without memory, can be terrifying. For the philosopher Alfred North Whitehead, loss is the ultimate evil, beyond our ability to prevent or ameliorate. He writes, "The world is thus faced by the paradox that, at least in its higher actualities, it craves for novelty and yet is haunted by terror at the loss of the past, with its familiarities and its loved ones."[4] It may seem odd that Whitehead, a philosopher who made process more basic than substance, should find the prospect of losing the past in the flux so horrifying. He found the solution, however, as many thinkers have, in theological construction: he imagined God as a salvational deity, who takes "a tender care that nothing be lost."[5] The salvation is both ontological and epistemic, preserving existents and their truths. In the long history of philosophy, God is an epistemic deus ex machina at least as often as an ontological deus ex machina.

The future is also unknowable—but for different reasons. We can *predict* many aspects of the future (to *predict* is to *foretell*; etymologically, "to say before"), but predictions are elaborations of our knowledge of the present, not knowledge of the future. The facts of the future remain but possibilities from our perspective—even if there are no alternative possibilities. Even the most ardent of determinists, who believe the future is theoretically predictable from complete knowledge of the present and of the laws of nature, must admit that our individual and collective knowledge of the present state of the world is woefully incomplete—and the state of the world is continually in flux. Moreover, underlying it all is the assumption that the laws of nature will not change.

In addition, there are facts that await a framework of conceptualization that does not yet exist. Galileo could not have known that solar flares produce bursts of radiation, because the framework of theoretical concepts that define electromagnetic radiation was not developed until centuries later. Hippocrates could not have known about vaccinations, because the entire realm of microbiology, the identification of pathogens and antigens, and the technique itself awaited discovery for two millennia. It appears a certainty that new theoretical paradigms, new concepts, will arise in the future—indeed, in the future beheld from any given moment. Not only do we not know what these will be, we cannot even imagine many of them. Like our ability to see with the beam of headlights as we drive on a dark road, our ability to know what lies ahead is limited. Once again, only the prospect of time travel—and then, only time travel in which the traveler's identity, especially memory, is not altered by the trip—would challenge these limits.

The opacity of the future is also the unknowability of our personal future. We cannot know our future self—rather, selves—for life surprises us. We are ignorant of things that will have an impact on our life and ways in which they will alter us. The recognition of this limit may be a source of trepidation: it confronts us with the fragility of our happy life and even our identity. But it can also be a source of hope: it is an argument advanced against suicide, especially those cases not motivated by terminal illness. One who contemplates suicide would deny the unknowability of the future, robbing a future self of its choices and its life.[6]

Finally, our knowing is obviously limited by our life span. As individual knowers, each of us has our own past and, as our time moves on, much of our personal history is lost to us. I mean "lost" in the sense that it has moved from the merely forgotten to the irretrievable; it has become unknowable. Even further beyond our cognitive reach and more profoundly unknowable to us are the events that will occur after we die. We can learn a lot in the time we have; but death is a sure and final limit of coming to know. Human knowing flourishes and vanishes with human life.

Biological Limits

Besides the absolute limit of our life span, our biology sets other important, individual limitations to knowledge. One is the capacity of the human brain. Even our roughly one hundred billion neurons can process and store only so much information. As a species, we transcend these individual limits by a division of cognitive labor resulting in a specialization of knowledge—which we then may store for others' access. But, of course, there are limits to this too. And we should not rush to assume that storing digitized information is our salvation from ignorance. Unfortunately, having access to information is not the same as knowing. Ask any student who owns a textbook. Just because one has access to vast Internet resources does not mean that one knows everything on the web.[7]

Moreover, we forget much of what we learn. This is not simply a biological flaw; it is a benefit too—psychologically and physiologically. The rare cases of people who remember everything, who cannot forget, reveal what an affliction it is to be unable to forget.[8] If we remembered every sensation we experienced, our cognitive processes would soon be overwhelmed. Forgetting is, in a sense, a cognitive ability. But we no longer know what we cannot remember.

Another important set of limitations is inherent in the very biological systems we use to gain knowledge: our sensory systems. All such systems operate within parameters. Take sight, our dominant sensory system: our eyes register only a tiny range of the electromagnetic spectrum as visible light, roughly wavelengths between 380 and 760 nanometers. Other creatures have eyes that see beyond this range: bees, for example, see a bit further into the ultraviolet range; so-called bee purple designates a color we humans cannot experience. In addition, the average human can use our complex network of three types of photoreceptor cells to discriminate about ten million different shades. But there is (contested) evidence that some humans are tetrachromats, and the effect of an extra type of photoreceptor means these people might actually see up to a hundred million different shades. The mantis shrimp has a visual system with at least twelve types of different photoreceptors—one of the most complex visual systems known. The point is that humans with normal chromatic vision are ignorant of the color experiences of creatures with greater discrimination.

In addition, our vision functions only within other constraints. We can see objects only within a certain distance and of a certain size. Our retinas have blind spots. All these limits apply even to someone with "perfect" human eyesight—and that is a minority. It is well known how inferior our olfactory and auditory systems are compared to that of many other creatures. And we lack whole sensory systems that other animals possess, including especially systems used for navigation, like the pigeon's ability to sense magnetic fields.

Thus, the parameters of our sensory systems, the mediation involved in perception, and the particular sensory systems we use all impose limits on our experience, and hence on what we can know. As Immanuel Kant, who carefully charted the limits of human reason, revealed, we can know that we have such limits, and that we ourselves structure our experience of the world; but we cannot know things-in-themselves, cannot know just what lies beyond or beneath our cognitive reach.

In the history of philosophy, interestingly, skepticism has arisen from the faults of our senses—illusions, variations, inconsistencies, debilitations—more often than from their parameters. But faults are detected and have meaning only by reference to correctness or accuracy. Parameters would limit knowledge even if our systems were fault-free.

In addition, to the extent that our knowledge is constituted in our ability to express it, we are limited by the resources of our language(s), syntactic and semantic. All symbol systems select salient aspects of experience; they become internalized as the lenses through which we experience the world. Some languages have only three different color terms; some modern languages do not distinguish green from blue—yet their speakers all have human eyes. All that is distinctive about humanity and *enables* our learning—our brain, our perceptiveness, our reason, our language—also serves to *structure and to limit* our knowledge as well.

Conceptual Limits

The attempt to state what we know, to frame our knowledge in propositions, can sometimes result in tangles that reveal our limits or that are self-limiting. Perhaps the most troubling are cases in which we can never exemplify a true claim. I have noted that such claims are true but "noninstantiable" (chapter 3), which is to say that we cannot cite a single instance. Nicholas Rescher has analyzed this phenomenon in two related books and has given it the name *vagrant reference*.[9] Consider these examples, poached from Rescher with slight modifications:

a.   There is an event that no one ever mentions.
b.   There is a number that no one has ever named or specified.

c.   There is a topic no one has thought about since the seventeenth century.

d.   There is a person whom no one now remembers.

And there are the formulations that underlie this chapter:

e.   There are facts that no one knows, knowledge no one has.

f.   There are unknown unknowns.

"Name one," we might ask in response to each of these. But any attempt to cite an instance or example will be self-defeating. The problem with these propositions is that an existential claim is made about something that is described obliquely and—although it may be true—the reference is made in such a way that it precludes identification of any item that meets the description. There are two loci of epistemic concern: one is the necessity that we must remain permanently ignorant of instances that fit such descriptions; the other is the limits on our ability to verify the propositions themselves. In some cases (such as (e) and (f)), the propositions may admit of logical proofs; but an empirical approach is ruled out for all.[10] These are not merely problems of formulation; these are not cases of linguistic gymnastics. Consider this noninstantiable claim: "There are at least two hundred unreported rapes in this city every year." Such a claim is genuinely cognitive and factive, but it is laden with inexorable ignorance.

There are many other circumstances in which we can justifiably claim knowledge of a general sort without being able to specify instances. As an example, imagine that a deadly disease has taken 25,000 lives each year among approximately 200,000 cases of infection. A vaccine is discovered and a program of mandatory inoculation and education is mounted. In the following year, there are only 2,000 cases of infection, of which 200 are fatalities. Assuming a discounting of other factors, we have reason to claim that the program dramatically reduced infection by 180,000 cases and saved over 24,000 lives that year alone. But *whose* lives were saved? *Whose* infection was prevented? We cannot identify anyone specifically— and we will never know. Ironically, our knowledge may sometimes range over great and broad statistical generalizations, while we remain ignorant of the individual cases that comprise that profile.

Proving causal relationships would, of course, be difficult. Identifying all the causal factors in play that produce any actual state of affairs in a society is an infinite task and a misplaced hope. But in the matter of "lives saved" and similar cases, we would need to identify all the causal links in a *hypothetical* state of affairs as well: what exactly would have happened *if* there had been no inoculation program, and to whom. I've already discussed the erosion of our knowledge of the past, but that discussion was about the *actual* past. To retrieve and account for the lost *possibilities*, the *what-if-this-had-happened-instead* scenarios, lies beyond our knowledge as well. Though we can speculate, we are facing both reconstructive and predictive problems and their inherent limits. Noninstantiability is thus as a conceptual limit to knowledge.

Counterfactual conditions may mark yet another limit to our knowledge. In a reflective moment, we may ask, "How different would our country be today if President Kennedy had not been assassinated?" or "If I could alter one crucial early decision I made, what would my life be like now?" This sort of "what if" question specifies scenarios that deviate from actual events. The exploration of such hypothetical scenarios has become a literary and historical genre called "alternate (or alternative) history." Attempts to answer these questions range from the historically serious, in which careful and scholarly responses are framed, to the creative, in which the question is used simply as a premise for imaginative fiction. Even for the most earnest inquiries, however, the outcome is not truth, but plausibility. We can only speculate—wistfully or gratefully or with other feelings—about the impact of "what might have been." We can know that certain things are possible, but we cannot know all that would flow from them, were they actual. Counterfactuals invite us to go beyond what is known, yet they embody conceptual limits to what can be known.

James Frederick Ferrier, the Scot whose *Institutes of Metaphysic* I cited in chapter 1, asserted the following as nearly the most important proposition of his tract: "We can be ignorant only of what can possibly be known; in other words, there can an ignorance only of that of which there can be knowledge." For Ferrier, if we are ignorant of X, X must be knowable—and he expands this to include things knowable in practice and in principle, not only to humans but to other "orders of intelligence." What are not knowable, he says, are necessarily (logically) false propositions like "a part is greater than the whole" or "two plus two equals five."[11] Such propositions are conceptually self-contradictory; they do not represent a limit to knowledge in either the completion or exhaustion interpretation. But since they lie outside all possible knowledge, we cannot be ignorant of them.

I turn next to limits that arise from the obstacles to predictive accuracy: chance, forms of indeterminacy, and free choice. We will find inherent limits there as well.

The Limits of Science and Mathematics

In the first half of the twentieth century, the vision and the dream of a complete knowledge of the world were dashed forever. The unkindest cut was that the blows came from within the very disciplines that had advanced the model of a completed science: physics and mathematics.

The theorists who developed quantum mechanics postulated and then demonstrated that the subatomic world was not fully knowable. Quanta behave in ways that are inherently random and therefore unpredictable. Ernest Rutherford's work on radioactive decay showed that we cannot predict which atoms in a sample will release radiation and transmute into a stable element. When any particular atom decays is not a function of how long it has been charged; the release of radiation is random, yet regular en masse: we can plot the rate of decay across large numbers of atoms. In 1907, Rutherford introduced the concept of *half-life*, the time span in which one-half of the atoms on average will lose their charge. Here again we confront a truth that we cannot instantiate—but for different, empirical reasons: we cannot know which atoms will decay.

Werner Heisenberg demonstrated in 1927 that it is impossible to measure the position and momentum of a particle simultaneously; the more precisely one measures one variable, the more the other is distorted. The uncertainty principle (or indeterminacy principle) presents the paradox of measurement: the observer's attempt to measure is an intervention that alters the phenomenon itself; in this case, as accuracy is increased for one variable, the other is pushed beyond reach. Thus, measurement, the fundamental activity of quantifying the world, both generates and limits our knowledge.

In 1935, Erwin Schrödinger described the *superposition of states*, in which two conflicting states occur simultaneously—a bizarre aspect of the quantum world. But when an observer views or makes accessible such a phenomenon, the superposition is lost and the state becomes simply one or the other. His illustrative thought experiment, "Schrödinger's cat," has become a meme of popular culture. A live cat is placed in a steel container with a lethal substance that can be triggered by the radioactive decay of a single atom. We cannot know whether an atom has decayed, so the cat is both dead and alive—until we open the container to check, of course, when we can determine whether the cat is alive or dead. In such cases, there is no single outcome unless the observation is made.

The world revealed by quantum physics presents not merely bizarre and elusive phenomena but inherent and ineluctable limits to human knowledge. While there are some scientists who hold out hope that these apparently random, inaccessible, paradoxical phenomena can be tamed into traditional causal frameworks, they are a fading minority. Still more weirdness arises and seems to thwart even basic assumptions about the world. This year, quantum scientists claimed to have shown that future events may determine events in the past. A team of Australian physicists announced they have demonstrated that what happened to certain particles in the past depends on observation and measurement of them in the future—a kind of backward flow of causality. One of the researchers declared: "It proves that measurement is everything. At the quantum level, reality does not exist if you are not looking at it."[12] (I find it difficult in this arena to separate the ontological from the epistemological—claims about what exists from claims about whether we can know what exists—and this time-warping claim will no doubt receive scrutiny by other scientists.)

In 1931, Kurt Gödel published his incompleteness theorems. He demonstrated that, for any formal system at least as complicated as arithmetic, there will be theorems known to be true on independent grounds that cannot be derived within the system; there will always be at least one true but unprovable proposition. Any consistent formal system that is sufficiently powerful to comprehend arithmetic will, therefore, always be incomplete; we will always encounter formally undecidable propositions.[13] Mathematics is the language of science, and the ultimate goal of scientific research, it was assumed, was to explain phenomena as instances of laws that can be expressed mathematically. Gödel's proofs—never refuted—show that any science modeled as a formal system must always be incomplete. We cannot capture everything in any single explanatory system, however complex we make it.

Taken together, these intellectual developments exploded the idealized model of human knowledge: "completed" science, especially scientific knowledge as represented in the mathematical precision of physics. If the physical world contains discontinuous movement ("quantum leaps"); if basic particles behave randomly; if the observer, in attempting to obtain knowledge, necessarily alters the phenomena, sometimes destructively; and if all mathematical explanatory systems are necessarily incomplete— we confront profound limits to our knowledge, to what is knowable even in theory.

The End of Knowledge

In his study of ignorance, Nicholas Rescher makes important observations about the limitations of human knowledge. Understanding his claims requires definitional stipulations for several terms. *Facts* are actual aspects of the world's state of affairs; they are features of reality. *Propositions* are claims regarding facts. *Statements* are *propositions formulated in a language* (the same proposition may be formulated in different languages, different statements). Facts may thus be represented through statements; *truth* is a property of correct statements. But facts "outrun linguistic limits." Facts about even one physical object are inexhaustible. Rescher says, "Its susceptibility to further elaborate detail—and to potential changes of mind regarding this further detail—is built into our very conception of a 'real thing.'"[14] Facts are infinite in number because the detail of the world is inexhaustible.

Though we humans are finite beings, we can know universal truths. We can also know generalizations about vast swatches of the world. And we can know many facts about individual things. But we can never know *fully* all the individual entities about which we generalize. Indeed, we can never fully know *even one individual*. Its facts are infinite, an infinitude that protects its opacity.

Though our knowledge does expand, the possibilities for further expansion are now contested. As science advances, its epistemic structure becomes more elaborated and filigreed. Though progress is always possible, Rescher says, results are more and more difficult to achieve. "In moving onward we must be ever more prolix and make use of ever more elaborate symbol complexes so that greater demands in time, effort, and resources are unavoidable."[15] Going further, the science writer Peter Horgan has argued that indeed we live in the twilight era of scientific discovery. The title of his controversial book states his conclusion: *The End of Science: Facing the Limits of Knowledge in the Twilight of the Scientific Age.*[16] Horgan believes that the fundamentals of scientific knowledge, our contemporary understanding of the universe, will not change dramatically: the nature of the solar system, the evolution of life, the natural elements of the world, and so on, are well and truly known. We possess a well-confirmed and deeply embedded understanding of the world. Only details remain. The time for profound discoveries is past. Yes, technology and other forms of applied science will continue to make major strides. Horgan thinks the most transformative form of applied science will be human immortality, the conquering of aging. But even this would not alter our understanding of the universe in any deep way. Most of what is knowable about the natural world and relevant to human life is already known; and at the frontiers of physics, scientists are approaching the limits of what is knowable. Since a completed science—a "theory of everything"—is impossible, contemporary physicists now offer only speculative metaphysical theories that defy confirmation or falsification (theories Horgan calls "ironic" and "theological"). Human beings have a limited capacity to understand the universe of which we are a tiny part—and we are now approaching it.

Rescher believes that although science will advance more slowly and major discoveries will be fewer, real progress will continue—and there will still be surprises.[17] He observes that previous generations have also thought they understood all the important stuff—and they were wrong. Horgan accuses Rescher of trying to retract a "depressing scenario" with "a happy coda." Horgan repeats a reviewer's metaphor: Rescher is whistling in the dark.[18]

I agree with Rescher on the inexhaustibility of facts and our inability to know all the facts about even a single object. But I am at odds with both Rescher and Horgan on the potential for new knowledge—and these two points are not unrelated. First, I believe both men underestimate the effects of the interpenetration of scientific theory and technology, and the potential for discovery that results from this dynamism.[19] Second, while it is true that most discoveries complexify our understanding, now and then a discovery unites, connects, and simplifies. Newton's discovery of the laws of gravitation is the obvious, paradigmatic example. It is an essential part of Horgan's thesis that such coherence-bringing breakthroughs are behind us. I see this, however, as an attempt to map our unknown unknowns from too low an altitude. It is simply not possible to fix the nature of unknown unknowns at such a level of specificity. Horgan and perhaps Rescher claim to know the range of the remaining unknown unknowns. Disguised as an affirmation of limits to our knowledge, these claims actually constitute an overreaching of what one can claim to know.

Omniscience

Regardless of varying prognoses for scientific progress, it is generally agreed that human knowledge will always be incomplete. We might consider more closely, however, what *complete* knowledge would be. *Omniscience* is the term for possessing complete knowledge, for the state of knowing all that is knowable, for possessing all truth. It is the annihilation of all ignorance, the freedom from all epistemic limits.

For monotheistic religions, omniscience is typically one of the divine perfections, an aspect of the perfect being of God. In Abrahamic religions, it is a crucial property, directing God's omnipotence, enabling God's providence, and informing God's wisdom and justice. These perfections are mutually supporting, for to be omniscient but impotent would be a kind of hell: knowing everything yet being unable to do anything about it. To explore the concept of omniscience, however, let us set aside theological presuppositions and other divine attributes unless and until we are led to them by the necessity of understanding.

First, it is clarifying to distinguish between (1) omniscience as the capacity to know any knowable truth one chooses, and (2) omniscience as the state of actually knowing all that can be known. Thomas Aquinas added a feature to the second interpretation: this actual knowing is *nondiscursive*, meaning that everything is known simultaneously—it is not the thinking of one thing, then another, and so on.[20] That may be considered a necessary condition, since otherwise a discursive omniscience would seem to require an infinite amount of time to know all the facts about even one momentary state of the world. But this has radical implications: it seems to imply that omniscience is not an infinite set of justified true beliefs, but rather an immediate, intuitive comprehension: knowing without believing. Under most interpretations, omniscience entails not only propositional knowledge (*knowing that*) but also direct knowledge (*knowing what it is like*) and profound understanding (although most analytic epistemologists treat omniscience purely in terms of propositional knowledge).[21]

Actual omniscience would mean that a single intelligence—for convenience and theistic neutrality, call it "Omni"—would know every detail of all the states of the world; the thoughts and feelings of all sentient creatures; all relationships, properties, laws, theories; all languages, texts, artworks, and communications; all subjects; all that each person knew and did not know; and more. For all these objects of knowledge, Omni would also know their past and their future. The shadowy implications of God's foreknowledge for humanity's free will have generated an entire literature of theological and philosophical gyrations. (Does foreknowledge imply predestination? Does free will repudiate omniscience?) In trying to reconcile omniscience and free will, some have argued, for example, that God can learn new facts as autonomous humans make their choices.[22] But whether Omni would be able to learn or not, it surely would never forget—which means it has no need to remember.

There are further entailments. Omniscience implies the knowledge of all *possibilities* for every epistemic object at every moment, not just their actualities. So, whatever knowledge Omni has of this world must be expanded modally to all possible worlds. Moreover, Omni would possess no false knowledge, since it would know that false beliefs were false, though it would know of the false knowledge held by others. That means Omni is *infallible*, since no epistemic errors are possible.[23] In addition, such a being would necessarily have total self-knowledge, metaknowledge, and transparency: Omni knows it is omniscient. And that, in turn, implies that it knows that there are no other truths to know. Omni must know there are no unknown unknowns.

Some philosophers have argued that because the truths of the world change, Omni's knowledge must change with them: earlier it was true that I was going to write this sentence; now it is true that I have written it. From a related concern, some have argued that Omni's knowledge must incorporate indexical truths, for example *de se* truths (truths about oneself affirmed in the first person), such as "I am writing this sentence." The indexical term "I," like "here" and "now," shifts reference according to the context of utterance. "I am writing this sentence" is a different truth from "Dan DeNicola is writing this sentence." Still others have argued that omniscience is impossible because it wrongly implies that there is a complete set of all truths. That implication is false because, no matter how we circumscribe the (supposed) set of all truths, there will be additional truths about the set of all its subsets that we must then include, and so on ad infinitum.[24] These arguments are presented as challenges to the concept of omniscience and its relation to other perfections. They are introduced and usually discussed in the framework of propositional knowledge, but there may be analogues for the framework of experiential knowledge and understanding. Suppose Omni understands all things: it follows that Omni must understand what it is to be ignorant, what it is to be me and to be ignorant of specific things, and what it is to learn. But these experiences and this understanding are incompatible with Omni's omniscience. (We pass by the question of whether a good God could truly know what it is to be evil.)

The point of all this—a piling on of epistemic attributes, implications, assumptions, and challenges—is to show that omniscience is a contested and unstable concept. It is threatened by mutability, perspectival knowledge, incompatibility with other attributes, and even logical incoherence. It is the outer limit to knowledge that seems impossible to reach by imagining a set of propositions that are justified, true beliefs—even an infinite set. The difficulty may arise from focus on the completion model of limit, rather than on the exhaustion model.

But the age-old ascription of omniscience to God meant that the universe was thoroughly and completely known by a single intelligence: the Mind of God. All that was knowable was known—and all was knowable to God. The death of God, therefore, carries the implication that the universe is no longer thoroughly known; indeed, there is no longer any assurance of its knowability. The universally unknown, the range of unknown unknowns, and the domain of the unknowable become an epistemic black hole, massive and forbidding.[25]

Arguments from Ignorance

For finite humans, what is knowable is limited: some things are unknowable in practice, others in principle, and even all that is knowable in practice is not knowable for finite, mortal creatures. What can we learn, what can we infer from our ignorance?

Making inferences from what is *not* known or from the *absence* of evidence or proof has long been considered a fallacy in logic textbooks. It is formally called *argumentum ad ignorantiam*, an argument from ignorance or an appeal to ignorance. In its basic structure, the argument may claim that because a claim has not been disproved, it is true; or because some purported fact has not been proved (or because there is no evidence of its truth), the alleged fact is false. For example, an art dealer claims that because a painting has not been proved to be a forgery, it is genuine. An inquisitor concludes that a man is a traitor, because there is no evidence he is loyal. A believer says the Loch Ness monster must exist, because no one has disproved its existence. The first assumes truth because contrary evidence is absent; the last two put the burden on proving the negative ("Prove there is no monster!").

In the austere formulations of logic texts and in the stark reasoning of these examples, the problematic inference is easy to see. The fallacy is obvious. But in many real-world situations, the use of this sort of argument actually seems valid. In medical research, a drug may be deemed safe for human use because there is no evidence of side effects—no evidence that it is unsafe. In court, we judge a person "not guilty" when we do not know of any evidence of guilt. These are judgments of practice, of course, and subject to practical conditions, but the arguments on which they rest are appeals to ignorance, nonetheless.

These judgments seem to have implications about the knowledge base and the sampling on which they rest. Suppose I have a bag with ten balls of various kinds, and you ask, "Is my tennis ball in that bag?' I look at each of the ten balls in turn and say, "It is not here." I found no ball that is your tennis ball, so you would certainly judge that I am entitled to that conclusion; the inference is unquestionably valid. But now suppose I have one hundred balls in the bag and examine only ten, and I say, "Your ball is not in the bag—and that's true because I have found no ball that is your tennis ball." The inference is now dubious.

Sorting out the epistemic and contextual factors in which *argumentum ad ignorantiam* is a legitimate type of argumentation is quite complex and beyond my scope here. I can only point to a comprehensive treatment of the range of such arguments by Douglas Walton.[26] But I can observe that there are indeed situations in which our ignorance is proper evidence for knowledge claims. And I can commend a general wariness of such arguments: their broad use enables willful ignorance and conspiracy theorists. Fanatics have ignored evidence of President Obama's Christian beliefs and claim that there is no proof that he is not a Muslim. Doubters have demanded that researchers prove there is no link between vaccines and autism. (And researchers reply that there is no evidence of such a link— itself another *argumentum ad ignorantiam*.) Members of Congress have asked the Secretary of State to prove that Iran will not violate a nuclear treaty. The demand for negative proof frequently issues from one who is committed to a belief as irrefutable, immune from evidence. It is a demand that is meant to close dialogue; it is not expected to be met; and, unless there is a specifiable, finite database to draw on, it never will be met.

10   Managing Ignorance

Ignorance is not such a bad thing if one knows how to use it.
—Peter Drucker

In the previous chapters, we have seen that despite learning, the ignorance that remains is infinite; that, while some portion of our ignorance is known to us, an immeasurable portion is not; and that, although simple ignorance is "natural," there are many forms of intentional and constructed ignorance. Moreover, as the last chapter chronicled, our capacity to know is limited in many ways. Ignorance is thus a fixture of our lives; it is part of the human condition. Now what are we to do about it?

Much of our ignorance is benignly irrelevant to our lives; our daily existence is unaffected by it. But relevant ignorance manifests itself, and we are regularly faced with the unknown. Early on, I spoke of the terrible cost exacted by ignorance; but, unfortunately, it is difficult to know which unknowns will remain benign and which will confront us and become costly. When we suddenly encounter the unknown, our biologically based, hardwired, responses—largely physiological—are engaged. But, smart creatures that we are, we have gone beyond these to develop additional ways of coping with the unknown: emotional, intellectual, practical, and social ways. These coping mechanisms include arrays of sophisticated conceptual tools and techniques, whole new fields of knowledge (ironically), and even special cultural institutions and social practices—all aimed at managing our ignorance.

I propose to catalog some of the most important of these, beginning with primitive responses and moving to those of increasing complexity. This presents no shocking discoveries or technological advances, and my treatment of each of these responses is necessarily brief. But there is a cumulative effect, I believe, in seeing them as a set of tools for ignorance management. On the one hand, this account will illustrate the ways in which even irremediable ignorance may inspire knowledge; on the other, it will show how our knowledge is embedded within a silent recognition of our ignorance. The progression from recognizing ignorance to responding to it, to coping with it, to managing it suggests that we may gain increasing control. Since ignorance is a permanent fixture of our lives, learning to manage it is a worthwhile, even fundamental, epistemic aim and a practical imperative.

Responding to the Unknown

An encounter with the unknown may pose three sorts of problems for us: emotional, intellectual, and practical. Basic emotional responses will often be activated before our reason is engaged. Like other primates, humans may react to the unknown with fear or aversion, but also with curiosity and fascination. This is especially true of sudden or surprising encounters. These two disparate tendencies form a polar tension: our need for safety and our inquisitiveness. Observing at a safe distance is often an intelligent compromise. When our reason kicks in, when we can safely observe, we can decide whether fear or caution are justified; and our curiosity can lead to cogitation—identifying, associating, classifying, inquiring, researching, computing, assimilating, comprehending, explaining—activities that render the unknown, known. This intellectual processing helps with practical issues: how to treat or use this unfamiliarity, how to apply it, whether to share it with others.

Early humans regularly encountered unpredictable, powerful, and unfathomable forces—especially the forces of nature and dangerous animals; and they often responded in fear and awe by attempting to appease these powers and ingratiate themselves through sacrifice and supplication. The rituals they developed may be understood as ways of coping with the mystery of supernatural forces, ways of living with gods. Various forms of fortune-telling and divination, especially haruspicy, became popular techniques. Still widely practiced, they employ indirect evidence and signs to reveal one's fate or god's will. Soothsayers generally claim insight into the future, not genuine knowledge of it; but we should recognize these activities, more plausibly, as attempts to cope with ignorance.

A contrasting approach (made with greater confidence) is to harness these forces for human purposes through craft and technique. The recipes that result do not rest on deep theoretical understanding; they are transmittable instructions for producing a desired result. The ancient glassblower or brewer knew little of chemistry, but could follow age-old instructions that were developed by trial-and-error methods. Recipes yield products; through serendipity and experiment, they may be improved. Recipes are externalized forms of *knowing how*; they do not require *knowing why*. They too may be understood as another way of managing processes and forces of which we are, in fact, ignorant.

Rituals reflect an attitude of humility toward the unknown; recipes reflect an assertion of human purpose and will to channel if not control natural processes. Ritualism establishes roles: priests, acolytes, supplicants, and others, who have special authority and play a specific part in the ceremonies—think of religious weddings and masses. Sacred objects and hallowed places are often required, and the sequence of actions and events is critical. Recipes, by contrast, are transferable—though a master will be more effective that an apprentice, often because of tacit knowledge. But the issue for a successful craft process is not so much *who* does it as *how* it is done. Recipes require tools and instruments, not sacred objects; and while sequence is important, the dominant temporal concern is for "just the right moment"—the precise moment for blowing and bending the glass or picking the grapes. As written culture evolved, both sacred rituals and recipes became textual; and it is true that blending, combining, and confusing of ritual and recipe occurs. Even today, we may begin or conclude the use of a recipe with a ritual: the toast offered for a new wine; the smashed champagne bottle to christen a new ship; the singing and blowing-out-of-candles before eating a birthday cake.

Note, however, that neither rituals nor recipes are attempts to *understand* the world. Nonetheless, they do help us cope with our ignorance: they address the emotional and practical dimensions. They offer a form of order and predictability; they impart a sense of security through continuity; and they help make the world a familiar place in which we may feel at home. But it is left to philosophy and science to address our wonder and intellectual curiosity about the unknown.

Coping with Ignorance

Among the aspects of ignorance that cause us concern are uncertainty, risk, error, and harm. Uncertainty occurs when we lack decisive determinants for thought or action. Future events are unpredictable, and so are people's actions. About the past and present too we often lack information, or have incomplete or conflicting information. Uncertainty leaves us at risk for error through action, inaction, or obliviousness, and real harm that may range from the trivial to the catastrophic. The emotional burden is stress and anxiety or a hope that may be false; and the regret or guilt that may follow.

The primitive responses have a legacy. Superstition or magic is a persistent, if misguided, way of coping with our ignorance; this is the belief in supernatural agencies that control events and can be influenced toward good or bad outcomes. Special objects, it is thought, may magically determine events: good luck charms or talismans to influence outcomes positively; amulets and apotropaics to ward off evil and prevent harmful outcomes; and poppets and cursed objects to cause harm to another. Blessings and curses or hexes are ritualized verbal techniques for trying to direct future events through magic. Magic combines ritual and recipe in arts that do not attempt to understand the world (because the world is governed by ineffable forces), but rather to influence, even to control, events. While all such superstitious practices seem to exemplify human ignorance, they also represent in their attempts to shape events a strategy for coping with our ignorance.

Fortunately, uncertainty may instead generate inquiry. Thinking is a multipurpose ability, but it is particularly useful in coping with the unknown, the strange, and with situations in which one must respond despite uncertainty. The routine situations of daily life we negotiate by habit, but (as the American Pragmatists emphasized) thought arises out of problems, situations in which we have neither certainty nor a comfortable routine. We may cope with pressing ignorance by intellectual activity that seeks to understand, and perhaps thereby gain the power of knowledge to control or act wisely. We've developed three basic intellectual strategies to cope with ignorance: (1) vanquish it with learning; (2) identify, map, and target our ignorance; (3) reduce the range and impact of specific residual ignorance. We all know about the first. It is the other two that call for examination here. They employ the tools and practices that have moved us from recognizing and coping to managing our ignorance.

In chapter 5, I discussed the idea of mapping our ignorance. The technique, begun in medicine and medical pedagogy, is now infiltrating other professions. "Ignorance management," largely defined in terms of identifying and mapping, has become a trendy term in management circles, leading to articles, consultants, seminars, and workshops on how to manage organizational ignorance. A team of British scholars led by John Israilidis, using the language of the management classroom, explains it this way: "Ignorance Management is a process of discovering, exploring, realising, recognising and managing ignorance outside and inside the organisation through an appropriate management process to meet current and future demands, design better policy and modify actions in order to achieve organisational objectives and sustain competitive advantage."[1] The core of this approach is the use of the four-part grid of second-order epistemic categories introduced in chapter 3 (known knowns and known unknowns; unknown knowns and unknown unknowns) as categories for identifying and mapping organizational ignorance. The ultimate aim, of course, is to treat these as resources for knowledge creation.

Psychologists and behavioral economists have been conducting empirical research on the ways in which we make decisions under conditions of uncertainty.[2] Uncertainty is not identical to ignorance; yet ignorance is its characteristic property. Uncertainty implies that one already possesses some salient knowledge, but the relevant information may be incomplete, ambiguous, or conflicting. This research is interesting because it often reveals cognitive biases, apparently irrational tendencies that pattern our choices. What is generally less clear is whether these patterns are, like visual illusions, inescapable even when we understand how they work, or whether they are tendencies that are correctable with proper information and alertness. Most likely, they are a mix of both. This work is descriptive of actual decision making; what is needed for ignorance management is to set these data against a normative account of decision making. For the latter, one may look to rational choice theory. Unfortunately, the field of choice theory has been limited in application because of its initially simplistic and controversial assumptions (such as assuming the sole motivation to be universal individual self-interest) and its need for mathematically precise specifications. In a deeper sense, all human decisions are made under conditions of uncertainty, because of the necessary limits to our knowledge.

Transformations in the Dark

Some of the most personally significant decisions we make must be made in conditions of radical uncertainty and fateful consequence: they are transformative. The contemporary philosopher L. A. Paul has called attention to two types of transformations: (1) *epistemic transformations*, in which we come to know what something is like—what it is like to live in a very different culture, perhaps, or to face death in battle; to gain cognitive abilities or a new sensory system, as to experience sight when one has been blind; and (2) *personal transformations* in which one's values and even one's identity are altered, in which one changes "how you experience being who you are."[3] The first can lead to the second, of course, and both can happen to us whether we desire them or not. But Paul's interest is in the cases in which we are presented with a choice. (Her opening thought experiment involves being presented with the choice to become a vampire!)

The difficult issue with personal transformative choices is that *we cannot know* what the change would be like until we experience it. Yes, we can study what others have said; we can accumulate objective evidence. But the subjective experience, the *knowing what it is like*, is unavailable to us. The decision to become a parent, to change gender, to retire in a distant land, or to undertake an education—we make these and other life choices without really knowing what we are in for or how we would be changed by it. Moreover, such decisions are usually irreversible: once you are a vampire, there is no going back. Such choices are irrational or nonrational in that they cannot conform to the norms of rational choice: we have no basis on which to assign comparative values to the alternatives. Yet they may open us to new and wondrous forms of life.

So, when it matters most, we feel our ignorance most keenly. If rational choice theory fails us in such matters, how can we manage? We have our subjective values, which involve more than valuing pleasure or happiness. Either we choose the status quo and affirm our current life and its conditions, or we choose to discover a new intrinsic nature and to evolve in our preferences and outlook—along with all the possible emotions and insights it will bring. Though some temperaments may make such choices in fear and trembling, others embrace openness. Paul's ultimate conclusion is this: "A life lived rationally and authentically, then, as each big decision is encountered, involves deciding whether or how to make a discovery about who you will become. ... One of the most important games of life, then, is the game of Revelation, a game played for the sake of the play itself."[4]

Unpredictability and Commitment

Our concern may not be with ourselves, however; it may be with others. Unpredictability is a troubling source of uncertainty, and the actions of other people are often unpredictable to us—not just the actions of strangers, but sometimes of intimates as well. We cannot, to use a Woody Allen phrase, "peer into the soul" of another person. Indeed, we are not very transparent to ourselves! Yet social interaction and the benefits of cooperation depend on people's reliability. If we cannot rely on others or reliably predict their actions, we can't trust them. We do not know what they will do.

An ancient, basic strategy to address this uncertainty is to constrain others' actions through exacting commitments that are formal and public. Oaths and promises, for example, are speech acts that create obligations. We use them to remove or reduce our uncertainty about what someone will do. The more complex version—usually in more durable, written form—is a contract. A contract is a mutual pact that declares specific commitments and voluntarily constrains the future behavior of both parties, usually under the prospect of penalty for breaching the agreement. Advanced social systems support contracts with adjudication of disputes and enforcement of provisions and penalties. As these sorts of commitments become established institutions, our uncertainty diminishes, along with the risk of ignorance.

In contemporary society, less formal commitment practices serve the same purpose of reducing uncertainty; for example, the making and taking of reservations, in which explicit commitments from customers and businesses are exchanged—for dining or lodging, for admission to events or attractions, for renting vehicles or vacation homes, for seats on airplanes or trains, for wedding venues and free-range turkeys. Commitments in all these forms constrain future behavior; they increase predictability and reduce risk; they build confidence in what will happen. These commitments are performative speech acts in which we create new facts through appropriate utterance: "I promise," "I agree to these stipulations," or "I consent."

These sorts of commitments are enabled by special features of language. Discussing the unknown and unpredictable requires language that can indicate and describe states of affairs that are doubtful, possible, imagined, or desired, but not factual. For this purpose, we have developed linguistic tools that enable a discourse of the uncertain. Individual words may signal these conditional states (like *perhaps* or *maybe* or *suppose*, in English); and we regularly distinguish between hypotheses and facts, between assumptions and observations. Hypothetical (or conditional) clauses also serve this purpose: they are the *if* portion of *if-then* sentences. Conditional sentences assert that a specific factual outcome follows from a hypothetical condition: "If you build it, they will come." In English and many other languages, the subjunctive mood is used for contrary-to-fact or nonfactual discourse. And in logic, new forms were invented to deal with *modalities*, including possibilities and statements for which the truth is variable.

Chance

We commonly use the word *chance* to refer both to random events and to events the causes of which are so complex as to defy explanation or prediction. Rolling dice violates no law of physics, but the mechanical forces in play are too many and too subtle for us to predict their outcome reliably. The same is true for the tornado that may sudden veer from its path and leave a lone house standing. Chance is the default cause of striking and inexplicable events, like the convergence of two causal streams: "The man happened to bend down to tie his shoe just when the bullet was fired." Some such convergences are chancy; some we call *coincidences*. Imagine: a distant, exotic location; you hail a cab and, upon entering, meet an old friend who is opening the opposite door. It is striking that, without foreknowledge or coordination, two friends should be in the same faraway place, reaching for the same cab at the same moment. Though no laws of nature were violated and each can reasonably explain his presence, the circumstances that led to that moment of intersection of their lives are so complex that we cannot explain their synchrony. We are baffled at such an unpredictable coincidence; so we say, "They met by chance."

(Some, of course, would say such coincidences are "fated.") When chance events affect us either positively or negatively, we may call them a matter of luck—either good or bad. The point is that the unpredictability and inexplicability of all these sorts of events and the ascription of chance or luck are functions of our ignorance.

Chance is also applied to events in the past ("By chance, this was the only manuscript to survive the fire") as well as in the future; however, it is the future that occupies our decisions and our actions. The future represents possibility and potential, but it also combines our ignorance (uncertainty) with risk. And the number of rational strategies available to us is distressingly small.

The simplest is to anticipate bad outcomes and prepare for them: saving money for unexpected expenses; stocking supplies in case of violent storms; practicing fire drills and other emergency responses. Preparation can involve a backup "Plan B": selecting a second-choice restaurant in case our first choice is closed or fully booked; including a "safe school" among one's college applications, in case the first-choice institutions send rejections; issuing "if that approach fails, then do this" instructions to employees. These plans, which often begin as consideration of "preferred-case, worst-case" outcomes, can grow into complex and formal documents as multiple scenarios are imagined: governmental disaster plans, military battle plans, and institutional long-range plans are examples. Anticipating bad outcomes and arranging contingent responses to them, at least in pure forms, do nothing to reduce the likelihood and little to reduce the costs of those events (the "harm"). In fact, preparation and planning represent additional costs.

A more proactive strategy is to reduce the impact of our residual ignorance, to reduce the risk of incurring harm from unforeseen events. And where we cannot reduce the likelihood or risk, we may try to reduce loss. Societies have developed instrumentalities, corporations, even whole industries designed to reduce loss: *insurance*, in its various forms, is paradigmatic. Other forms include warranties, guarantees, prenuptial agreements, and bail bonds.

Think of the historically important example of insuring ships and their cargo. Both the shipping company and its insurers are ignorant of future events, and there is considerable risk of loss of property and lives on the high seas. So, the two parties agree to a special form of contract in which

the insurer "underwrites" the voyage. In exchange for payment of a premium, the insurer takes on some of the risk by guaranteeing payment in
the event of damage or loss. The shipping company agrees to pay in order
to reduce its risk of much greater financial losses.

Like gambling, insurance is based on the calculation of odds regarding
future events. In the case of insurance, however (assuming no criminal
manipulation), both parties desire the same outcome: a safe and sound
voyage, in my shipping example. In the preferred outcome, the shipper
would deliver the goods intact, having felt protected against loss, for which
payment of a premium was worthwhile. At the same time, the underwrit-
ers would gain a profitable payment and, thankfully, have had to expend
no reimbursement for losses. The calculation each makes starts with the
riskiness of the voyage: the premium rises as the perceived risk increases,
and some voyages may be deemed simply too risky to insure. In all cases,
the shipping company must determine whether the risk is sufficiently high
to pay the premium asked. Calculations of risk and premiums are made by
actuaries, based on statistics regarding past events and trend lines. Where
scientific laws are insufficient to predict outcomes, the historical record of
like events is the best source of information. Insurance is thus an instrument for managing our ignorance and its effects, and actuarial calculation
is its defining technique.

Because so many aspects of future events are important to us, and
because underwriting can be quite profitable (especially as technology and
safety measures reduce risk), the insurance industry has grown and diversi-
fied in startling ways. One may now insure against damage and loss regarding a wide range of personal and corporate property, from automobiles
and homes to jewelry, livestock, and smartphones. Insurers now distinguish the causes for potential losses, so, for example, we must insure our
homes separately for losses from fire or storm, from flood, or from theft.
We may insure our "beneficiaries" against the financial impact of our own
death. These are tame, familiar examples. What some people hold to be
precious, however, and what risks some have worried over, have led to
quite exotic insurance policies, the stuff of tabloids. In the 1940s, as a pub-
licity stunt (at least in part), Twentieth Century Fox insured each of Betty
Grable's shapely legs for $1 million. Decades later, Rolling Stones guitarist
Keith Richards insured one finger, his middle finger, for $1.5 million. An
Australian cricket player, Merv Hughes, whose handlebar mustache is a

personal trademark, claims to have insured it for $400,000. It has recently been reported that over $10 million has been spent in the United States to insure against abduction by aliens—with higher payouts for repeated abductions.[5] What a sideshow!

A stock market is a temple of calculated risk-taking. What sort of insurance could there be against significant financial loss in the market? Having a diverse investment portfolio was the traditional wisdom, but it was a prophylactic, hoping to avoid loss rather than offering real protection against actual loss. So-called hedge funds, however, have often been promoted as investment vehicles that attempt to return a profit regardless of whether the market was up or down. Historically, the term *hedging* referred to the attempt to reduce the risk of a bear market, usually by "shorting" the market.[6] Today, however, most of these funds aim to maximize return on investment; and because they are often aggressively managed and trade in devices like derivatives, it seems they may actually involve more risk than conventional market investments. While some investors have profited by hedge funds during downturns, others have lost disastrously—and in nearly all cases, hedge fund managers have fared better than their clients.[7]

From Possibility to Probability

Essential to all whose profession is trading in uncertainty—insurers, stocker brokers, gamblers—are the mathematical tools developed to manage ignorance and minimize risk. All such tools are refinements of the concept of *probability.*

Our plight can be described simply: we are ignorant of future outcomes, yet we want to anticipate (predict) them to reduce risk; we know there are many *possible* outcomes, but we don't know the *likelihood* that a particular outcome will actually occur. What mathematics offers us is the quantification or measurement of that likelihood, which we call *probability.* The concept of probability shaped a theory that has blossomed into a rich and complex field of mathematics. On the surface, it seems to replace our ignorance with quantitatively precise knowledge, but—as we shall see—our ignorance is managed, not vanquished. The theory has contested alternative versions, and all of them are freighted with persistent philosophical problems.

In this section, we will discuss briefly four interpretations of probability. (A mathematically challenged reader need not panic: a very basic discussion will be sufficient to illustrate the relevant points.)

(1) The *classical interpretation* is derived from the situations for which probability theory was originally constructed: gambling. Rolling dice is an easy example. There is a precise number of possible outcomes in rolling a die: each of six sides of a fair die, 1 through 6. *Which* number will actually be rolled on any throw is unknown. In the classical interpretation, the alternative outcomes are assumed to be *equally probable*. How probable is it that the player will roll, say, a 6? It is one out of six, or 1/6, or 16.667 percent. Thus, an impossible outcome (like rolling a 0) has a probability of 0; a certain outcome has a probability of 1.0 or 100 percent.

Here is the *classical interpretation* as summarized by Pierre-Simon Laplace in 1814:

The theory of chance consists in reducing all the events of the same kind to a certain number of cases equally possible, that is to say, to such as we may be equally undecided about in regard to their existence, and in determining the number of cases favorable to the event whose probability is sought. The ratio of this number to that of all the cases possible is the measure of this probability, which is thus simply a fraction whose numerator is the number of favorable cases and whose denominator is the number of all the cases possible.[8]

The process seems clean and clear. We could, by extrapolation, apply this method to determining the probability of betting on the right number in roulette, of drawing a royal flush, or of winning a lottery.

Note, however, that all this hinges on the assumption that each alternative outcome is in fact "equally possible," that the die (or roulette wheel or deck of cards or whatnot) is fair. There is the rub. We accept dice as fair because they are properly marked and are constructed symmetrically (except perhaps for the minuscule differences in weight produced by the varying number of dots). We see no relevant differences among the six sides. The "fairness" of a die is not a function of the numbers one actually rolls with it; no one at the factory tests dice for their fairness by rolling them and marking the results. Yes, in theory, a fair die is one that will, given an infinite number of rolls, roll each number an equal number of times. But of course no one can roll dice infinitely. There is a hint here of the circularity that makes philosophers uneasy: the classical theory requires *probability* to be calculated on the base concept of *equally possible* alternative outcomes, but the notion of events being "equally possible" seems itself to designate a measure of *probability*—equal probability.

(2) Most of life's choice situations are not as neatly defined as gambling problems. For these situations, the *frequency interpretation* may be applicable.

Earlier, I spoke of transformative choices in which we cannot know the nature and value of an alternative presented to us; but in many of life's decisions, we cannot *identify* all of the alternative outcomes or fix their number; and even when we can, we may not be able to establish the likelihood of each occurring. Every student knows that even the blithely unprepared have a one-in-two chance of correctly answering a true-false question. But the calculation for a fill-in-the-blank question is much more difficult: we cannot identify all the possible choices or establish their likelihood. Calculating life insurance rates requires estimating the probability that someone will die in a given period. But the actuary cannot assume that all people are equally likely to die in that given period. All of us will die, of course; the relevant question is *when*.

A different method of coping with uncertainty was developed for these cases—it is the method applied in underwriting insurance: the researcher examines the frequency of alternative outcomes in similar situations in the past. This method is *statistical inference*, which combines the analysis of numerical data with induction, thereby drawing inferences regarding a whole set of cases from a given sample. It holds that probability statements are about ways in which the future will reflect the past. In this view, probabilities refer not to an individual event but to classes of similar events. For useful guidance, one needs a large number of previous cases, a "valid sample size" to produce "statistically significant" results.[9]

Take this statement: "The probability that a sixty-five-year-old American male will die during the year is one in sixty-one (1.6389 percent)." It means that in the set of such men in recent years, one of every sixty-one died during the year. We should expect the set of such men this year to exhibit the same death rate, if other conditions remain constant. This interpretation makes probability statements empirical and inductive, not a matter of logic alone. These inferences presume that the whole is like the part, and that the future will be like the past.

Notice the difference between the classical and the frequency methods. In the case of dice, the probability is an abstract calculation based on an idealized notion of possible outcomes. The probability that anyone will roll a 6 is not derived from a statistical analysis of previous dice rolls. By contrast, the probability that males will die is inferred from historical data. Nonetheless, abstract games-of-chance mathematics is often used to express statistical inferences. The death rate of males between sixty-five and sixty-six years old in the United States, which is determined by statistical analysis, is 0.016389; this is roughly equivalent to 1/61.[10] The chance of any such male dying this year is therefore one in sixty-one. The gaming model of odds, which is the likelihood of possibilities, is thus used to express results in both methods.[11]

The frequency interpretation requires drawing inferences from a relevant set of previous outcomes, but a difficulty arises in delineating the sets so as to derive the information we seek. Grouping things as sets always requires us to ignore individual differences among its members, but it is possible that some of those differences may relate to the probability we seek. Imagine a patient learns that a certain surgical implant has a 30 percent rejection rate. If this means that 30 of every 100 patients receiving the implant suffered rejection and the implant had to be removed, then the presumption is made that one patient is like another for purposes of this comparison. And that may be false. Patients are unique, and there is no patient exactly like the current subject.

Another concern in both examples is the *ceteris paribus* requirement—"other things being equal," the stipulation that "other conditions remain the same." In the implant rejection case, there may now or soon be improved methods of implantation, antirejection drugs, advanced postoperative care, a younger and generally healthier group of patients needing the implant, and so on. The future context is never an exact match with the past.

Most importantly, notice also that *neither method will predict the outcome of a particular case*: knowing the odds doesn't predict the next roll of the die; knowing the death rate doesn't identify which individuals will die. Our ignorance regarding any specific case remains. This is the genius—and the limitation—of probability theory: because identifying determinative causal factors is so difficult, *it ignores them altogether*.[12] Dice are used as models of chance because the determinative factors in any roll are impossibly complex for our analysis and are not in our control. Similarly, causes of death are various and subject to individual factors; while they are not random, they cannot be processed so as make individual predictions. Using the statistical method, researchers may attempt to reveal causes by subdividing the population, testing different subsets, and applying regression analyses. For example, one might divide the relevant male population by race or smoking practices or marital status to determine whether there are differential correlations, different death rates for each group. But a high rate of correlation is still just that: a correlation, not a cause. Here is the takeaway point: probability theory allows us to claim knowledge of populations and series, large classes of events, and to manage—and mask—our ignorance of individual events that lie beyond our prediction or control.

(3) A third interpretation makes probabilities neither about logic nor about a pattern of past events in the world, but rather about one's degree of belief. It is usually termed the *subjectivist interpretation*. This account seems most plausible for statements like: "I will probably attend the concert" or "I am not likely to finish this project by tomorrow." In our previous cases, the intent was to assert something about the outcomes themselves, not about one's confidence that a particular outcome would occur. Moreover, it is true that one may be quite confident that an event is very unlikely, or unsure of whether an event is highly probable. Thus the concepts of probability and confidence are clearly distinguishable. Where they connect is when one is addressing the likelihood of one's choices or actions; one's intention and one's level of commitment to a belief then become relevant factors in determining the likelihood of outcomes.

The three theories sketched here have been ably summarized by Herbert Weisberg in his discussion of the history of probability theory:

There are three main ideas that have been subsumed in what we generally regard today under the heading of probability. First, probability is assumed to obey certain *mathematical rules* that are illustrated in their purest form by games of chance. Second, *statistical regularities* observed in natural and social phenomena are regarded as examples of probability in action. Third, probability reflects in some sense a *degree of belief* or measure of certainty.[13]

All three interpretations (and there are other variations)[14] report probabilities in quantitative terms, but the first two offer a basis for precision in objective (or, rationally debatable) factors; they conceive of probability itself as an inherently mathematical notion. The subjectivist's "degree of belief" is inherently less quantitatively precise. (How does one measure the difference between a confidence of 75 and 80 percent?) But it reveals more openly the underlying ignorance that the first two interpretations disguise.

(4) Finally, an older, even ancient, notion of probability is still operative in some arenas today. I will term it the *judgment interpretation*. It is neither formalized nor quantized, but rather takes probability to be a matter of the weight of salient evidence. We find this notion today in the application of the legal term "probable cause." A judge, asked to issue a warrant or subpoena, does not determine whether there is a 1/6 cause or a 5/6 cause; the determination is made more loosely based on an assemblage of relevant evidence, argument, and legal considerations. Since probability in this context is a matter of judgment, it is easy to see how the focus can morph from the weight of evidence into the (judge's) degree of confidence in belief (the subjectivist interpretation). But the concept of probable cause points to objective factors—the factors the judge weighs. Admittedly, the judicial standard of "beyond a reasonable doubt" for a guilty verdict seems to point ambiguously toward the evidence and also toward the jury's degree of confidence in their belief. Both embody claims about whether a probability is sufficient for a particular judicial action; both assist us in the management of ignorance.

The Chance of Rain

As we have seen, nagging questions remain about the concept of probability under its varying interpretations: vicious circularity, assumptions of statistical inference, unfounded quantification of confidence, the imprecision of judgment, and so on. These issues leave us with the vexing problem of understanding what exactly we mean by a statement of probability. Assertions of probability are commonplace, but do we really know what they mean? For example: what does a weather forecaster mean by the statement, "There is a 20 percent chance of rain tomorrow"?

National Public Radio asked this very question with hilarious results. The responses from the public revealed wildly different beliefs and the admitted uncertainty of many, including a mathematician and a respected meteorologist![15] The total number of respondents was 42,143—quite a good sample. Among the interesting results:

• Over four percent of the respondents thought the forecast meant that "it will rain tomorrow for 20 percent of the time."

• Over seven percent thought it meant "20 percent of the weather forecasters believe it will rain tomorrow."

- One in five interpreted the statement as meaning that "it will rain tomorrow in 20 percent of the region."
- Half of the respondents thought it meant "it will rain on 20 percent of the days like tomorrow."
- The remainder had still other interpretations or simply didn't know.

Note first that in all of the interpretations (except perhaps those unspecified), the implication is that we could replace "it will rain" with "it will certainly rain": for example, "it will (certainly) rain tomorrow for 20 percent of the time." In other words, these interpretations attempt to eliminate or cash out the uncertainty involved in probability by its expression as a statistical fact. This uses redirection to transform ignorance into apparent certainty. Second, these interpretations are still plagued by vagueness: where will it rain; who count as "weather forecasters"; what are the boundaries of "the region"; what exactly are "days like tomorrow"? The fourth interpretation has a verification problem: it projects an infinite number of "days like tomorrow"—but in practice, we cannot observe an infinite number of trials. And all of them are imprecise about what is meant by "rain"—a few drops, a drizzle, a short and scattered burst, a sustained deluge, and so on. Forecasters are aware of this problem and usually supplement the probability statement with additional descriptions, such as "scattered showers," or "thunderstorm around noon."

Setting aside audience perceptions, what is the intended meaning of the forecast? To answer this question, the National Weather Service published an official definition, though they used "a 40 percent chance of rain" (which might seem to double the odds):

Mathematically, PoP [Probability of Precipitation] is defined as follows:

PoP = C × A where "C" = the confidence that precipitation will occur *somewhere* in the forecast area, and where "A" = the percent of the area that will receive measureable precipitation, *if it occurs at all.*

So … in the case of the forecast above, if the forecaster knows precipitation is sure to occur (confidence is 100%), he/she is expressing how much of the area will receive measurable rain. (PoP = "C" × "A" or "1" times ".4" which equals .4 or 40%.)

But, most of the time, the forecaster is expressing a combination of degree of confidence *and* areal coverage. If the forecaster is only 50% sure that precipitation will occur, and expects that, *if it does occur*, it will produce measurable rain over about 80 percent of the area, the PoP (chance of rain) is 40%. (PoP = .5 × .8 which equals .4 or 40%.)

In either event, the correct way to interpret the forecast is: there is a 40 percent chance that rain will occur at any given point in the area.[16]

So we now know that "rain" means "measurable precipitation"—which is elsewhere stipulated as "at least .1 inch." And we see that the affected portion of the "forecast area" is indeed a factor ("how much of the area will received measurable rain"). This reduces the probability to a fact: a percentage of area.

But the other factor is quite odd: the *degree of confidence* of the forecaster (singular, not plural) that precipitation will occur *somewhere* in the area. This is very troublesome. First, combining these two factors creates an ambiguity: any given percentage (say, our initial 20 percent) could represent either the product of a small area and high confidence (20 percent of the forecast area and 100 percent confidence) or a large area and low confidence (or 100 percent of the area, and a measly 20 percent confidence)— and any combination in between. But the prediction would read the same: "20 percent chance of rain."

Second, how does one quantify a degree of confidence? It seems a strange approach to make the percentage a function of both the degree of belief and a geographical area. Indeed, it is hard to see how "correctness" could be applied to a quantified statement that refers to a subjective level of confidence—and with the implied singular forecaster. The combination of ambiguity and vagueness leads me to conclude that the official attempt to interpret this probability statement has failed.

Given the widespread meteorological use of computer modeling, one might well have expected that a forecaster's prediction would be based on computer simulations, which are, in turn, derived from the patterns of past weather records.[17] In short, my expectation was that a version of the frequency interpretation, grounded in statistically based modeling, would have informed the definition. My suspicion is that this omission is an unfortunate mistake, but I am astonished that is *no mention* of a frequency interpretation in this official account. Even so, every weather day is unique; so one would need to set parameters, necessarily deciding to ignore individual differences, in order to construct a class of past weather days like today and examine the tomorrows that followed.

However one unpacks the definition, the result would not cash out the inherent uncertainty in the statement. The assertion that "there is a 20 (or 40) percent chance of rain tomorrow" will not be confirmed or refuted by whether it rains or shines on me tomorrow. So the forecaster can claim a correct prediction either way.

Despite their vagueness, ambiguity, and residual uncertainty, we often are guided by such probability statements, especially when the probability stated is high or low—and rightly so: we are more likely to carry an umbrella if the chance of rain is 90 percent than if it is 20 percent. Where probabilities are cashed out as patterns or percentages of actualities, they are descriptively verifiable only as statements about a class of previous events; but where they are derived from such facts, yet offered as predictions, forecasts, odds, or chances of future events, they are indexes of our ignorance.

Other Intellectual Tools

Though I have focused on probability theory, mathematics offers numerous concepts and techniques for ignorance management. The statistical concept of *margin of error* is an example. It is a measure of sampling error, the likely variation from the sampling result one should expect if the whole class were surveyed. If a political candidate receives 33 percent voter support among the sample in a political poll with a ±3 percentage point margin of error, we should expect between 30 and 36 percent of the entire population to support that candidate. But the likelihood of the whole-population result being "within the margin of error" is itself a probability. Today, a researcher strives for a 95 percent *confidence level*, which is a statistical measure of the *reliability* of results—in this case, there is a probability of at least 95 percent that the results are accurate (true). This too can be read as an index of uncertainty.

One could argue that the entire discipline of algebra is a tool for gaining knowledge by managing ignorance. Algebra abstracts mathematical relationships from numbers, allowing the manipulation of unspecified quantities, using letters (a, b, c ... x, y, z) to represent unknowns. It is from its use in algebra that X became a common symbol for "the unknown."

This meaning of the letter X may be traced to the Arabic word for *thing*, or *šay*. Early Arabic texts such as Al-Jabr (820 CE), which established the principles of algebra (and gave the discipline its name), referred to mathematical variables as *things*. So, we might read an equation as "3 things equal 21" (the *thing* being 7). Much later, when Al-Jabr was translated into Old

Spanish, the word *šay* was written as *xei*, which was soon shortened to *X*. Today we find *X* used to designate phenomena that are mysterious (X-rays, *The X Files*, *The X Factor*, *X the Unknown*) or the unknown or forgotten (as when Malcolm Little honored his ancestors by changing to his name to Malcolm X). *X* is the symbol of our ignorance.

The devices of ignorance management that have been developed in other disciplines and in social use are endless. For policy and planning, we use projective scenarios, simulations, and feedback loops. In science, replication of experiments by others is used to increase confidence in the results. Special protocols of confirmation for important military orders are designed to reduce uncertainty. Passwords and related security devices serve to reduce uncertainty, both to identify those entitled to information and those excluded from it. We manage our individual ignorance about esoteric matters by consulting certified experts: it is the premise of television's *Antiques Road Show* and of services such as jewelry appraisals, home inspections, and financial audits. The list is endless.

In closing this chapter, I should note once again that we often use ignorance constructively, especially to create conditions of fairness. To decide fairly who should receive the initial kick-off in a football game, we toss a coin. To determine who wins a door prize, we draw a ticket from an unseen pile in an opaque jar. To assign a high-risk mission, we may draw lots. In such cases, we turn over the decision to chance, to events so complex we cannot predict or control the outcome. This is quite different from John Rawls's use of the veil of ignorance or from "blindfolded" justice in the courtroom: while these, too, use ignorance to assure fairness, they do not opt for chance or unpredictability; they choose the exclusion of specific information, purposefully bounded ignorance.

I also close with a nod to the game of baseball for my appropriation of its rich terminology. It was Muddy Ruel or Bill Dickey, depending on your source, who first applied the term *tools of ignorance* to the catcher's equipment: mask, chest protector, shin guards, cup, and glove—a good metaphor for the instruments of this chapter.

V Ignorance as Horizon

So that, as rational metaphysics teaches that man becomes all things by understanding them, this imaginative metaphysics shows that man becomes all things by not understanding them; and perhaps the latter proposition is truer than the former, for when man understands, he extends his mind and takes in the things, but when he does not understand he makes the things out of themselves and becomes them by transforming himself into them.

—Giambattista Vico

11 The Horizon of Ignorance

It may be that what is "right" and what is "good" consist in staying open to the tensions that beset the most fundamental categories we require, to know unknowingness at the core of what we know, and what we need, and to recognize the sign of life—and its prospects.

—Judith Butler

Although the idea of a horizon retains something of the images of boundary and limit, it is, by contrast, apparent and perspectival. Our horizon moves with us, the line of our outermost reach. It moves, that is, against the objective epistemic terrain, circling the domain of our knowledge. It is "our" horizon because its range and compass are relative to our position and our visionary resources: we see farther in flat landscapes, or from a great height, or with the aid of a telescope. When we picture ignorance as a horizon, we recognize that it not only changes with our knowledge but is constructed by our knowing. Moreover, while we may remove a boundary or cross it, our horizon is always with us and yet always out of reach. Nevertheless, the horizon does beckon us: it attracts our reach, our yearnings. Dawnings and sunsets, like awakenings and forgettings, happen at the horizon, illuminating and darkening our plain of understanding.

The horizon image embodies the fusion of the constantly shifting with the eternally present that is the relationship of knowledge and ignorance. We pursue learning, we research, we comprehend and discover, but—as I remarked at the outset—the vast surround of ignorance remains. Our individual horizon of knowledge may be absorbed within the known terrain of the human race, but collective human knowledge at any moment in time has its own circumscribing horizon. Our learning responds to (some) ignorance, eliminates (some) ignorance, manages (some) ignorance, creates a refined and restructured ignorance, and grows knowledge within that vast surround. We grasp the epistemic aspects of the human condition only when we understand the *interaction* between our knowing and the unknown.

Epistemic Luck

Luck is a term we use to describe an event or state that usually has three properties: it occurred by chance or was not foreseen; it was not under human control; and it was of significance—positive or negative—to the individual. Luck is a philosophically significant concept, mostly because philosophers intuitively want to exclude it from normative assessment. In ethics, for example, the moral worth of an action or the virtues and vices of a person's character should be based not on matters of luck but rather on deeper expressions of the self in desires, intentions, and wills. Similarly, the ideal of justice is based on what one deserves, not on luck. Achieving something by luck undermines its quality as a genuine achievement.

In the last chapter, we discussed various tactics and tools for managing the impact of chance and unpredictable events, techniques of using knowledge to cope with ignorance. But epistemologists have recently noticed that luck can undermine our knowledge; it can disqualify as counterfeit what otherwise seems to be genuine knowledge. Let us take a moment to consider this point.

"Genuine" knowledge, as I have noted before, must traditionally meet three criteria: (1) it must be believed; (2) the belief must be true; and (3) the believer must have adequate justification or warrant for believing it. Since Plato, the analysis of knowledge has been framed as "justified true belief." Because this account is focused on propositional knowledge (*knowing that*), it is commonly summarized in a simple schema:

S knows that p if and only if:

1. S believes that p;
2. p (is true); and
3. S has adequate justification or warrant for believing that p.

Centuries of epistemology have been devoted to the attempt to spell out just what is involved in each of those three conditions, with increasingly elaborated results. But the assumption has been that *if* these three conditions were met (however one defined them), they would yield genuine knowledge (for S).

In 1963, this game was shockingly disrupted by a tidy, three-page article. It is Edmund Gettier III's one and only publication.[1] He simply presented cases in which even justified true belief was not sufficient for knowing something "in the strong sense," that is, for genuine knowledge. How could that be?

Imagine, for example, that Jim believes the Red Sox beat the Yankees today by a score of 4 to 3, and in fact they did; Jim learned this by watching the game on TV. Thus Jim's belief is in fact true and he has reasonable justification for his belief. Here is the problem: unbeknownst to Jim, what he watched was a rebroadcast of yesterday's game—in which it also happened that the Red Sox beat the Yankees by the same score. So, Jim does not really know who won today's game, not in the "strong sense."

In Gettier's problematic situations, there is a mere coincidence between one's epistemic judgment and the facts: we do not really possess the knowledge we think we do. In Jim's case, unknown unknowns were in play; his justified true belief was a matter of *epistemic luck*. Typically, Gettier cases postulate both one's ignorance of relevant factors and one's luck in meeting the justified, true belief conditions notwithstanding that ignorance. How can we exclude such circumstances? Unfortunately, Gettier did not develop a solution; he just let loose the force of his examples.

An immediate response—one made by various philosophers—is that we need to tighten the standard for proper warrant or justification. So, in the baseball case, contrary to first glance, we might say Jim did not in fact have sufficient justification for his belief about today's game. But surely he did have reasonable evidence. Then perhaps we need to introduce a distinction: one might distinguish between *entitlements to belief* and *justifications for belief*. In the case above, Jim would have had *entitlement* for his belief about the game, but not a genuine *justification* for it. But that is a tricky business. The higher we set the bar for genuine justification, the more we risk a hollow tautology: one's belief would be justified only if one genuinely knows it to be true. I know only if I know.

Another approach is to require greater precision in formulating the belief proposition. Instead of saying "Jim believed that the Red Sox beat the Yankees today by 4 to 3," we should say, "Jim believed he saw a game on TV today in which the Red Sox beat the Yankees, 4 to 3." That justified true belief is not undermined by the epistemic luck that afflicted the earlier belief. This is a dubious move as well. First, that more precise statement does not capture fully what Jim actually believes: he believed it was today's game. We only state it that cautious way because we are aware of the Gettier threat. And second, other Gettier conditions may be in play that affect even this refined statement—how would one know?

Many epistemologists, therefore, have simply adopted a fourth criterion for genuine knowledge, an amendment to the schema:

4.   Gettier-type circumstances do not obtain.

In other words, genuine knowledge also requires that epistemic luck is not a factor. That formulation is only a placeholder, of course. It labels and excludes but does not present a general characterization of the undermining Gettier circumstances. The literature has blossomed with new and more contrived Gettier-type cases, proposals for their general characterization, and attempts at a resolution that would eliminate the need for a Gettier asterisk in the analysis of knowledge.

We should mark several points in this matter. Gettier-type cases are matters of epistemic luck; they involve coincidental interactions between knowledge and ignorance. Knowledge is embedded in the justification: Jim knew he saw the game, and he knew the Red Sox won 4 to 3 in the game he saw. He was ignorant of the fact that he watched a rebroadcast; for Jim, it was an unknown unknown. By luck he could form a justified true belief despite relevant ignorance. Second, we should note that luck undermines our sense of achievement, so if we are trying to achieve knowledge, we cannot get there by luck.

Nonetheless, in common human experience, luck is indeed a factor in our coming to know, and our ignorance is also often a matter of luck. Duncan Pritchard, drawing on the work of Peter Unger, has identified three types of "benign" epistemic luck and has proposed a fourth.[2] (1) There is *content epistemic luck*: it is lucky that the proposition is true, that the Red Sox won, in my example. (2) Second, there is *capacity epistemic luck*: it is lucky that Jim is capable of knowing the outcome of the game. (3) There is *evidential epistemic luck*: it is lucky that Jim happened to see the game on TV. This condition presumably describes cases like those discussed earlier (chapter 9) in which some historical traces have survived by luck, despite the loss of others. (4) Pritchard also teases out *doxastic epistemic luck*, in which it is lucky that the believer believes the proposition: it is lucky that Tim believes the Red Sox won. These are, Pritchard asserts, unproblematic for genuine knowledge. But another type is of concern: (5) *veritic epistemic luck*, in which it is a matter of luck that the belief is true.[3] Veritic luck is at play in Gettier-type cases, and Pritchard thinks it is fatal to genuine knowledge and must be eliminated. While it seems clear that Gettier-type cases do involve veritic luck—it was a matter of luck that Jim's belief about who won the game was true—we might also analyze the case as a matter of (bad) evidential luck: perhaps it was unlucky that Jim didn't happen to watch the screen when the notice appeared that it was a rebroadcast.

Since Pritchard's purpose is to protect knowledge from luck, he understandably gives less attention to the "benign" forms. They seem not to threaten the genuineness of knowledge; nonetheless, they do affect the knowledge and ignorance we possess. Evidential luck is particularly significant. Moreover, no matter how we formulate the criteria to secure genuine knowledge, we simply cannot in practice rule out the salience of unknown unknowns. Our Jim may acknowledge that unknown unknowns are always with us; but, by definition, he cannot state what they are or whether any of them would undermine his claim to knowledge by revealing that he was simply lucky in his belief.

We work purposefully within the surround of ignorance to gain knowledge. But the horizon of unknown unknowns is always with us. Not only can we not capture and tame it; it infuses even the circle of light we claim as knowledge. Epistemic luck is continuously at work in the interaction of the known and the unknown. Our horizonal perspective is not something we can autonomously determine or reduce, and the range and reach of our knowledge is not a luck-free zone. Moreover, paradoxically, it seems that the very pursuit of knowledge creates ignorance. Every epistemic advance serves to expand the horizon of the unknown.

How Learning Creates Ignorance

We have discussed the ways in which individuals, organizations, and governments may construct and protect ignorance (chapter 6). But how does the very process of coming to know something *create* ignorance or—as some would say—"improve" it? What is an *improved* ignorance?

Let us look at a couple of examples. First: in recent years, advances in submersibles and underwater photography have resulted in deeper dives and the discovery of many new species. Photos and videos now show fascinating, bizarre creatures never before observed. Pondering these images, a marine biologist may now be curious about the function of an odd-looking structure, about the evolutionary advantage of strange behavior, or about the adaptations that allow such a delicate organism to survive under the great pressure of deep waters.

The second example: in tracing her family genealogy, a woman knows that her maternal great-grandparents came to the United States from Scotland, but she doesn't know exactly when. She discovers they are listed in the Scotland Census of 1861, but she cannot locate them in the Scotland Census of 1871. She draws the reasonable, if only probable, conclusion that they emigrated sometime in the decade between the dates of the two censuses.

In the latter example, the ignorance was "improved" or "refined" by narrowing the search, specifying more precisely a known unknown: the possible emigration date—though still uncertain—has been narrowed to a ten-year span. In the former example, however, new knowledge has generated new questions, questions that could not have been asked previously because the organisms were unknown. New knowledge may "create" ignorance by making unknown unknowns into known unknowns; it is a transformation at the metalevel. It is not just that there was no reason to ask these new questions previously; rather, it is that there was no epistemic basis to ask them, no known subject about which to formulate them.

There are more startling cases. A discovery may reveal new relationships among elements of previous knowledge, altering their theoretical connections. Occasionally, an important breakthrough launches new concepts, or even a new conceptual framework or paradigm. In such discoveries, our understanding of a field may be irreversibly altered. The discovery of new sea creatures, despite its significance, does not portend a conceptual revolution. We apply well-embedded biological concepts (species, adaptation, reproduction, and so on) to raise questions about the newly discovered organisms. Contrast that with the impact of new knowledge like the original discoveries of microorganisms, subatomic structure, and evolution. Each introduced new knowledge that reinterpreted our previous knowledge and generated whole conceptual structures within which new sorts of questions might be framed. Sometimes, long-established concepts are given new meanings (in the way that Einstein's concept of *mass* altered Newton's *mass*). And each such discovery restructures and refines our ignorance, extends its horizonal span, and sets a new agenda for inquiry.

Yet we need to push still further to grasp fully the creation of ignorance. My language may suggest that Nature simply awaits curious humans to uncover its secrets, to discover what is already there but hidden, and thereby to "acquire" knowledge. This outlook, adopted with good effect by the "natural philosophers" of the early Enlightenment, is nonetheless misleading. It underplays the role of the imagination, of theory construction, of creativity, in the search for knowledge. I am not suggesting that there is no reality except what we create—though certainly some do take that position. That view turns scientific research into a convoluted exercise of self-expression by the self-deceived researcher. It leaves us with an unsatisfying account of Nature's stubbornness, of the surprising refutation of dearly held hypotheses.[4] Nevertheless, the linguistic and quantitative systems we employ, our conceptual frameworks, the metaphors that underlie them, the theory-laden instruments we construct, the techniques we develop for research—these are all human creations. Insofar as human knowledge is a social construct in this profound sense, *so is ignorance*. This means that our new knowledge *creates* our ignorance: it does not simply identify unknowns that were lurking among the unknown unknowns all along; as we grasp for them, we formulate them, and thus we create their manifestation.

So much of our ignorance is rightly thought of negatively; but when we think of ignorance *only* negatively, the picture is demoralizing, paralyzing, even terrorizing. It is the epistemic paradox: while we work to learn in order to remove ignorance, we cannot reduce its infinite sea, and—as in the Greek myths of self-defeating actions—our very efforts to learn, even when successful, may increase our ignorance. This dark and stultifying view, however, fails to reflect the full importance of ignorance in our lives. As debilitating and tragic and reprehensible as ignorance can be, as devastating as may be the errors it enables, ignorance, especially when it is acknowledged, also contributes enormous positives to human life. It is to those I now turn.

Freedom, Creativity, and Ignorance

Neurobiologist Stuart Firestein, in *Ignorance: How It Drives Science*,[5] argues not only that scientific research is propelled by ignorance, but that the goal of science is to refine and improve our ignorance. Yes, curiosity is necessary for scientific research; but curiosity arises only in the presence of ignorance. The felt presence of the unknown can summon us to inquiry. Ignorance, Firestein argues, sets the agenda for research; furthermore, the fecundity of a discovery is largely in the ignorance it creates. We can broaden the thesis, for the same claims apply in the social sciences, in archaeological research, and also in most forms of scholarly research in the arts and humanities.

It is, indeed, the presence of the horizon of ignorance that provides room for imagination, free thought, and creativity. Knowing—and I mean the sort of genuine knowing that carries conviction—is the culmination of thought; it carries no more epistemic yearning on the matter. Only new doubt, new uncertainties can subvert this contentment and spur learning. Only recognition of the possibility of our own ignorance opens a cognitive space for unlearning false knowledge and for genuine learning (or an improved ignorance).

The work and play of imagination and creativity are ventures into the unknown. They are inimical to the repetition of facts, the regurgitation of knowledge. Ingenuity, inventiveness, originality, spontaneity—they all require forays into the unknown.

While all forms of human creativity presume the unknown, some give it a place of honor. Improvisational performance is such an escapade in the unpredictable. Improvisational jazz, for example, uses just enough of the "known" (perhaps a basic melody, a time signature, and a cycle of spotlighted moments by individual musicians in the ensemble) to structure a venture into the free performance space of the unknown. Aleatoric art goes even further, opening the performance or the artwork to chance or random elements. John Cage's *Radio Music* (1956), a work for eight radios, was composed using random operations: it involves tuning the radios to fifty-six different frequencies, programmed by eight individual musicians, with or without intervening silences. The same principles are applied in avant-garde theatrical works, painting and other visual arts, dance, and poetry. Films may, of course, include scenes that are not structured in detail, such as recording whatever happens outside a particular window over fifteen minutes. But other aleatoric films use different gateways for chance: *Six Reels of Film to Be Shown in Any Order* (1971), directed by Barry Salt, was distributed with a special die to be rolled by the projectionist at each showing to determine the order of the reels.

In literature and film, mysteries are emblematic of our love of the unknown. Obviously, no story would be a mystery without the reader's ignorance of some crucial matter: who committed the murder or, in "locked-room mysteries," how the crime was committed. There is yet a more fundamental and pervasive role in literature and film for the unknown. Narrative itself has its mesmerizing effects because it moves forward into the unknown: what will happen next; how will things turn out; who is this character? In narrative, as in research, in art, and in life, adventure requires the push into the unknown. (It is true, of course, that especially as children, we love to hear or certain familiar stories read again and again; they become as cherished poetry, and their reading becomes a ritual. Yet it is the delight of the first reading that we rehearse in reexperience, but inevitably find ourselves reading or listening in a different way. The same is true of the favorite films of childhood.)

Ignorance and knowledge, we might say, have a *yin-yang* relationship: it is the balance and interaction of the two that give us the life of the mind. It is the mutually prehending relationship of the known to the unknown that provides the matrix of learning, the challenge of discovery, the quest of the research lab, the anticipation of turning the next page of the narrative, the exhilaration of risk, the yearning of hope, and the thrill of surprise.

The horizonal presence of ignorance has affective impact; it inspires feelings. One of the most eloquent portrayals of this sense of ignorance is found in John Dewey's early landmark text, *Psychology*. Dewey presents ignorance as a state of mind with a distinctive feeling. It is worth quoting at length:

A feeling of knowledge is necessarily accompanied by one of ignorance, and will so continue until the whole organic system of knowledge is mastered. ...

A feeling of ignorance is, therefore, strictly correlative to one of knowledge. A feeling of knowledge is one of the realized self; a feeling of ignorance is one of the unrealized self. One is the feeling of the objective and universal self, so far as this has been made to exist in individual form; the other is the vague and indefinite feeling of this universal self as not realized. An animal may be ignorant, for example, but we cannot conceive it to be conscious of this ignorance, unless we attribute to it a true self-consciousness. Ignorance is the feeling of the division or conflict in our nature.

A feeling of the unknown must be distinguished, therefore, from one of the un-knowable. The latter would be a feeling of something utterly unrelated to self, and hence is a psychological impossibility. The feeling that something is unknown, or of ignorance, is the feeling of self, but of self as still incomplete. A feeling of the unknowable would be possible only if we could transcend wholly our own being; a feeling of the unknown is possible, if we can transcend our *present* being, and feel our true being as one which is not yet completely realized. The true function of the feeling of ignorance is, therefore, to serve as an inducement, as a spring, to further action, while a feeling of the unknowable could only paralyze all action.[6]

In Dewey's vision, the horizon of ignorance is felt as the unrealized self. Its knowability moves us to transcendence of the present, to a knowing that is self-actualization.

Ignorance and the Possible

Lovers of mysteries know that a fact is just a fact, a node in our web of knowledge—until it points us to our ignorance. Then the fact becomes a *clue.* Hunches, guesses, estimates, inferences, conjectures, and hypotheses are projectiles launched from a base of the known into the possible. Inti-mations and hints are revelations, graspable fringes, prehensions, of the unknown. The very concept of *evidence* links a known to uncertain pos-sibilities; its etymology identifies *evidence* as *that which makes visible.* When we form a question we use our knowledge to cast a grappling hook into our ignorance. Asking questions is in fact the greatest (and most common) expression of the link between knowledge and ignorance. Questions, in their very framing, convey a sense of what is possible; they anticipate the sort of answer that will satisfy our seeking.

Some questions may be answered only by sophisticated knowledge or research: *What is the antidote for this toxin?* Some questions may be posed meaningfully only by those with sophisticated knowledge (though the answer may not be difficult to locate): *What "obscenity" was John Stuart Mill arrested for distributing?* Some questions meet both conditions: *What are the advantages and pitfalls of the Sveshnikov Variation in chess?* But it is easy to discern the implicit knowledge that frames not only all these sorts of questions, but simpler, everyday questions: *Can I post a .jpg file to Facebook?*

We are capable not only of factual knowledge, but also of *modal* knowledge; that is, we can have knowledge of actualities, but also of possibilities, necessities, and impossibilities. We can know what is the case, what might be, what must be, and what could not be the case—though there may be variations in the sources and justification of such knowledge. And we can, of course, be ignorant (and have false knowledge) in all these realms. To be clear: we cannot know that which is impossible, but we can know *that* it is impossible. We can also lack that knowledge or mistakenly believe it *is* possible. The realm of the actual is the domain of *realized* possibilities, some of which we know, much of which we do not. Everything that is knowable, however, is in that respect possible. All that is knowable but unknown—the horizon of our ignorance—is unrealized possibility.[7] If a question is not merely rhetorical, it seeks to actualize an epistemic possibility.

Although questioning, the verbal manifestation of curiosity, is elemental in all fields of inquiry, it has a special place in philosophy. Philosophy is not a science: its task is not to assemble and validate a set of facts, not even to produce new propositional knowledge of the world in a narrow sense. It may offer insight; it makes intellectual progress; but it rejoices in its questions. The philosopher's task is, in the first instance, to maintain, sustain, and expand our sense of the possible. It entails the recognition of our ignorance and our collusion in its creation. And second, it involves the elucidation of specific possibilities and their interrelations.

Wonder and the Shepherd of Possibilities

The philosopher is the shepherd of possibilities. I borrow the image from the French philosopher, Michel Serres. He writes:

It is the function of the philosopher, the care and passion of the philosopher to protect to the utmost the possible, he tends the possible like a small child, he broods over it like a newborn babe, he is the guardian of the seed. The philosopher is the shepherd who tends the mixed flock of the possibles on the highlands. …

The philosopher keeps watch over unforeseeable and fragile conditions, his position is unstable, mobile, suspended, the philosopher seeks to leave ramifications and bifurcations open, in opposition to the confluences that connect them or close them. …

The function of the philosopher, the care and the passion of the philosopher, is the negentropic ringing-of-the-changes of the possible.[8]

This does not mean that philosophy floats untethered to empirical reality. It is an irresponsible philosophy that is uninformed by what is known; but it is a suicidal philosophy that confines itself to empirical facts, or that aims simply to add to their store. Philosophers find insight into the possible to be as interesting and precious as knowledge of *what is*: the possible inspires action (*what might be*), opens the future (*what could be*), and thereby creates space for the normative (*what should be*). It is an orientation that frustrates those who are impatient with openness, those who see value only in the closure of clear facts that can be added to the hoard of knowledge. "What use is it?" ask the unimaginative, who do not look to the horizon.

Philosophia is not *the love of knowledge*; it is *the love of wisdom*. Wisdom entails knowledge, of course, but it expects much more, and it begins in wonder. It is Socrates, as depicted by Plato, who first says that "wonder is the feeling of a philosopher, and philosophy begins in wonder."[9] Not surprise, not curiosity—wonder.

Surprise involves a sudden, unexpected revelation. An unknown unknown has, in a blink, become known. Although being surprised implies a state of ignorance, it is constituted by the extinguishing of that state, and therefore is a state of knowing. Though generally short-lived, surprise is a response to awareness—whether that response morphs into shock and horror or relief and joy. Surprise admits of degrees, and where one's cognitive expectations (beliefs, habits of thought, expectations of others, etc.) are violated by the revelation, one might be *astonished*. It is characteristic of these emotions, that their object (the stimulus) is inchoate in the instant of their occurrence.

Curiosity, as we have seen (chapter 8), is both a state of mind and a trait. It involves awareness of one's ignorance, a specific known unknown, and the felt pull of discovery. Though it bridges knowledge and ignorance, it is felt as a yearning state of ignorance. Whether it is virtue or vice, whether the state is good or bad, it is a desire that is fulfilled in its own extinction. Curiosity impels us to know, to "satisfy" our puzzlement and to leave us in happy possession of the knowledge we seek. Complete knowledge is the extinguishing of curiosity.

Wonder, however, beholds the unknowable. Wonder does not seek the knowledge that will quench it. It does not follow the arc or assume the possibility of such a completed knowing. The *pathos* of wonder does, however, have effects. There are three alternative paths: wonder may open the door to endless questioning; it may stun and paralyze; or it may lapse into curiosity. The first is the philosophical dwelling in wonder; it activates a spiritual quest or the ceaseless dialectic Socrates modeled. The second is an epistemic torpor, a cognitive languor that is derided as a vice: to be "lost" in wonder. The third is the surcease of wonder, its replacement by the purposeful narrowness of curiosity: philosophy devolves to science; the sublime devolves to analysis; spirituality devolves to religious creeds.[10]

When Aristotle echoed Socrates's view that philosophy begins in wonder, he seemed to give the idea a historical turn: "For it is owing to their wonder that men both now begin and at first began to philosophize." But he may have had curiosity as I have described it in mind rather than wonder: he says, "[A] man who is puzzled and wonders thinks himself ignorant (whence even the lover of myth is in a sense a lover of wisdom, for myth is composed of wonders); therefore since they philosophize in order to escape from ignorance, evidently they were pursuing science in order to know, and not for any utilitarian end."[11] Aristotle's wonder seeks closure in knowledge, in understanding for its own sake, and it seems premised on the aim of "escape" from ignorance. His comment seems more suited to ignorance as a place or as a boundary. He seems to maintain this outlook even in the face of ignorance as a limit: "The possession of [knowledge] might be justly regarded as beyond human power; for in many ways human nature is in bondage."[12] Yet Aristotle wavers, for his inclusion of myth as "composed of wonders" does not yield to curiosity. It is wonder, not curiosity, that suits the recognition of ignorance as a horizon, the eternal surround of the unknown.

I am not demeaning science. Philosophy has given birth to most of the natural and social sciences, parturition through partition, as areas of inquiry developed appropriate research methods. The wonderful became the empirical, and the pursuit of knowledge has continuing urgency despite increasingly sophisticated tools. I have celebrated the liberation that knowledge can provide and bemoaned the terrible consequences of individual, political, and collective ignorance. Curiosity feeds learning. The point here, however, is that genuine philosophical understanding recognizes an ultimate "escape from ignorance" as an impossibility, a vain attempt to clutch the horizon.

Aristotle's well-ordered cosmos was self-contained and stable in its cycles and equilibrations: a snow-globe world. But, as the contemporary European philosopher, Peter Sloterdijk, has written: "Spheres are constantly disquieted by their inevitable instability: like happiness and glass, they bear the risks native to everything that shatters easily."[13] Fatefully, as Sloterdijk describes, modernity not only displaced humanity from the privileges of cosmic centrality, it shattered the protective globe. The sky fell. Moderns and postmoderns have found themselves not inside a sheltering sphere, but on the outer surface, staring into the infinite void of space.

Ever More: A Conclusion

The horizon of the unknown, darkest ignorance in all its splendor, is the horizon of our finitude. "Whereof one cannot speak, thereof one must be silent."[14] We can point to, but not even point out, unknown unknowns, let alone understand them. We have only intimations despite a surety of their presence. The dread of ultimate incomprehensibility, existential angst, and radical skepticism of this surround is counterpoised by the openness, freedom, and possibility, and transcendence it creates.

At the outset, I observed that the infinite unknown has turned some to skepticism and nihilistic despair. For others, like Blaise Pascal, it is a source of existential anxiety: "The eternal silence of these infinite spaces frightens me."[15] Some find liberation and rich possibility, as we have seen in this chapter. Still others have surrendered to the unknown, and pursued an apophatic approach. For theologians, this is *via negativa*, the grasp of what God is *not* as our meager mode of understanding. For mystics, the yielding is an opening to transcendence.

In *The Lure of the Transcendent*, Dwayne Huebner writes:

There is more than we know, can know, will ever know. It is a "moreness" that takes us by surprise when we are at the edge and end of our knowing. There is a comfort in that "moreness" that takes over in our weakness, our ignorance, at our limits or end. It is a comfort that cannot be anticipated, a "peace that passeth all understanding."

In language that echoes Dewey's description of the feeling of ignorance, he continues:

One knows of that presence, that "moreness," when known resources fail and somehow we go beyond what we were and are and become something different, something new. There is also judgment in that "moreness," particularly when we smugly assume that we know what "it" is all about and we end up in the dark on our behinds. It is this very "moreness" that can be identified with the "spirit" and the "spiritual."... Spirit is that which transcends the known, the expected, even the ego and the self. It is the source of hope. It is manifested through love and the waiting expectation that accompanies love. It overcomes us. ... One whose imagination acknowledges that "moreness" can be said to dwell faithfully in the world.[16]

Within that horizon, however, we may come to understand a great deal about what we do not know, about its intricacy and impact. Within that horizon, we are epistemic agents in community with others, participating in the creation of knowledge and ignorance, and drawing on the traits that help or hinder us in the achievement of learning. Within that horizon, we may come to seek a learned ignorance, to understand our search for knowledge not as a quest for certainty, but as an attempt to refine, improve, and moralize our ignorance.

Epilogue: Ignorance and Epistemology

... that collapsed circus tent of epistemology—those acres of canvas under which many of our colleagues still thrash aimlessly about.
—Richard Rorty

The study of ignorance is an exercise *in* epistemology; but it is also an exercise with implications *for* epistemology as a field of study. It implies a critique and expansion of traditional, analytical epistemology. I have noted those implications throughout; they have formed a subtext to my discussion. For scholarly impact, they require a systematic and appropriately technical presentation that is, however, not the focal purpose of this book. What I can attempt here is to distill these implications in this epilogue for readers with special interest in meta-epistemology.

The present is an exciting time for epistemology. Happily, each of the elements of this critique has already been advanced by other philosophers in works of influential scholarship. I have referred to their projects throughout this text: social epistemology, "knowledge-first" epistemology, virtue epistemology, feminist epistemology, and resistance epistemology. But what *is* new, I believe, is the recognition that these developments, especially in tandem, open the conceptual space required for any adequate understanding of ignorance; the converse claim that ignorance can open new lines of inquiry in all these approaches; and the ultimate vision of an epistemology that is centered on the *interaction* among understanding, knowledge, and ignorance.

Epistemology: Context and Content

Epistemology, under standard definitions, has a capacious portfolio: it studies the nature, scope, and limits of human knowledge. In theorizing knowledge, it sustains a subsidiary interest in our cognitive faculties: perception, memory, imagination, emotion, reason, intuition, and the mind itself—especially insofar as these relate to the acquisition, possession, and retention of knowledge. This subsidiary work, however, is often shelved under philosophy of mind; and epistemology proper (as practiced by Anglophone epistemologists, at least) has held a much narrower focus.

It is fair to say that modern epistemology has been haunted by the insolent skepticism that is the legacy of Cartesian doubt. The highest priority has been the assurance of the *possibility* of knowledge. (No one has doubted the possibility of ignorance.) Knowledge has had to be characterized defensively, so as to ward off the demons of doubt. Thus, epistemologists have concentrated on explicating the sources, structure, and justification of genuine knowledge, especially in contrast to mere belief. Certainty has been the gold standard for "knowledge in the strong sense"; anything less is dross. Epistemic analysis is, therefore, pointedly normative or regulative; and the primary, likely the sole, epistemological value—is truth.

Although skepticism has been a philosophical stance since the ancient Greeks, the crucible in which modern epistemology took form was much later. The necessity of distinguishing genuine knowledge from belief was burned into Western thought by the conflicts among religious doctrines during the Reformation and Counter-Reformation, and especially by the conflict between religion and science. It gained traction with the elevation of mathematical science (formal systems) as the idealized model of knowledge. And in the early twentieth century, positivism and Reichenbach's dictum that epistemology should concentrate exclusively on the context of justification (leaving the context of discovery to psychologists) secured the focus.

I do not denigrate this history. The public culture of ignorance and contemporary conflicts that arise from religious beliefs, conspiracy theories, pseudo-science, image manipulation, and disinformation campaigns show us that distinguishing genuine knowledge from belief is of high priority.

During the past century, vigorous debates on the problem of knowledge were conducted largely within the traditional schema: belief, truth, justification, and (since 1963) the absence of Gettier conditions—all directed toward and expressed in propositions. This schema has enabled an extensive research agenda; the vast literature it has generated displays technical refinement with increasingly sophisticated formulations and elaborations.

It has also imposed a severely limited vision of epistemology. For some, it may still be a circus tent with a great show; but for others, it is collapsed—a dull preoccupation. As a comprehensive account of knowledge, I believe its potential for illumination has largely been exhausted. Although continued elaboration may yield surprises, I think its best value going forward is not as the commanding paradigm for the field, but rather as a finely honed heuristic instrument to be deployed within an expanded vision of epistemology.

In what ways does this traditional schema impose a "severely limited vision"? I have claimed that it is restrictive in that it:

• attends only to propositional knowledge, or incorporates other forms only by reduction;
• excludes such concepts as *understanding* and *wisdom*;
• ignores *ignorance*, or takes it only as the negation of "*S* knows that *p*";
• frames key scalar concepts as bivalent;
• dismisses issues in the context of discovery that shape the nature of the knowledge achieved;
• examines only the individual knower in solo acts of cognition, and ignores the dynamics of epistemic communities; and
• ignores many values issues that arise from the process, content, purpose, and context of knowledge.

One could insist, of course, on restricting the term *epistemology* to the narrower focus; but that would be arbitrary and clearly incomplete as a theory of knowledge. Let us begin the unpacking with the first two of these claims, and then pursue the remained in the order listed.

Beyond Propositional Knowledge

The interpretation of knowledge as a specially certified set of propositions is reflective of philosophy's fixation with language. But we recognize there is a difference between a set of such propositions and all that is involved in knowledge—say, one's knowledge of mathematics. The schema cannot bridge that gap. What more is required?

If we point out that knowledge also involves coherence among our multiple beliefs, theorists may reply that tests of propositional coherence are built into the warranting condition (which is likely to be reduced to known propositions as well). But knowledge clearly involves more than propositional coherence: it involves conceptual integration, conceptual frameworks, cognitive structures within which concepts can be grasped and propositions formed, for example.

A comprehensive epistemology would surely embrace more forms of knowing than propositional knowledge. Some stalwarts defend the intellectualist position, demanding that *knowing how, knowing what something is like*, and *knowing an individual* must be reduced to or cashed out as a set of propositions if they are to be regarded as having any genuine knowledge content. It is a view suitable for the Age of Assessment, but most philosophers accept all of these as distinct ways of knowing.[1]

Moreover, there are important epistemic concepts that are undertheorized by and alienated from the traditional schema, such as *expertise, understanding*, and *wisdom*. Richard Mason and Catherine Elgin have independently argued that our central epistemological focus should shift from knowledge or belief to *understanding*—or, at minimum, that epistemology should now attend to understanding understanding.[2] (I have titled this book "*Understanding* Ignorance," not "*Knowing Things about* Ignorance.") As Mason explains, that project cannot be based on the traditional schema: understanding incorporates tacit or knowing as well as explicit propositional knowledge, and it also admits of degrees. Jonathan Kvanvig has argued that although knowledge has immense value, so does understanding; and a case can be made that it has even more value.[3] He believes that understanding is not a form of knowledge, but that knowledge incorporates understanding. For me, understanding is both a broader and more basic concept than knowledge, not narrower, and it points to the concept of wisdom.

It is a nice question whether knowledge or understanding is more basic. Earlier I noted Williamson's view that knowledge is primitive and logically prior to belief, and the thin interpretation of ignorance that results.[4] Williamson does not discuss *understanding* in *Knowledge and Its Limits*, but presumably his analysis would require him to take understanding to be a derivative mental state, normative to truth. But I find it equally or more plausible that *understanding* is the primitive concept, logically prior to *knowledge* and *belief.*

The upshot of these claims is that epistemology properly includes more forms of cognition than propositional knowledge. As this purview becomes more inclusive, the role of ignorance may be further revealed and elaborated.

Negation and Complexity

Even if one accepts the standard schema as the commanding analysis of knowledge, it follows that ignorance has a richer structure than a single, simple negation of knowledge. If genuine knowledge requires the meeting of four criteria, the failure of any one of the four criteria (belief, truth, warrant, and the absence of Gettier conditions) or any particular combination of failures represents a *different* way of *not knowing*, a situation in which S does *not* have knowledge of p. It is worth sorting out these epistemic failures.

(1) If the belief criterion alone fails, there are several possible scenarios, revealing an important ambiguity. What does "S does not believe that p" mean? It might mean that S simply does not have the belief that p, having no opinion on the matter or no knowledge of the domain or conceptual framework in which p occurs. But it might also mean that S refuses to believe p; or even that S disbelieves p, which is say that S believes p is false (more precisely stated as "S believes that $\sim p$"). The result of any of these scenarios, however, is ignorance.

(2) If the only factor that fails is the truth criterion, the hapless believer is unfortunate indeed, for despite sufficient warrant of no Gettier issues, the belief is false. One might be tempted to call this *justified ignorance*. But how could this happen? Suppose David believes his family is of Lutheran heritage, a belief for which he has adequate warrant (testimony from relatives, a few generations of Lutheran baptisms, etc.). An unexpected event—perhaps a discovered diary or DNA analysis—leads to the realization that his ancestors were in fact German Jews. What was once warranted is no longer. Perhaps one would prefer to say that the justification criterion had failed in the first place, not just the truth criterion: David's warrant for his belief in his Lutheran heritage was insufficient all along. It is precisely at this point that the trickiness of stringent standards of justification is revealed. If we draw those standards so tight that *any* false belief *must* arise only from insufficient warrant, there would then be no logical space between adequate

justification and certainty. Under any interpretation, David was ignorant of his Jewish ancestry.

(3) Suppose the failure lies only in the third criterion: the believer lacks
sufficient warrant. In such a case, the fact that one's belief is true may
be a matter of coincidence or luck (as with Gettier factors); but it may
include an astute hunch, a correct guess, the acceptance of accurate
hearsay, or well-placed trust in an expert. There are two targets of ignorance in such cases: S is ignorant of p, and S is ignorant of whatever
might comprise adequate justification for p. (If possessing adequate justification is interpreted as knowing other propositions, there is a threat
of vicious circularity: we end up defining knowing one proposition [in
part] as knowing other propositions—which leaves us in the dark about
what knowing any proposition involves.)

(4) I discussed the Gettier-type epistemic failure earlier (chapter 11). Once
again, there are two targets of ignorance: S is ignorant that conditions
of epistemic luck are in play, and therefore does not know that p. Ignorance of particular circumstances constitutes the Gettier effect only
when they are relevant to p and the other three criteria are met.

My larger point in detailing these cases is to show that, although the
schema may suggest a single, unified way of *knowing p*, it also allows for
several varieties of *not knowing p*; and the differences are epistemically significant, in part because they point to the particular sources of ignorance.
They foreshadow, at least partially, the structure of ignorance.

A second point: there is an asymmetry in the way the criteria implicitly relate to S. Both belief and justification seem to require some sort of
"cognitive possession" by the believer. S must *believe* and *have* warrant. It
is not simply that warrant must exist; S must "possess" it, if S is to have
knowledge. (But it would open the trapdoor to circularity if that means
S must *know* that she believes p and must *know* the facts of the warrant
and that they are epistemically compelling.) By contrast, S cannot be the
authority for affirming the truth of p; that would simply reassert S's belief.
And, by definition, the absence of Gettier conditions in affirming p can
never be claimed by S; they are always unknown unknowns. Thus neither of these criteria is "cognitively possessed" by the believer; each states
S-independent, objective facts. This asymmetry reflects the subjective and
objective perspectives implicit in the schema.

In a recent series of articles, the Dutch philosopher Rik Peels has argued that "contrary to what one might expect and to what nearly all philosophers assume, being ignorant is not equivalent to failing to know," at least on the four-criterion traditional interpretation.[5] Rather, Peels claims that ignorance is a lack of true belief. (He does not claim that having true belief is sufficient for genuine knowledge; for him, knowledge and ignorance are asymmetrical in a way quite different from the asymmetry I just described.) Now there is no doubt that a lack of true belief is a failure to know; either the belief or truth criterion or both have failed. (In my account, these conditions create three different forms of ignorance.) The salient claim for Peels is that the failure of the warrant condition will not by itself constitute ignorance.

I reject this interpretation. Note that if Martha, who lacks justification for her true belief that a sliced onion will reduce the pain of a bee sting, has her belief confirmed by medical authorities or discovers an explanation for the palliative effect, she will have *removed her ignorance* on that point. Similarly, a detective who correctly believes she has identified the killer but lacks sufficient evidence will continue her investigation to discover motive, means, and opportunity. If she succeeds, she both gains a justification for her belief and removes her ignorance. I believe that the lack of warrant for true belief does indicate ignorance. Moreover, Peels has reopened the door to epistemic luck: on his account, Gettier conditions do not create ignorance. According to Peels, Jim would not be ignorant of the outcome of today's baseball game, because he holds a true belief. This seems counterintuitive. What term would one use to describe epistemic defects like Jim's failure to know the outcome of today's baseball game or our detective's missing knowledge? To discount the relevance of warrant and luck for ignorance also disvalues the securing of justification and the achievement of knowing without epistemic luck.

A brief pause to note an odd case: can one be ignorant of something that is, in fact, false?

Putative examples are suspicious. Suppose Sherman is ignorant of the principles of phrenology. Suppose Miriam is unaware of a false report in the local paper. Suppose Ian is unaware that the Piltdown Man is thought to have supplied the "missing link." Such cases seem to involve double targets of ignorance. Sherman is ignorant of the principles of phrenology, and did not know they had been debunked. Miriam did not know about the report, so did not know that it was false. Ian had never heard of the Piltdown hoax. More generally, one might be ignorant of certain impossibilities; but that is better understood as one's being ignorant of the truth that such-and-such is impossible, not of the falsehood that such-and-such is possible. Ignorance is never a lack of ignorance.

The overarching claim in this section is that, even within the confines of the traditional schema, one finds evidence of the more complex structure of ignorance.

Bivalency and Scalar Gradience

Because the aim of the traditional schema is to secure genuine knowledge against doubt, it adopts an absolutist model; that is, its logic treats key concepts as though they are bivalent (on/off) properties: either S knows that p or S does not. Yet two of its criteria center on concepts that admit of degrees. *Belief* is one such term: there is an epistemic difference between a belief that I do not realize I have until asked ("Why yes, I believe my desk lamp in the study is on now") and a deep conviction ("I believe that life is more important than property"). Earlier, we encountered "degree of belief" as an interpretation of probability (chapter 10). I also noted the difference between not having a belief and refusing to believe. In short, belief can involve gradations of conviction and awareness.

There is a similar problem with the concept of warrant. Treating *warrant* or *justification* as bivalent concepts denies the scalar reality: a belief might be more or less justified, and the strength of its warrant might alter over time. In addition, it is misguided to imagine that the requirement for "sufficient warrant" is identical for all types of knowledge claims, or that we should believe only claims that have the strongest warrant or are certain. Such follies occur when epistemologists idolize mathematical knowledge, extending its model to empirical sciences, and thence to all forms of "genuine" human knowledge.

Are *knowing* and *not knowing* therefore also a matter of degree? If the two key components of belief and warrant have gradations, surely the target concept (knowledge) must also have gradations. In our consideration of ignorance as a boundary (chapter 5), I contrasted the "disjunctive" and "scalar" interpretations of knowing, presenting various "borderline" cases of knowing that involve degrees of recall, recognition, articulation, awareness, and so on. Admittedly, these matters, at least *prima facie*, are indicators of knowledge, not essential components of the logical structure of knowledge, but they do bear on the affirmation that "*S* knows *p.*" They indirectly reflect the gradualism of knowing.

Knowing how and *knowing what it's like* do not have the same sort of traditional schema; the conditions for their certification are far less standard. But it is clear that there are degrees of skill—one can be more or less skilled at rope-jumping or organ-playing. It is not an either/or designation. It is controversial whether the same is true for *knowing what it's like*, but I think even here, at least in many cases, the knowing can be gradual. I can learn what it is like to fly a plane somewhat by piloting a model airplane. But I learn more by sophisticated simulation programs. I learn still more by sitting with a pilot during flight. And I come to "really" know by piloting in various aircraft under varying conditions.

Any adequate epistemology should accommodate a gradualist understanding of key terms like *belief, warrant,* and *knowing.* The bivalent interpretations of the traditional scheme reflect the pull of certainty and its absolutist demands.

Discovery and Justification

The traditional adherence to Reichenbach's boundary between discovery and justification has had the negative consequences of disconnecting the theory of knowledge from the process of learning, and of divorcing normative epistemology from educational practice. Treating knowledge only as a fait accompli, a structure of certified propositions, has also severed knowledge from the capacities and virtues that are required for its acquisition and the vices that may thwart it.

During my exposition, I have turned to several approaches that cross or open Reichenbach's boundary between discovery and justification. Making this boundary at least more permeable is necessary for a better understanding of ignorance.

Perhaps Michael Polanyi is the twentieth century thinker who has rejected this bifurcation most directly. I cited him (first in chapter 3) for his advocacy of tacit (proposition-resistant) knowledge. But it is a different aspect of his work that I have in mind here. The thesis of his classic 1958 book, *Personal Knowledge,*[6] is that "impersonal knowledge" is a fiction, that scientists necessarily "participate in" the knowledge they possess and create, and that such knowledge requires a personal commitment and results in personal transformation. Scientific knowledge bears the marks of the human enterprise that produced it.

Gettier, in showing that epistemic luck can undermine apparently situations of knowing, is addressing the context of discovery—the context of coming-to-know—as well. Luck is a matter not of the structure of knowledge, but of how one came to believe it was true.

The most direct and sweeping challenging to Reichenbach's barrier, however, is the rise of virtue epistemology. Taking knowledge to be an achievement opens the connection between the ways in which one pursues knowledge and the quality of the knowledge one obtains.

My point here is that these assaults on the Reichenbach distinction move us in a positive direction. It is not that I believe epistemology should become or replace cognitive psychology; the two fields properly have different aims and methods. But if there are epistemically relevant issues that arise within the process of coming to know, any adequate epistemology should be inclusive of them and attend to them. For me, all these approaches are useful in part because they also reveal the interaction with ignorance (though they are not normally presented in that way). Thus, Polanyi's notion of tacit knowledge is one of unknown knowns. And Gettier describes epistemically erosive conditions of which the believer is ignorant. Virtue epistemology opens up space to consider the role of ignorance as motivator and as a factor in such virtues as intellectual humility, epistemic restraint, and discretion.

Individual Knowers and Epistemic Communities

The "*S*" of "*S* knows that *p*" might as well stand for *Solo*. Knowing is understood to be a mental state of individuals, and knowledge is possessed by individuals. As a corollary, *epistemic autonomy* is taken as ideal, while *epistemic dependence* is regarded as deficient. Thus, first-hand knowledge—seeing with one's own eyes, checking the proof for oneself, directly verifying purported facts—is preferred if one's knowledge is to be sterling. The best knowledge is literally self-evident—evident to oneself. Reliance on the authority or testimony of others for information and knowledge is *déclassé*. Such dependence risks crediting hearsay, even gossip, and other mediated information, even if it is common practice and the basis of didactic teaching.

This framing of thought is, of course, traceable to Plato: the model of knowing-as-seeing, culminating in *noesis,* the moment of intellectual insight experienced only by a well-prepared individual. But this model can have both authoritarian and democratic forms. It suited well the Reformation and the rise of liberalism. Descartes's method of doubting all inherited knowledge to believe only ideas he himself found indubitably clear and distinct is a radical version. The impulse to epistemological foundationalism betrays an atomistic individualism and a certain self-importance; it seeks to shed the messy structure others have made so as to build a superior version oneself. W. K. Clifford's dictum that our beliefs not exceed our direct evidence is a stringent rule for the autonomous, individual knower.[7] In the democratized form, every rational human is equally capable of discerning the truth, of possessing and being a source of knowledge; and each individual carries the epistemic responsibility of verification, of knowing *first-hand.*

Yet in life as we live it, knowledge is constructed within an epistemic community; it is possessed and justified or rejected in the epistemic interactions of a community. We all hold membership in different, plural, and overlapping epistemic communities, and most of anyone's personal "storehouse of knowledge" is derived from other sources. It is a distortion to lump all testimony into a tainted category: it not only ignores practice, it also obscures the rich and varied epistemic relationships of trust, authority, and expertise that are exhibited in the giving and receiving of testimony. Epistemic dependence is not only frequently necessary, but in some situations, such as the deferral to experts, it may be epistemically virtuous or even obligatory.[8]

The appropriate response is now coalescing: a shift from the individual knower to the epistemic community, with a correlative shift from epistemic autonomy to forms of epistemic dependence. One place to begin is the reassessment of the epistemic value of testimony: C. A. J. Coady produced a provocative analysis that branded "autonomous knowledge" an "illusory ideal," and bolstered testimony as a common and legitimate source of knowledge.[9] In the groundbreaking work of Alan I. Goldman, the value of testimony is placed within the larger context of other practices, such as argumentation and a set of traditions that represent epistemic communities such as law and science.[10]

Social epistemology and especially feminist epistemology have inspired reflection on the ethical dimensions of epistemic communities. I earlier cited Miranda Fricker, who has identified practices of "epistemic injustice" (chapter 7), such as the systematic devaluation of the testimony of certain groups, which creates an epistemic oppression usually tied to other forms of prejudice and marginalization. Social epistemologists of varying stripe have brought attention to sources and forms of socially constructed ignorance, to the privilege and power that permit certain types of willful ignorance, and to the need for an "epistemology of resistance" that reveals and disrupts structures of epistemic oppression.

I find the concentration on epistemic communities particularly fertile *when it is linked with virtue epistemology.* In that juncture, intellectual virtues are not merely characteristics of the learner as an autodidact and individual knower; they are intellectual qualities and capacities that sustain the functioning of an epistemic community. Just as moral virtues require communal supports, arenas, and forms of engagement for their display and refinement, epistemic virtues also require the support, arena, and forms of participation of an epistemic community.

Understanding a culture of ignorance requires the insights of social, virtue, and feminist epistemologies. These approaches may be integrated; only their integration allows us fully to understand and the dynamics and the multiple forms of ignorance in our culture.

Epistemic Value

Traditional epistemology is normative and regulative in its placement of genuine knowledge as the sole intrinsic, epistemic value (dependent, of course, on the value of truth). *Knowing*—discovering and possessing knowledge—is the epistemic good: the more knowledge, the better. This is affirmed whether knowledge is valued intrinsically or instrumentally.

Interestingly, none of the new approaches cited to this point has challenged that presumption. Nonetheless, I argue that this presumption is problematic; it may be challenged within their more expansive vision of the field. Of course, knowledge *is* of enormous value. And although true beliefs are useful, we are all confident that genuine knowledge is more precious (though spelling out the rationale for that judgment may be difficult).[11] The question is whether knowledge is *always* of value and is the *only* epistemic value, or whether it is responsive to other values.

How might the assumption of monistic epistemic value be challenged? One response is that it precludes the possibility that it might sometimes be better *not to know*. It therefore treats conditions of privacy or confidentiality, matters of dangerous or harmful knowledge, along with decisions *not to know*, as of ethical concern only, not of epistemological interest. Surprisingly, even virtue epistemology has usually characterized virtues and vices only in relation to the acquisition of knowledge, a valued goal. Virtues like discretion and intellectual humility, and vices like nosiness, tattling, and betrayal—qualities that reflect the value of restraining or withholding knowledge—are largely ignored. Yet these traits become important when we theorize a normative epistemic community.

A second, related response is that it fails to give proper attention to ignorance. As we have seen, ignorance may have value, as in rational and strategic ignorance (chapter 6). In recent literature, the strongest case for ignorance as a positive epistemic value has been made by Cynthia Townley, who argues both for its value for individual knowers and commends its role in optimal epistemic communities.[12] In her account, the individual knower becomes an epistemic agent, acting within an epistemic community. A well-functioning community has pluralistic epistemic values, of which knowledge is only the primary one; ignorance under certain conditions is valued as well.

The view that epistemology should value both knowledge and ignorance (polar opposites) can be made coherent only if there are deeper, governing values at work—values that determine when the valence properly switches from one to the other. I quite agree with Townley that when we shift from the individual knower to the role of responsible agents in epistemic communities, we find that epistemic values other than knowledge are in play. Epistemic agents are responsible as believers, as testifiers who pass on knowledge, as receivers of information, as confidantes and authorities, and so on.

I would go a bit further and claim that we learn a great deal by thinking of epistemology as an arena of value theory and ethical concern. Just as we consider justice in the distribution of rights, privileges, and rewards, so we may consider justice in the distribution of epistemic roles and values like knowledge, ignorance, expertise, and sharing. The concern is broader than the ethics of belief, though that is important. It includes the ethics of curiosity, secrecy, confidentiality, transparency, accuracy of testimony, and other practices. Once we make this transition in perspective, new norms of epistemic flourishing may be articulated and familiar ones may take new forms.[13]

Conclusion

If Anglophone epistemology has too often been locked in Cartesian concerns, Enlightenment affirmations, and structural models of knowledge, it nonetheless has generated analytical progress. The critique summarized here does not aim to overthrow that progress, nor does it jettison the formal schema (though I believe that its continuing creative possibilities seem limited). Rather, it argues for a grander, more inclusive framing of epistemology within which the traditional analysis would occupy a particular place. In the innovative approaches I have cited, that reformative task has begun.

The excitement I find in epistemology is the vision of a study that embraces various forms of knowing and gives proper place to understanding; of an inquiry that links the ways in which we come to know and the structure of knowledge; of an epistemology that in all these dimensions addresses the interactions between knowledge and ignorance in community and the values that govern them; of a field that illuminates our epistemic predicament as we move among the known, the knowable, the unknown, and the forgotten, within the horizon of the unknowable.

Notes

1 The Impact of Ignorance

1. Oscar Wilde, *The Importance of Being Earnest* (1895), act 1 (Project Gutenberg, 1997), https://www.gutenberg.org/files/844/844-h/844-h.htm.

2. A 2014 study by the US Department of Education and the National Institute of Literacy found that 32 million adults in the United States cannot read (14 percent of the population). But 21 percent of adults read below a fifth-grade level. Many factors, however, complicate measuring literacy rates, beginning with the contested term "literacy." Recent studies focus on *functional literacy* (and *illiteracy*), which includes more factors than the ability to read words and write letters; it targets levels of reading comprehension and written expression required for functioning in contemporary society, along with other relevant communication skills. Historical comparisons are therefore difficult. What was required for functional literacy in colonial America would differ from today's requirements. Lawrence Cremin made an influential argument for the favorable comparison in *American Education: The Colonial Experience* (New York: Harper & Row, 1970); a still-authoritative historical text is Kenneth A. Lockridge, *Literacy in Colonial New England: An Enquiry into the Social Context of Literacy in the Early Modern West* (New York: W. W. Norton, 1975).

3. For a synopsis of public ignorance in many domains of knowledge, see Sheldon Ungar, "Ignorance as an Under-Identified Social Problem," *British Journal of Sociology* 59, no. 2 (2008): 301–326.

4. Claude Adrien Helvétius, *Treatise on Man* (1810; New York: Burt Franklin, 1969), vol. 2, sec. VI, chap. II, 79.

5. The National Constitution Center regularly publicizes its surveys on its website: http://constitutioncenter.org/.

6. Ilya Somin, *Democracy and Political Ignorance: Why Smaller Government Is Smarter* (Stanford, CA: Stanford University Press, 2013). Chapter 1 describes the shocking extent of current political ignorance.

7. John Walters, "No Good Deed Goes Unpunished," *Vermont Political Observer*, blog post, January 19, 2015, https://thevpo.org/2015/01/19/no-good-deed-goes -unpunished/. The errors of grammar and spelling are original; respondents' names are not cited here to protect the ignorant.

8. Kyle Dropp, Joshua D. Kertzer, and Thomas Zeitzoff, "The Less Americans Know about Ukraine's Location, the More They Want U.S. to Intervene," *Washington Post*, *The Monkey Cage*, blog post, April 7, 2014, https://www.washingtonpost.com/blogs/ monkey-cage/wp/2014/04/07/the-less-americans-know-about-ukraines-location-the -more-they-want-u-s-to-intervene/.

9. "Gunman Kills 6 at Sikh Temple Near Milwaukee," *New York Times*, August 6, 2012. http://www.nytimes.com/2012/08/06/us/shooting-reported-at-temple-in -wisconsin.html. For the record of crimes against Sikhs to that date, see Nick Carbone, "Timeline: A History of Violence against Sikhs in the Wake of 9/11," *Time*, August 6, 2012, http://newsfeed.time.com/2012/08/06/timeline-a-history-of -violence-against-sikhs-in-the-wake-of-911/.

10. For a provocative examination of contemporary American culture with a sense of history, see Susan Jacoby, *The Age of American Unreason* (New York: Pantheon Books, 2008).

11. I take this brief definition as a received, provisional starting point. It will ulti- mately prove insufficient once the various forms and implications of ignorance are described.

12. For an imaginative, postmodern elucidation of stupidity, see Avital Ronell, *Stupidity* (Urbana: University of Illinois Press, 2002).

13. Scott Adams, *When Did Ignorance Become a Point of View?* (Riverside, NJ: Andrews McMeel Publishing, 2000). Ironically, Adams himself embraces this point of view regarding his decision to switch from the Democratic to the Republican candidate. Adams writes:

There are many things I don't know. For example, I don't know the best way to defeat ISIS. Neither do you. I don't know the best way to negotiate trade policies. Neither do you. I don't know the best tax policy to lift all boats. Neither do you. … So on most political topics, I don't know enough to make a decision. Neither do you, but you probably think you do. … Given the uncertainty about each candidate—at least in my own mind—I have been saying I am not smart enough to know who would be the best president. That neutrality changed when Clinton pro- posed raising estate taxes. I understand that issue and I view it as robbery by government. (Scott Adams's blog, September 25, 2016, http://blog.dilbert.com/post/150919416661/why-i-switched -my-endorsement-from-clinton-to)

14. Stefan Halper and Jonathan Clarke, *The Silence of the Rational Center* (New York: Basic Books, 2007).

15. For a discussion of this phenomenon, see Lisa M. Heldke, "Farming Made Her Stupid," *Hypatia* 21, no. 3 (2006): 151–165.

16. Nicholas of Cusa, *On Learned Ignorance* (*De docta ignorantia*), in *Renaissance Philosophy*, vol. 2: *The Transalpine Thinkers*, trans. and ed. Herman Shapiro and Arturo B. Fallico (New York: The Modern Library, 1969), 4. Alternately named Nicholas of Kues or Nicolaus Cusanus, Nicholas's lifespan, 1401–1464, places him on the cusp of the transition from the medieval world to the Renaissance.

17. James Frederick Ferrier, *Institutes of Metaphysic: The Theory of Knowing and Being* (1856), reprinted in edited form in *James Frederick Ferrier: Selected Writings*, ed. Jennifer Keefe (Charlottesville, VA: Imprint Academic, 2011), 157. See also n. 20 below.

18. The following works are exemplary in those fields, respectively: Shannon Sullivan and Nancy Tuana, eds., *Race and Epistemologies of Ignorance* (Albany, NY: SUNY Press, 2007); Jonathan Mair, Ann H. Kelly, and Casey High, eds., *The Anthropology of Ignorance: An Ethnographic Approach* (New York: Palgrave Macmillan, 2012); Michael Smithson, *Ignorance and Uncertainty: Emerging Paradigms* (1989; New York: Springer Science & Business Media, 2012); Donald W. Katzner, *Time, Ignorance, and Uncertainty in Economic Models* (Ann Arbor: University of Michigan Press, 1999); Erik Malewski and Nathalia Jaramillo, eds., *Epistemologies of Ignorance in Education* (Charlotte, NC: Information Age Publishing, 2011); Bill Vitek and Wes Jackson, eds., *The Virtues of Ignorance: Complexity, Sustainability, and the Limits of Knowledge* (Lexington: The University Press of Kentucky, 2008); Stuart Firestein, *Ignorance: How It Drives Science* (Oxford: Oxford University Press, 2012); Nancy Tuana, "Coming to Understand: Orgasm and the Epistemology of Ignorance," *Hypatia* 19, no. 1 (2004): 194–232; and Nicholas Rescher, *Ignorance (On the Wider Implications of Deficient Knowledge)* (Pittsburgh: University of Pittsburgh Press, 2009). A useful multidisciplinary set of articles is gathered in Matthias Gross and Linsey McGoey, eds., *Routledge International Handbook of Ignorance Studies* (London: Routledge, 2015).

19. Robert Proctor tells us: "My hope for devising a new term was to suggest ... the historicity and artifactuality of non-knowing and the non-known—and the potential fruitfulness of studying such things. In 1992, I posed this challenge to the linguist Iain Boal, and it was he who came up with the term *agnotology*, in the spring of that year." Robert Proctor, "Agnotology: A Missing Term to Describe the Cultural Production of Ignorance (and Its Study)," in Robert N. Proctor and Londa Schiebinger, eds., *Agnotology: The Making and Unmaking of Ignorance* (Stanford, CA: Stanford University Press, 2008), 27. As the preface of that volume declares, its purpose is "opening a door to a broader realm of inquiry."

20. The term *agnoiology* was coined by James Ferrier—who also coined the term *epistemology*—in his 1856 *Institutes of Metaphysic* (n. 17 above). Ferrier defined *agnoiology* as "a systematic doctrine of ignorance," and argued for its essential role as a distinct field that bridges epistemology and metaphysics (ontology). Ferrier's concept is of a field within the discipline of philosophy; Proctor's notion of *agnotology* is a new discipline or interdisciplinary field, with a focus on socially constructed ignorance.

2   Conceiving Ignorance

1. An influential article that has spawned theories of holes is D. K. Lewis and S. R. Lewis, "Holes," *Australasian Journal of Philosophy* 48 (1970): 206–212; reprinted in D. K. Lewis, *Philosophical Papers*, vol. 1 (New York: Oxford University Press, 1983), 3–9.

2. Jean-Paul Sartre, *Being and Nothingness*, trans. Hazel E. Barnes (London: Methuen, 1957), 9–10.

3. Timothy Williamson, *Knowledge and Its Limits* (Oxford: Oxford University Press, 2000). On his account, which he terms a "knowledge-first" epistemology, the mental state of knowing is unanalyzable and logically primitive—hence, more basic than belief. Williamson also claims that we are never in a position to be certain that we are in the mental state of knowing (or any other mental state); all mental states are therefore, as he puts it, "non-luminous."

4. Williamson wrote a brief but thoughtful response to my email query. I had asked for his interpretation of ignorance, since he is not explicit on this point (the term is not listed in the index to *Knowledge and Its Limits*). Williamson does allow that conventionally, *ignorance* implies that knowing is a possibility; so he finds it true but pointless to ascribe the state to objects.

5. I will hyphenate the term *not-knowing* when I wish to emphasize the mental-state interpretation of ignorance.

6. Shoshana Felman, "Psychoanalysis and Education: Teaching Terminable and Interminable," *Yale French Studies* 63 (1982): 21–44.

7. We may bluntly say of someone that "he is ignorant" or "he is an ignorant person," without specifying particular objects, as a holistic and likely insulting ascription. But the dilated meaning is something like "he is ignorant of everything—or, of many important things." There are many parallel cases of usage: for example, "anger" always implies an object; one is necessarily angry at something or someone; but one can also say "she is angry (or an angry person)" and mean that "she is angry at everything" (or "… many things")—an ascription of a relatively stable and significant disposition of character or personality.

8. I use X rather than p to indicate any object of ignorance—even whole subjects; p refers only to a proposition.

9. This is the difference between "A knows X and B does not" and "A knows X and A *knows that* B does not."

10. Even to assert "I believe that p" implies "I know that I believe that p."

11. But Samuel Johnson in his landmark dictionary of 1775 includes this entry for "to ignore": "Not to know; to be ignorant of. This word Boyle endeavored to

introduce; but it has not been received." Johnson includes this citation from Boyle: "Philosophy would solidly be established, if men would more carefully distinguish those things that they know from those that they ignore." Quoted in Jack Lynch, ed., *Samuel Johnson's Dictionary: From the 1755 Work That Defined the English Language* (Delray Beach, FL: Levinger Press, 2004), 257.

12. Large dictionaries, such as the *Oxford English Dictionary* or *Webster's Third New International Dictionary*, list "to not know" or "to be ignorant of" as an archaic meaning of *ignore*. In Italian, the word *ignorare* retains both meanings. Further discussion of *ignoring* will be held until chapter 5.

13. There are objections to this equation of ignorance with a lack of knowledge. I will discuss the dissident but quite different views of Jacques Rancière and Rik Peels in chapter 8 and the epilogue, respectively. In the meantime, using the simple, dictionary-based account is provisional and harmless.

14. Michael Smithson, for example, uses a typology that classifies error as a type of ignorance, both in his *Ignorance and Uncertainty* and in the materials for his MOOC titled Ignorance (offered in 2015 by the Australian National University on https://courses.edx.org.) This classification is itself an error and, I believe, a serious conceptual confusion.

15. For a provocative philosophical examination of error, see Nicholas Rescher, *Error (On Our Predicament When Things Go Wrong)* (Pittsburgh: University of Pittsburgh Press, 2009).

16. For the introduction of the *knowing that* versus *knowing how* distinction, see Gilbert Ryle, *The Concept of Mind* (New York: Barnes & Noble, 1949), 25–61. This neat distinction of types of knowing has, admittedly, been challenged by others.

17. See, however, the most sophisticated defense of the reductionist position: Jason Stanley, *Know How* (Oxford: Oxford University Press, 2011).

18. The example is drawn from the first section of David Hume's *A Treatise of Human Nature* in which he famously asserts: "We cannot form to ourselves a just idea of the taste of a pine-apple, without having actually tasted it." David Hume, *A Treatise of Human Nature*, 2nd ed., ed. L. A. Selby-Bigge and P. H. Nidditch (1739; Oxford: Oxford University Press, 1978), 5. The fact that pineapples would have been more exotic in mid-eighteenth-century Britain surely enhanced, but does not now diminish, his point. Recently, another exotic fruit, the durian, has been used to make this same point: L. A. Paul, *Transformative Experience* (Oxford: Oxford University Press, 2014), 15.

19. *Qualia* are the phenomenal qualities of our experience, accessible by introspection—what we experience when we smell a rose, see its color, or are pricked by its thorns.

20. It is a vexed question whether understanding necessarily presupposes knowledge or the reverse. For a perceptive examination of this topic, see Richard Mason, *Understanding Understanding* (Albany, NY: SUNY Press, 2003).

21. See the discussion in Josef Pieper, *Leisure: The Basis of Culture*, trans. Gerald Malsbary (1948; South Bend, IN: St. Augustine's Press, 1998), 40–41.

22. Plato calls his doctrine that learning is remembering, *anamnesis* (literally, "unforgetting"). He develops this view in several of his dialogues, but the elaborate story, the Myth of Er, is told in the final passages of the *Republic*, Book X, 614b–621d.

3   Dwelling in Ignorance

1. Jean-Jacques Rousseau, *Emile, or On Education,* ed. R. L. Archer (Hauppage, NY: Barron's Educational Series, 1964), 56. The meaning of *stupid* in this passage—in accord with my distinction in chapter 1—would better be expressed by *ignorant.*

2. Glen MacDonough and Victor Herbert, *Babes in Toyland* (New York: M. Witmark & Sons, 1903).

3. *Republic*, Book VI, 514a–520a. The quotations given in this section are from the translation by C. D. C. Reeve, 3rd ed. (Indianapolis: Hackett, 2004). I use this translation unless otherwise noted.

4. Plato, *Republic*, 516d, quoting Homer, *Odyssey*, Book XI, ll. 489–490. My translation.

5. Cf. N. Rescher, *Ignorance*, 2.

6. Al-Ghazzali, *On the Treatment of Ignorance Arising from Heedlessness, Error and Delusion*, trans. Muhhammad Nur Abdus Salam (Chicago: Great Books of the Islamic World, 2002).

7. Reeve translates *phusei* as "naturally," but this adverb also means "by chance or happenstance" or even "accidentally."

8. In other dialogues, especially *Symposium*, Plato implies that *eros* provides the initial impulse and the sustaining motivation for pursuing the good, the true, and the beautiful.

9. "Then the prisoners would in every way believe that the truth is nothing other than the shadows of those artifacts." *Republic*, Book VII, 515c.

10. *Republic*, 516c–d.

11. A radical skeptic might assert this as our universal condition—though she could not claim to *know* it to be so.

12. More on this point will come in chapter 9.

13. Secretary Rumsfeld made these remarks at a press briefing on February 12, 2002. He was responding to the issue of a lack of evidence that Iraq possessed weapons of mass destruction. Perhaps because of this context, he was criticized for using gobble-dygook. Independent of his intended use, however, it seems to be a succinct and apt distillation of rather complex epistemological issues. A more incisive criticism would have been that Rumsfeld used it to make an argument from ignorance (see chapter 9). An excellent piece on this quote is David A. Graham, "Rumsfeld's Knowns and Unknowns: The Intellectual History of a Quip," *Atlantic*, March 27, 2004, http://www.theatlantic.com/politics/archive/2014/03/rumsfelds-knowns-and-unknowns-the-intellectual-history-of-a-quip/359719/.

14. The term *noninstantiable* is borrowed from Nicholas Rescher, who has offered a proof that there are always unknown unknowns: see Rescher, *Ignorance*, 5.

15. Ann Kerwin, "None Too Solid: Medical Ignorance," *Science Communication*, 15 (1993): 166–185.

16. Though the term has since become the title of a documentary film about Secretary Rumsfeld: *The Unknown Known: The Life and Times of Donald Rumsfeld*, directed by Errol Morris (Los Angeles, CA: The Weinstein Company, 2013).

17. Žižek writes: "If Rumsfeld thinks that the main dangers in the confrontation with Iraq were the 'unknown unknowns,' that is, the threats from Saddam whose nature we cannot even suspect, then the Abu Ghraib scandal shows that the main dangers lie in the 'unknown knowns'—the disavowed beliefs, suppositions and obscene practices we pretend not to know about, even though they form the background of our public values." Slavoj Žižek, "What Rumsfeld Doesn't Know That He Knows about Abu Ghraib," *In These Times*, May 21, 2004, http://www.lacan.com/zizekrumsfeld.htm.

18. Michael Polanyi, *Personal Knowledge: Toward a Post Critical Epistemology* (Chicago: University of Chicago Press, 1958). The physical principle followed by the successful bicyclist, e.g., is: "For a given angle of unbalance, the curvature of each winding is inversely proportional to the square of the speed at which the cyclist is proceeding" (50). Polanyi elaborated the concept in *The Tacit Dimension* (New York: Anchor Books, 1967).

19. Psychological research on introspection is collected in David Dunning, *Self-Insight: Roadblocks and Detours on the Path to Knowing Thyself* (New York: Psychology Press, 2005). One of the strongest philosophical challenges is set forth in William E. Lyons, *The Disappearance of Introspection* (Cambridge, MA: MIT Press, 1986).

20. Diogenes Laertius, *Life of Pyrrho*, 9.62, translated by Brad Inwood and L. P. Gerson, in *Hellenistic Philosophy: Introductory Readings* (Indianapolis: Hackett, 1988), 173. It doesn't matter for our purposes whether the account is historically accurate—and Diogenes is notoriously gossipy. The portrayal can be taken as a thought

experiment, a playing out of the practical consequences of complete suspension of judgment.

21. For a forceful presentation of this sort of skepticism, see Peter Unger, *Ignorance: A Case for Skepticism* (Oxford: Clarendon Press, 1979).

4 Innocence and Ignorance

1. The story is told in Genesis 2–3. Quotations are from the *New International Version* (NIV).

2. Some theologians retroactively project the plural "us" as foreshadowing the Trinity. But for a classic discussion of the issue, see A. E. Whatham, "The Polytheism of Gen., Chap. 1," *Biblical World* 37, no. 1 (Jan. 1911): 40–47.

3. John Milton, *Paradise Lost*, Book IV, 516–517 (Project Gutenberg, 2011), http://www.gutenberg.org/cache/epub/20/pg20.html (accessed October 2016).

4. There are many other interpretations, of course. Some theologians believe Adam and Eve were immortal before the Fall, though this seems to violate their physical nature. Others distinguish between physical and spiritual death. Still others say they existed in a deathless state, but were given the choice of death or immortality. And since they were allowed to eat of every tree except one, they could have eaten from the tree of life and gained immortality; unfortunately they succumbed to temptation. (That interpretation makes the garden a sort of game show set in which the couple would be rewarded if they happen to pick from the right tree.) The view I have expounded is reminiscent of the Gnostics, or better, of theologian Paul Tillich, who said the Fall represented "a fall from the state of dreaming innocence" in psychological terms, a transition from essence to existence, an awakening from potentiality to actuality, and a necessary step in the development of humanity. Paul Tillich, *Systematic Theology*, 3 vols. (Chicago: University of Chicago Press, 1963), vol. 2, part 3, chap. 1, sec. B, 33–36.

5. Interestingly, Eve does seem to have a glimmer of awareness, for she "saw that the fruit of the tree was good for food and pleasing to the eye, and also desirable for gaining wisdom," based only on the serpent's claim (Genesis 3:6).

6. The etymological discussion in this section is drawn from the *Oxford English Dictionary, Compact Edition*, 2nd sub. ed., ed. E. S. C. Weiner and J. A. Simpson (Oxford: Oxford University Press, 1991).

7. A wonderful essay on this topic is Herbert Morris's "Lost Innocence," in his *On Guilt and Innocence: Essays in Legal Philosophy and Moral Psychology* (Berkeley, CA: University of California Press, 1976). Roger Shattuck has a richly nuanced discussion of both the Genesis and Miltonian accounts of the expulsion from the Garden in

Forbidden Knowledge: From Prometheus to Pornography (New York: St. Martin's Press, 1996).

8. The full *OED* definition of this sense is: "Freedom from cunning or artifice, guilelessness, artlessness, simplicity, hence want of knowledge or sense, ignorance, silliness."

9. For our ambivalence regarding *cunning*, see Don Herzog, *Cunning* (Princeton, NJ: Princeton University Press, 2006).

10. Martha C. Nussbaum has discussed this phenomenon with great sensitivity in *Love's Knowledge: Essays on Philosophy and Literature* (Oxford: Oxford University Press, 1990), especially in the essays "Flawed Crystals: James's *The Golden Bowl* and Literature as Moral Philosophy" and "'Finely Aware and Richly Responsible': Literature and the Moral Imagination." It is in the latter essay that she writes, "Obtuseness is a moral failing" (156).

11. John Milton, *Paradise Lost*, Book IV, l. 516.

12. For a recent exploration of the relationship between ignorance and vulnerability, see Erinn Gilson, "Vulnerability, Ignorance, and Oppression," *Hypatia* 26, no. 2 (2012): 308–332.

13. The term *epistemic community* is used in more specialized ways, especially in the fields of international relations and policy analysis. See Peter Haas, "Epistemic Communities and International Policy Coordination," *International Organization* 46, no. 1 (1992): 1–35.

14. *Republic*, Book II, 359a–360d.

15. Niklas Luhmann, *Social Systems*, trans. John Bednarz Jr. and Dirk Baecker (Stanford, CA: Stanford University Press, 1996), especially chapter 3, "Double Contingency," 103–136.

16. John Rawls, *A Theory of Justice* (Cambridge, MA: Harvard University Press, 1971), chapter 3.

17. This succinct summary is from John R. Searle, "The Chinese Room," in *The MIT Encyclopedia of the Cognitive Sciences*, ed. R. A. Wilson and F. Keil (Cambridge, MA: MIT Press, 1999), 115. Searle introduced this *"Gedankenexperiment"* in "Minds, Brains, and Programs," *Behavioral and Brain Sciences* 3, no. 3 (Sept. 1980): 417–424.

18. Frank Jackson, "Epiphenomenal Qualia," *Philosophical Quarterly* 32, no. 127 (1982): 127–136. This thought experiment has generated a sizeable set of elaborations and responses, many of which have been collected in *There's Something About Mary: Essays on Phenomenal Consciousness and Frank Jackson's Knowledge Argument*, ed. Peter Ludlow, Yujin Nagasawa, and Daniel Stoljar (Cambridge, MA: MIT Press, 2004).

19. More accurately, Jackson would originally have made this argument. His views have since changed.

20. Harry Frankfurt, "Alternate Possibilities and Moral Responsibility," *Journal of Philosophy* 66, no. 23 (Dec. 1969): 829–839.

5 Mapping Our Ignorance

1. A succinct but rich treatment of *border* and *boundary* is Massimo Cacciari, "Names of Place: *Border*," in *Contemporary Italian Philosophy: Crossing the Borders of Ethics, Politics, and Religion*, ed. Silvia Benson and Brian Schroeder (Albany, NY: SUNY Press, 2007), 277–283. Cacciari defines the two terms differently, focusing on *border*; and he thinks of boundaries as "rigid."

2. Ronald Duncan and M. Weston-Smith, *The Encyclopedia of Medical Ignorance: Mind and Body in Health and Disease* (Oxford: Pergamon Press, 1983).

3. The remark by Lewis Thomas is quoted by his former student, Marlys Witte, in "Q & A with Founder" at http://ignorance.medicine.arizona.edu/about-us/qa -founder (accessed June 2016).

4. That was in the 1980s. Today the program is federally funded.

5. The information on these programs is drawn from their websites. The CMI learning goals are drawn from: http://msrp.medicine.arizona.edu/medical_ignorance/. Information on SIMI may be found at http://ignorance.medicine.arizona.edu/ (both accessed October 2016).

6. Dr. Witte bills herself as "the Ignorama Mama." See, e.g., these University of Arizona websites: http://ignorance.medicine.arizona.edu/ and http://womensplaza .arizona.edu/honor/view.php?id=405 (accessed October 2016).

7. Donald Schoen, *The Reflective Practitioner: How Professionals Think in Action* (New York: Basic Books, 1984).

8. This need for awareness and the ability to recall and articulate applies not just to the proposition believed and to the warrant or justification one has for it, but also to the metalevel claims of knowing that one knows!

9. Sheldon Ungar, "Ignorance as an Under-Identified Social Problem," *British Journal of Sociology* 59, no. 2 (2008): 301–326, at 303. This seminal article has shaped my presentation of this issue of public ignorance in the following section.

10. Ungar, "Ignorance," 301–302.

11. "Politically-Challenged: Texas Tech Edition," video posted by PoliTech (October 28, 2014), https://www.youtube.com/watch?v=yRZZpk_9k8E (accessed October 2016).

12. Ungar, "Ignorance," 321.

13. Daniel R. DeNicola, *Learning to Flourish: A Philosophical Exploration of Liberal Education* (New York: Continuum/Bloomsbury, 2012).

14. Ungar, "Ignorance," 301, 315–316.

6 Constructed Ignorance

1. Aristotle, *Metaphysics*, Book I, chap. 1, 980b23, in *The Complete Works of Aristotle: The Revised Oxford Translation*, 2 vols., ed. J. Barnes (Princeton, NJ: Princeton University Press, 1983).

2. Typologies of ignorance and terminologies vary in the literature. I have tried to stay in the mainstream in usage, but occasionally I note a variation. What is counted as willful ignorance is variable; some writers include what I later describe as "inadvertent" but constructed ignorance.

3. Apparently, the term was coined by Anthony Downs in *An Economic Theory of Democracy* (New York: Harper & Brothers, 1957). The term is misleading because it suggests that other forms of ignorance are necessarily irrational—which is false. But the usage is now standard.

4. I champion the skill of wisely deciding what not to learn as an important goal of contemporary liberal education in DeNicola, *Learning to Flourish*.

5. A friend reported that a grandson in elementary school, proficient in reading, asked her to "translate" his birthday card. The greeting was in cursive writing—a skill no longer taught in his school.

6. Because the ignorance is chosen cunningly as an advantageous tactic for oneself, it does not fit the *willful ignorance* category described later in this chapter.

7. Psalm 139:4 (NIV).

8. The Impartial Spectator figures centrally in Adam Smith, *The Theory of Moral Sentiments*, ed. D. D. Raphael (Oxford: Oxford University Press, 1976). The Ideal Observer is proposed by Roderick Firth in "Ethical Absolutism and the Ideal Observer," *Philosophy and Phenomenological Research* 12, no. 3 (1952): 317–345.

9. Psalm 139:6 (NIV).

10. Chapter 10 considers techniques of ignorance management. Blindfolding justice is a tactic for managing our lack of omniscience.

11. "As the history of science has shown us, the discovery of truth is hard, but the acceptance of truth can be even harder." Lee McIntyre, *Respecting Truth: Willful Ignorance in the Internet Age* (New York: Routledge, 2015), 1.

12. In earlier etymological comments (chapter 2), I noted that the use of "to ignore" in the sense of "to be ignorant of" is archaic. The central meaning entails an act that rejects or refuses attention, though perhaps the level of one's awareness of the matter might rise and fall.

13. Charles W. Mills, "White Ignorance," in *Race and Epistemologies of Ignorance*, ed. Shannon Sullivan and Nancy Tuana (Albany, NY: SUNY Press, 2007), 35. See also Charles W. Mills, *The Racial Contract* (Ithaca, NY: Cornell University Press, 1997).

14. Jennifer Logue, "The Unbelievable Truth and the Dilemmas of Ignorance," *Philosophy of Education Archive* (2008): 54–62.

15. Harry Frankfurt, *On Bullshit* (Princeton, NJ: Princeton University Press, 2005).

16. For fuller consideration of the issues of privacy and intimacy, see Ferdinand David Schoeman, ed., *Philosophical Dimensions of Privacy: An Anthology* (Cambridge: Cambridge University Press, 1984), especially Robert Gerstein, "Intimacy and Privacy," 265–271.

17. A classic treatment of these concepts and related ethical issues is Sissela Bok, *Secrets: On the Ethics of Concealment and Revelation* (New York: Vintage Books, 1989). My definitions are not identical to hers.

18. A bare profile of the Tartu library's collection is presented on the University of Tartu website: https://utlib.ut.ee/kogud (accessed October 2016).

19. See, e.g., Stanton A. Glantz et al., eds., *The Cigarette Papers* (Berkeley, CA: University of California Press, 1998); and Naomi Oreskes and Erik M. Conway, *Merchants of Doubt: How a Handful of Scientists Obscured the Truth on Issues from Tobacco Smoke to Global Warming* (New York: Bloomsbury Press, 2010). For a discussion of the relation of this campaign to the construction of ignorance, see David Michaels, "Manufactured Uncertainty: Contested Science and the Protection of the Public's Health and Environment," in *Agnotology*, ed. Robert N. Proctor and Londa Schiebinger, 90–107.

20. See, e.g., Andre Mayer, "Soft-drink Makers Accused of Using 'Big Tobacco Playbook,'" *CBCNews*: http://www.cbc.ca/news/health/soft-drink-makers-accused-of-using-big-tobacco-playbook-1.1362598 (accessed October 2016).

21. See Bok, *Secrets*.

22. See, e.g., Nancy Tuana, "Coming to Understand: Orgasm and the Epistemology of Ignorance," *Hypatia* 19, no. 1 (2004): 194–232.

23. John Addington Symonds, *On a Problem in Greek Ethics: Being an Inquiry into the Phenomenon of Sexual Inversion Addressed Especially to Medical Psychologists and Jurists* (London: privately printed, 1883).

24. For a fascinating study of these practices, see Arthur M. Melzer, *Philosophy between the Lines: The Lost History of Esoteric Writing* (Chicago: University of Chicago Press, 2014).

25. Quoted in *The Sacramento Daily Union*, October 25, 1866.

26. Paul Berg et al., "Summary Statement of the Asilomar Conference on Recombinant DNA Molecules," *Proceedings of the National Academy of Science (USA)* 72, no. 6 (June 1975): 1981–1984. A twenty-fifth anniversary conference was held to discuss the application of "the Asilomar process" to issues in contemporary genetic engineering. See Marcia Barinaga, "Asilomar Revisited: Lessons for Today?" *Science* 287 (2000): 1584–1585.

27. CRISPR is an acronym for "Clustered Regularly Interspaced Short Palindromic Repeat." For a discussion of the technique and the issues, see Hank Greely, "Of Science, CRISPR-Cas9, and Asilomar," Stanford Law School, *Law and Biosciences Blog* (April 4, 2015), https://law.stanford.edu/2015/04/04/of-science-crispr-cas9-and -asilomar/.

28. Bill Joy, "Why the Future Doesn't Need Us," *Wired Magazine* (April 2000); reprinted in *Nanoethics: The Ethical and Social Implications of Nanotechnology*, ed. Fritz Allhoff et al. (Hoboken, NJ: Wiley, 2007), 47–75.

29. Ibid., 70.

30. Ibid., 72.

31. McIntyre, *Respecting Truth*.

7   The Ethics of Ignorance

1. This analytical terminology is from Neil C. Manson, "Epistemic Restraint and the Vice of Curiosity," *Philosophy* 87, no. 2 (April 2012): 239–259. Manson, however, applies these terms to the evaluation of epistemic dispositions or traits, not to knowledge or the state of knowing. In chapter 8, I will apply these terms in their original context: the moral evaluation of curiosity.

2. G. E. Moore, "Moore's Paradox," in *G. E. Moore: Selected Writings*, ed. Thomas Baldwin (London: Routledge, 1993), 207–212.

3. A comprehensive analysis of doxastic ethics is presented in Jonathan E. Adler, *Belief's Own Ethics* (Cambridge, MA: MIT Press, 2002). Adler argues for a "modified evidentialism."

4. W. K. Clifford, "The Ethics of Belief," in *The Ethics of Belief and Other Essays* (1876; Amherst, NY: Prometheus Books, 1999), 77.

5. William James, "The Will to Believe" (1896), in *William James: Writings 1878–1899* (New York: The Library of America, 1992), 457–479.

6. Clifford, *The Ethics of Belief*, 73.

7. For ineluctable ignorance, moral concerns are void. *"Ought* implies *can"* is a venerable principle of ethical theory, and there is nothing one can do about ineluctable ignorance, except recognize its presence.

8. Confusingly, these propositions may have negations as well, doubling the negative. Thus, it may be false that we do not have the option or the need or the desire to know, etc. These would be labeled ~A*n* to ~E*n*, respectively. The implications are complex. For example, if it is false that I have the right not to know (~D*n*), the implication is that I have the obligation to know (E), which entails the right to know (D).

9. Rachel Carson, *Silent Spring* (1962; New York: Houghton Mifflin, 2002). See especially the introduction by Linda Lear and afterword by E. O. Wilson.

10. See, e.g., George G. Lowry, *Lowrys' Handbook of Right-to-Know and Emergency Planning* (Chelsea, MI: Lewis Publications, 1989).

11. R. Andorno, "The Right Not to Know: an Autonomy Based Approach," *Journal of Medical Ethics* 30, no. 5 (2004): 435–439, at 435. The author defends the position I have outlined: a defense of the right not to know, qualified by the epistemic rights of others.

12. Barbara might claim she chose strategic ignorance; interested others are likely to see it as willful ignorance.

13. The documents cited and the quoted passages from them appear in Andorno, "The Right Not to Know."

14. Alfred North Whitehead, *The Aims of Education* (1929; New York: The Free Press, 1967), 14.

15. For a full treatment of these matters, see George Sher, *Who Knew? Responsibility without Awareness* (Oxford: Oxford University Press, 2009).

16. Amy Davidson, "Did Edward Snowden Break His Oath?" *New Yorker*, January 5, 2014; http://www.newyorker.com/news/amy-davidson/did-edward-snowden-break -his-oath.

17. Aristotle, *Nicomachean Ethics*, Book 3, secs. 1–2, 1109b30–1112a17.

18. My discussion here of the way in which ignorance affects our moral obligations is truncated. A comprehensive if controversial analysis is offered by Michael J. Zimmerman, *Ignorance and Moral Obligation* (Oxford: Oxford University Press, 2014).

19. Miranda Fricker, *Epistemic Injustice: Power and the Ethics of Knowing* (Oxford: Oxford University Press, 2007), 7.

20. José Medina, *The Epistemology of Resistance: Gender and Racial Oppression, Epistemic Injustice, and Resistant Imaginations* (Oxford: Oxford University Press, 2013).

21. Barbara Applebaum, "Needing Not to Know: Ignorance, Innocence, Denials and Discourse," in *Philosophy of Education 2015*, ed. Eduardo Duarte, 448–456, http://ojs .ed.uiuc.edu/index.php/pes/article/view/4529/1432 (accessed October 2016).

8 Virtues and Vices of Ignorance

1. Indeed, Reichenbach introduces this distinction to assert that "epistemology is only occupied in constructing the context of justification." Hans Reichenbach, *Experience and Prediction: An Analysis of the Foundations and Structure of Knowledge* (Chicago: University of Chicago Press, 1938), 7–8. The book's title exemplifies this view of epistemology, and Reichenbach was influential in its dominance.

2. More precisely, knowledge is the set of justified, true beliefs *that are not acquired by luck*. This provision, inserted to address what are known as "Gettier conditions," and broader notions of epistemic luck are discussed in chapter 11 and the epilogue.

3. Aristotle, *Nicomachean Ethics*, Book VI.

4. See the collected essays in Ernest Sosa, *Knowledge in Perspective* (Cambridge: Cambridge University Press, 1991), and his more recent consolidation: *A Virtue Epistemology: Apt Belief and Reflective Knowledge*, vol. 1, and *Reflective Knowledge: Apt Belief and Reflective Knowledge*, vol. 2 (Oxford: Oxford University Press, 2009, 2011).

5. Linda Zagzebski, *Virtues of the Mind: An Inquiry into the Nature of Virtue and the Ethical Foundations of Knowledge* (Cambridge: Cambridge University Press, 1996); Robert C. Roberts and W. Jay Wood, *Intellectual Virtues: An Essay in Regulative Epistemology* (Oxford: Oxford University Press, 2007).

6. P. G. Walsh, "The Rights and Wrongs of Curiosity (Plato to Augustine)," *Greece and Rome* 35, no. 1 (April 1988): 73–85.

7. Walsh notes that *Lucius the Ass* (an anonymous short story that appears with works of Lucian) has the same theme as Apuleius's *The Golden Ass*. While the Lucius story is light-hearted and portrays his fault as a mere social lapse, Apuleius "superimposes on the story the element of an impious or ungodly curiosity." Ibid., 75.

8. Thomas Hobbes, *Leviathan*, part 1, chap. 6. The citation for the critical edition is: *Thomas Hobbes Leviathan*, vol. 2, ed. G. A. J. Rogers and Karl Schuhmann (1651; London: Continuum, 2003), 47.

9. For a thorough and accessible history of curiosity, see Phil Ball, *Curiosity: How Science Became Interested in Everything* (New York: Vintage Press, 2013).

10. Note that *curiosity* can also designate an object that is *curious* in the sense of being odd or puzzling—again, strangeness that sparks curiosity—as once displayed in grand "curiosity cabinets."

11. Bertolt Brecht, *Galileo*, trans. Charles Laughton (1940; New York: Grove Press, 1966); all quotations in this paragraph are from scene 6, pp. 85–86.

12. Manson, "Epistemic Restraint and the Vice of Curiosity."

13. See Jason Baehr, *The Inquiring Mind: On Intellectual Virtues and Virtue Epistemology* (Oxford: Oxford University Press, 2011). For the discussion of intellectual courage, see his chapter 9, 163–190.

14. Thomas Aquinas, *Summa Theologiae*, 2, Q167; quoted by Manson, "Epistemic Restraint," 250.

15. There is, in this case, a risk of confusing the good, the right, and the virtuous, which typically have different sorts of objects. If we think of a virtue or vice as a trait, we would need to focus our attention on the disposition to have admirable or reprehensible motives, which is to pursue morally worthy or unworthy purposes, respectively.

16. Manson, "Epistemic Restraint," 255.

17. Sissela Bok, *Lying: Moral Choice in Public and Private Life* (1978; New York: Vintage, 1999), 31n.

18. President Ronald Reagan's use of the Russian proverb, "Trust, but verify," may suggest that although one extends appropriate credibility to the source, the information in this case is so significant that additional verification should be sought.

19. Bill Vitek and Wes Jackson, eds., *The Virtues of Ignorance: Complexity, Sustainability, and the Limits of Knowledge* (Lexington: The University Press of Kentucky, 2010).

20. *Basing* an action or a policy on ignorance would seem to be like Aristotle's *acting from ignorance* (chapter 7), which is hardly a good prescription.

21. Julia Driver, "The Virtues of Ignorance," *Journal of Philosophy* 86, no. 7 (July 1989): 373–384.

22. Owen Flanagan, "Virtue and Ignorance," *Journal of Philosophy* 87, no. 8 (August 1990): 420–428.

23. G. F. Schueler, "Why Modesty Is a Virtue," *Ethics* 107, no. 3 (April 1997): 467–485; Julia Driver, "Modesty and Ignorance," *Ethics* 109, no. 4 (July 1999): 827–834; G. F. Schueler, "Why IS Modesty a Virtue?" *Ethics* 109, no. 4 (July 1999): 835–841.

24. Nicolas Bommarito, "Modesty as a Virtue of Attention," *Philosophical Review* 122, no. 1 (2013): 93–117.

25. For example: Aaron Ben-Ze'ev, "The Virtue of Modesty," *American Philosophical Quarterly* 30 (1993): 238–246; Jason Brennan, "Modesty without Illusion," *Philosophy and Phenomenological Research* 75, no. 1 (2007): 111–128; and A. T. Nuyen, "Just Modesty," *American Philosophical Quarterly* 35, no. 1 (1998): 101–109.

26. Jacques Rancière, *The Ignorant Schoolmaster: Five Lessons in Intellectual Emancipation*, trans. Kristin Ross (Stanford, CA: Stanford University Press, 1991).

27. Jacques Rancière, "On Ignorant Schoolmasters," in *Jacques Ranciere: Education, Truth, Emancipation*, ed. Charles Bingham and Gert Biesta (New York: Bloomsbury, 2010), 1.

28. The phrase is take from the title of: Gert Biesta, "A New Logic of Emancipation: The Methodology of Jacques Rancière," *Educational Theory* 60, no. 1 (February 2010): 39–59. The article places Rancière's educational theory within the context of his political theory.

29. Richard Rorty, "Education as Socialization and Individualization," in *Philosophy and Social Hope* (London: Penguin Books, 1999), 114–115. See also Richard Rorty and Eduardo Mendieta, *Take Care of Freedom and Truth Will Take Care of Itself: Interviews with Richard Rorty* (Palo Alto, CA: Stanford University Press, 2005).

30. Rancière, *The Ignorant Schoolmaster*, 71.

31. This interpretation of *Birdman* is, of course, one of many possible—but published reviews usually seem to ignore the film's cryptic second title, *"The Unexpected Virtue of Ignorance."*

32. In contrast to my critical claims, see the analysis in Charles Bingham and Gert Biesta, *Jacques Rancière: Education, Truth, Emancipation* (New York: Bloomsbury, 2010).

33. "Ignorance is not a virtue," said President Barack Obama in his May 2016 Commencement Address at Rutgers University. Associated Press (May 15, 2016): http://www.telegraph.co.uk/news/2016/05/15/barack-obama-mocks-donald-trump -ignorance-is-not-a-virtue/.

9 The Limits of the Knowable

1. Immanuel Kant, *Prolegomena to Any Future Metaphysics* (1783; Indianapolis: Bobbs-Merrill, 1951), 101.

2. Proposition 5.6 in Ludwig Wittgenstein, *Tractatus Logico-Philosophicus*, trans. C. K. Ogden (1922; London: Routledge & Kegan Paul, 1981), 149.

3. In the last decade, though, a discipline of "olfactory studies" has emerged, with a special interest in the reconstruction of historic smells and the importance of odors in cultural history.

4. Alfred North Whitehead, *Process and Reality: An Essay on Cosmology* (1929; New York: Harper & Row, 1960), 516.

5. Ibid., 525.

6. This is but one argument traced by Jennifer Michael Hecht in *Stay: A History of Suicide and the Arguments Against It* (New Haven, CT: Yale University Press, 2013).

7. This is not the place to engage the vexed question of whether artificial intelligence is capable of "knowing" (strong AI). Our interest is with human knowledge and ignorance, though I will mention the role of AI in managing our ignorance in the next chapter.

8. Viktor Mayer-Schönberger, in *Delete: The Virtue of Forgetting in the Digital Age* (Princeton, NJ: Princeton University Press, 2011), 21, discusses the case of "AJ," who has hyperthymestic memory, and the problems it brings.

9. Nicholas Rescher, *Unknowability: An Inquiry into the Limits of Knowledge* (Lanham, MD: Rowman & Littlefield, 2010), especially chapter 6; and Rescher, *Ignorance*, especially chapter 2.

10. Rescher offers a proof of the claim that "The domain of fact is inexhaustible; there is no limit to facts about the real," and of the claim that "The manifold of facts is transdenumerably infinite." *Ignorance*, 49–51.

11. Ferrier, *Institutes of Metaphysic*, 160–161, prop. III.

12. The scientific paper is A. G. Manning, R. I. Khakimov, R. G. Dall, and A. G. Truscott, "Wheeler's Delayed-Choice Gedanken Experiment with a Single Atom," *Nature Physics* 11 (2015): 539–542, http://www.nature.com/nphys/journal/v11/n7/full/nphys3343.html. The press coverage included Richard Gray, "Does the Future Affect the Past? Physicists Demonstrate How Time Can Seem to Run Backwards," *Daily Mail*, June 9, 2015, http://www.dailymail.co.uk/sciencetech/article-3116792/Does-future-affect-PAST-Physicists-demonstrate-time-run-backwards.html.

13. Kurt Gödel, "On Formally Undecidable Propositions of *Principia Mathematica* and Related Systems" (1931), in *The Undecidable: Basic Papers on Undecidable Propositions, Unsolvable Problems and Computable Functions*, ed. Martin Davis (Hewlett, NY: Raven Press, 1965), 5–38.

14. Rescher, *Ignorance*, 48.

15. Ibid., 53.

16. John Horgan, *The End of Science: Facing the Limits of Knowledge in the Twilight of the Scientific Age*, new ed. (New York: Basic Books, 2015).

17. This is Rescher's position in *Ignorance*, but he articulated it more frontally in *Scientific Progress: A Philosophical Essay on the Economics of Research in Natural Science* (Pittsburgh: University of Pittsburgh Press, 1978).

18. Horgan, *The End of Science*, 22. The reviewer of Rescher's book was Bentley Glass.

19. I discussed these relationships in "Paradigms and Paraphernalia: On the Relationship of Theory and Technology in Science," in *New Directions in the Philosophy of Technology*, ed. Joseph C. Pitt (Dordrecht: Kluwer Academic, 1995), 85–94.

20. Thomas Aquinas, *Summa Theologiae*, 1, Q14, art. 7.

21. For example: "[Omniscience] is typically defined in terms of knowledge of all true propositions": Edward Wierenga, "Omniscience," *The Stanford Encyclopedia of Philosophy* (winter 2013 ed.), ed. Edward N. Zalta, http://plato.stanford.edu/archives/win2013/entries/omniscience/ (accessed August 2016). Wierenga provides an excellent summary of issues. I have drawn freely from it in this section, including in the selection of exemplary philosophical positions.

22. "Open Theism" is the view that God must learn about our choices as we make them. Versions of this view are articulated and defended in Charles Pinnock, Richard Rice, John Sanders, William Hasker, and David Basinger, *The Openness of God: A Biblical Challenge to the Traditional Understanding of God* (Downers Grove, IL: InterVarsity Press, 1994).

23. See, e.g., Norman Kretzmann, "Omniscience and Immutability," *Journal of Philosophy* 63 (1966): 409–421.

24. See, e.g., Patrick Grim, "Against Omniscience: The Case from Essential Indexicals," *Noûs* 19 (1985): 151–180.

25. In 1963, Frederic Fitch, analytic philosopher and logician, introduced a paradox the implications of which have since divided epistemologists (Frederic Fitch, "A Logical Analysis of Some Value Concepts," *Journal of Symbolic Logic* 28, no. 2 (June 1963): 135–142). According to the paradox, the view that every truth is, in principle, knowable (*the knowability thesis*)—a seemingly straightforward claim—implies that every truth is known (*the omniscience principle*)—which is not plausible. Suppose there is a truth, *p*, that is never known: then it is unknowable that *p* is a truth that is never known. The existence of unknowable truths denies the knowability thesis. A comprehensive analysis is offered in Jonathan L. Kvanvig, *The Knowability Paradox* (Oxford: Oxford University Press, 2006). There is no agreement on whether Fitch's proof is valid or what its implications are.

26. Douglas Walton, *Arguments from Ignorance* (University Park: The Pennsylvania State University Press, 1996).

10   Managing Ignorance

1. John Israilidis, Russell Lock, and Louise Cook, "Ignorance Management," *Management Dynamics in the Knowledge Economy* 1, no. 1 (2013): 71–85, http://www

.managementdynamics.ro/index.php/journal/article/view/4, at 76. Israilidis, in his doctoral dissertation and with later coauthors, cites the work of ignorance mapping by Dr. Witte and her colleagues at the University of Arizona (see my chapter 5).

2. See Michael Smithson, *Ignorance and Uncertainty*; and Donald W. Katzner, *Time, Ignorance, and Uncertainty in Economic Models*.

3. L. A. Paul, *Transformative Experience* (Oxford: Oxford University Press, 2014), 17.

4. Ibid., 178.

5. These examples are quoted from Terry Wood, "11 of the Most Unusual Things People Have Ever Insured," US Insurance Agents, https://usinsuranceagents.com/unusual-insurance-policies (accessed October 2016).

6. "Shorting the market" works roughly like this: Brokers lend clients stock to sell, crediting them with the proceeds as though they owned the stock. But the loan is conditional: the clients promise to buy back the stock at market price and "cover" the amount on which they are "short." The client's hope, of course, is for the price to have dropped, so they would pay less to buy than they did to sell.

7. For an expert's account of hedge fund risk, see Frank J. Travers, *Hedge Fund Analysis: An In-Depth Guide to Evaluating Return Potential and Assessing Risks* (Hoboken, NJ: Wiley, 2012).

8. P. S. Laplace, *A Philosophical Essay on Probabilities* (1814; New York: Dover, 1951), 6–7.

9. The formula for choosing minimum sample size includes several factors: *population size* (total count of cases in the whole set); *margin of error* (acceptable range of accuracy); *confidence level* or *Z score* (desired level of confidence in results); *standard deviation* (a measure of the variability of expected responses); and *response rate* (for survey studies, the percentage of those receiving surveys who actually respond).

10. Elizabeth Arias, "United States Life Tables, 2009," *National Vital Statistics Reports* 62, no. 7 (January 6, 2014): 6, table 2, http://www.cdc.gov/nchs/data/nvsr/nvsr62/nvsr62_07.pdf.

11. There are many excellent histories of probability theory; a recent one that illuminates these philosophical issues is Herbert I. Weisberg, *Willful Ignorance: The Mismeasure of Uncertainty* (Hoboken, NJ: Wiley, 2014).

12. Weisberg (ibid.) terms this *willful ignorance*. In my typology, it is a case of strategic ignorance, a subtype of deliberate ignorance.

13. Ibid., 73.

14. I have omitted discussion of the *logical interpretation* formalized by Rudolf Carnap, the *propensity interpretation* developed by C. S. Pierce and elaborated by Karl Popper, and the *"Best-System" interpretation* recently developed by David Lewis.

Though each is quite distinctive, each is derivative from one of the three interpretations included. For a brief discussion of the full roster of interpretations, consult the "Probability" entry by Alan Hájek in *The Stanford Encyclopedia of Philosophy*, http://plato.stanford.edu/entries/probability-interpret/ (accessed October 2016).

15. For the results, the program, and the script, see NPR Special Series, "Pop Quiz: 20 Percent Chance of Rain. Do You Need An Umbrella?" (July 22, 2014), http://www.npr.org/2014/07/22/332650051/there-s-a-20-percent-chance-of-rain-so-what-does-that-mean.

16. National Weather Service, "Explaining Probability of Precipitation," August 2009, http://www.weather.gov/ffc/pop/ (accessed October 2016).

17. Strictly speaking, however, there is a sharp difference between one's degree of confidence in a prediction and a frequency probability generated by a computer model: one might have little confidence in a particular model that predicted a 100 percent chance of rain, for example.

11 The Horizon of Ignorance

1. Edmund L. Gettier, "Is Justified True Belief Knowledge?" *Analysis* 23, no. 6 (1963): 121–123.

2. Duncan Pritchard, *Epistemic Luck* (Oxford: Oxford University Press, 2005), chapters 5 and 6. Pritchard draws on Peter Unger, *Ignorance: A Case for Scepticism*.

3. Pritchard also identifies a fifth type of epistemic luck as problematic: (5) *reflective epistemic luck*, in which, "given what the agent is able to know by reflection alone, it is a matter of luck that her belief is true" (*Epistemic Luck*, 175). This type is directed toward internalist accounts of knowledge—accounts that take the justification of beliefs to be solely a matter of the believer's internal, cognitive states.

4. For an astute analysis of these issues, see Israel Scheffler, *Science and Subjectivity*, 2nd ed. (Indianapolis, IN: Hackett, 1982).

5. Stuart Firestein, *Ignorance: How It Drives Science* (Oxford: Oxford University Press, 2012).

6. John Dewey, *The Early Works of John Dewey, 1882–1898*, vol. 2: *1887, Psychology*, ed. Jo Ann Boydston (Carbondale: Southern Illinois University Press, 1975), 261.

7. One of the ways in which understanding exceeds knowledge is its comprehension of the modal; to understand a thing is not only to know facts about it, but also to comprehend its possibilities.

8. Michel Serres, *Genesis*, trans. Genevieve and James Nielson (Ann Arbor: University of Michigan Press, 1997), 23. Unconventional punctuation is in the original. His image may be derived from Martin Heidegger's claim: "The human being is not the

lord of beings, but the shepherd of Being." Martin Heidegger, *Letter on Humanism* (1947), trans. Frank A. Capuzzi, in *Martin Heidegger: Basic Writings*, ed. David Farrell Krell (New York: Harper & Row, 1977), 210.

9. Plato, *Theaetetus*, 155d. From Plato, *Complete Works*, ed. John Cooper and D. S. Hutchinson (Indianapolis, IN: Hackett, 1997). Though this "Socrates" is a persona in a later dialogue by Plato (and therefore generally given less credence as an accurate report of the historical Socrates), it is likely Plato remembered hearing this particular claim directly, even repeatedly, from his mentor.

10. For a rich philosophical discussion of wonder to which I am indebted, see Mary-Jane Rubenstein, *Strange Wonder: The Closure of Metaphysics and the Opening of Awe* (New York: Columbia University Press, 2008).

11. Aristotle, *Metaphysics*, Book I, chap. 2, 982b12–22.

12. Ibid., 982b29–30.

13. Peter Sloterdijk, *Spheres*, vol. 1: *Bubbles: Microspherology*, trans. Wieland Hoban (Los Angeles, CA: Semiotext(e), 2011), 48.

14. Ludwig Wittgenstein, *Tractatus Logico-Philosophicus*, prop. 7, p. 189.

15. Blaise Pascal, *Pensées*, trans. W. F. Trotter (1670; New York: E. P. Dutton, 1958), §206.

16. Dwayne Huebner, *The Lure of the Transcendent: Collected Essays* (Mahwah, NJ: Erlbaum, 1999), 403.

Epilogue: Ignorance and Epistemology

1. It is true that many languages use different words for these different forms; English conflates them. In German, *wissen* is used for *knowing that*; *kennen* is used for *knowing by acquaintance*. But the use of different terms reflects their different meanings; it does not require that only one is *knowledge* and the other must be placed outside the purview of epistemology.

2. Richard Mason, *Understanding Understanding* (Albany, NY: SUNY Press, 2003); and Catherine Z. Elgin, "From Knowledge to Understanding," in *Epistemology Futures*, ed. Stephen Hetherington (Oxford: Oxford University Press, 2006), 199–215.

3. Jonathan L. Kvanvig, *The Value of Knowledge and the Pursuit of Understanding* (Cambridge: Cambridge University Press, 2003), especially chapter 8.

4. See chapter 2, notes 3 and 4.

5. See Rik Peels, "What Is Ignorance?" *Philosophia* 38 (2010): 57–67, at 57; "Ignorance Is Lack of True Belief: A Rejoinder to Le Morvan," *Philosophia* 39 (2011): 345–355; and "The New View on Ignorance Undefeated," *Philosophia* 40 (2012):

741–750. An effective refutation would require a fuller, more analytical response than I provide here, but I have indicated the direction of a partial rejoinder.

6. Michael Polanyi, *Personal Knowledge: Toward a Post-Critical Philosophy* (Chicago: University of Chicago Press, 1958).

7. Clifford, *The Ethics of Belief.* See my chapter 7.

8. For a rich and extensive analysis of these roles, see Linda Trinkaus Zagzebski, *Epistemic Authority: A Theory of Trust, Authority, and Autonomy in Belief* (Oxford: Oxford University Press, 2012).

9. C. A. J. Coady, *Testimony: A Philosophical Study* (Oxford: Oxford University Press, 1995).

10. Alvin I. Goldman, *Knowledge in a Social World* (Oxford: Oxford University Press, 1999).

11. Kvanvig, *The Value of Knowledge*, 205, claims this problem is insoluble.

12. Cynthia Townley, *A Defense of Ignorance: Its Value for Knowers in Feminist and Social Epistemologies* (Lanham, MD: Roman & Littlefield, 2011). Townley is a fellow-traveler in noting that the monistic theory of epistemic value has continued even in virtue epistemology and discussions of epistemic communities.

13. For example, see Beritt Brogaard, "Intellectual Flourishing as the Fundamental Epistemic Norm," in *Epistemic Norms: New Essays on Action, Belief, and Assertion*, ed. Clayton Littleton and John Turri (Oxford: Oxford University Press, 2014). Her characterization of the proposed norm of epistemic flourishing is, however, conducted within the perspective of the solo knower.

Bibliography

Adams, Scott. *When Did Ignorance Become a Point of View?* Riverside, NJ: Andrews McMeel Publishing, 2000.

Adler, Jonathan E. *Belief's Own Ethics*. Cambridge, MA: MIT Press, 2002.

Al-Ghazzali, Abu Hamid Muhammad ibn Muhammad. *On the Treatment of Ignorance Arising from Heedlessness, Error and Delusion*. Trans. N. A. S. Muhhammad. Chicago: Great Books of the Islamic World, 2002.

Andorno, R. "The Right Not to Know: An Autonomy Based Approach." *Journal of Medical Ethics* 30, no. 5 (2004): 435–439.

Applebaum, Barbara. "Needing Not to Know: Ignorance, Innocence, Denials and Discourse." *Philosophy of Education* 2015: 448–456. Ed. Eduardo Duarte. http://ojs.ed.uiuc.edu/index.php/pes/article/view/4529/1432.

Aquinas, Thomas. *Summa Theologiae. Prima Secundae*. Trans. Fr. Laurence Shapcote. Lander, WY: The Aquinas Institute for the Study of Sacred Doctrine, 2012.

Arias, Elizabeth. "United States Life Tables, 2009." *National Vital Statistics Reports* 62, no. 7 (January 6, 2014): 6, table 2. https://www.cdc.gov/nchs/data/nvsr/nvsr62/nvsr62_07.pdf.

Aristotle. *The Complete Works of Aristotle: The Revised Oxford Translation*. Ed. J. Barnes. 2 vols. Bollingen Series. Princeton, NJ: Princeton University Press, 1983.

Ashaer, Atef. "Poetry and the Arab Spring." In *Routledge Handbook of the Arab Spring: Rethinking Democratization*, ed. Larbi Sadiki. New York: Routledge, 2014.

Baehr, Jason. *The Inquiring Mind: On Intellectual Virtues and Virtue Epistemology*. Oxford: Oxford University Press, 2011.

Ball, Philip. *Curiosity: How Science Became Interested in Everything*. New York: Vintage Press, 2013.

Barinaga, Marcia. "Asilomar Revisited: Lessons for Today?" *Science* 287 (2000): 1584–1585.

Ben-Ze'ev, Aaron. "The Virtue of Modesty." *American Philosophical Quarterly* 30 (1993): 238–246.

Berg, Paul, David Baltimore, Sydney Brenner, Richard Roblin III, and Maxine F. Singer. "Summary Statement of the Asilomar Conference on Recombinant DNA Molecules." *Proceedings of the National Academy of Sciences of the United States of America* 72, no. 6 (June 1975): 1981–1984.

Biesta, Gert. "A New Logic of Emancipation: The Methodology of Jacques Rancière." *Educational Theory* 60, no. 1 (February 2010): 39–59.

Bok, Sissela. *Lying: Moral Choice in Public and Private Life*. Updated ed. New York: Vintage Books, 1999. First published in 1978.

Bok, Sissela. *Secrets: On the Ethics of Concealment and Revelation*. New York: Vintage Books, 1989.

Bommarito, Nicolas. "Modesty as a Virtue of Attention." *Philosophical Review* 122, no. 1 (2013): 93–117.

Brecht, Bertolt. *Galileo*. Trans. C. Laughton. New York: Grove Press, 1966. First published in 1940.

Brennan, Jason. "Modesty without Illusion." *Philosophy and Phenomenological Research* 75, no. 1 (2007): 111–128.

Brogaard, Beritt. "Intellectual Flourishing as the Fundamental Epistemic Norm." In *Epistemic Norms: New Essays on Action, Belief, and Assertion*, ed. Clayton Littleton and John Turri. Oxford: Oxford University Press, 2014.

Cacciara, Massimo. "Names of Place: *Border*." In *Contemporary Italian Philosophy: Crossing the Borders of Ethics, Politics, and Religion*, ed. Silvia Benson and Brian Schroeder. Albany, NY: SUNY Press, 2007.

Carbone, Nick. "Timeline: A History of Violence against Sikhs in the Wake of 9/11." *Time*, August 6, 2012, http://newsfeed.time.com/2012/08/06/timeline-a-history-of-violence-against-sikhs-in-the-wake-of-911/.

Carson, Rachel. *Silent Spring*. With introduction by Linda Lear and afterword by E. O. Wilson. New York: Houghton Mifflin, 2002. First published in 1962.

Clifford, W. K. "The Ethics of Belief." In W. K. Clifford, *The Ethics of Belief and Other Essays*. Amherst, NY: Prometheus Books. 1999. First published in 1876.

Coady, C. A. J. *Testimony: A Philosophical Study*. Oxford: Oxford University Press, 1995.

Cremin, Lawrence. *American Education: The Colonial Experience*. New York: Harper & Row, 1970.

Davidson, Amy. "Did Edward Snowden Break His Oath?" *New Yorker*, January 5, 2014. http://www.newyorker.com/news/amy-davidson/did-edward-snowden-break-his-oath.

DeNicola, Daniel R. *Learning to Flourish: A Philosophical Exploration of Liberal Education*. New York: Continuum/Bloomsbury, 2012.

DeNicola, Daniel R. "Paradigms and Paraphernalia: On the Relationship of Theory and Technology in Science." In *New Directions in the Philosophy of Technology*, ed. Joseph C. Pitt. Dordrecht: Kluwer Academic, 1995.

Dewey, John. *The Early Works of John Dewey, 1882–1898*, vol. 2: *1887, Psychology*. Ed. Jo Ann Boydston. Carbondale: Southern Illinois University Press, 1975.

Downs, Anthony. *An Economic Theory of Democracy*. New York: Harper & Brothers, 1957.

Driver, Julia. "The Virtues of Ignorance." *Journal of Philosophy* 86, no. 7 (July 1989): 373–384.

Driver, Julia. "Modesty and Ignorance." *Ethics* 109, no. 4 (July 1999): 827–834.

Dropp, Kyle, Joshua D. Kertzer, and Thomas Zeitzoff. "The Less Americans Know about Ukraine's Location, the More They Want U.S. to Intervene." *Washington Post*, April 7, 2014, *The Monkey Cage*, blog post. https://www.washingtonpost.com/blogs/monkey-cage/wp/2014/04/07/the-less-americans-know-about-ukraines-location-the-more-they-want-u-s-to-intervene/.

Duncan, Ronald, and M. Weston-Smith. *The Encyclopedia of Medical Ignorance: Mind and Body in Health and Disease*. Oxford: Pergamon Press, 1983.

Dunning, David. *Self-Insight: Roadblocks and Detours on the Path to Knowing Thyself*. New York: Psychology Press, 2005.

Elgin, Catherine Z. "From Knowledge to Understanding." In *Epistemology Futures*, ed. Stephen Hetherington. Oxford: Oxford University Press, 2006.

Felman, Shoshana. "Psychoanalysis and Education: Teaching Terminable and Interminable." *Yale French Studies* 63 (1982): 21–44.

Ferrier, James Frederick. *Institutes of Metaphysic: The Theory of Knowing and Being* (1856). In *James Frederick Ferrier: Selected Writings, Library of Scottish Philosophy*, vol. 3. Ed. Jennifer Keefe. Charlottesville, VA: Imprint Academic, 2011.

Firestein, Stuart. *Ignorance: How It Drives Science*. Oxford: Oxford University Press, 2012.

Firth, Roderick. "Ethical Absolutism and the Ideal Observer." *Philosophy and Phenomenological Research* 12, no. 3 (1952): 317–345.

Fitch, Frederic. "A Logical Analysis of Some Value Concepts." *Journal of Symbolic Logic* 28, no. 2 (June 1963): 135–142.

Flanagan, Owen. "Virtue and Ignorance." *Journal of Philosophy* 87 (8) (August 1990): 420–428.

Frankfurt, Harry. "Alternate Possibilities and Moral Responsibility." *Journal of Philosophy* 66, no. 23 (December 1969): 829–839.

Frankfurt, Harry. *On Bullshit*. Princeton, NJ: Princeton University Press, 2005.

Fricker, Miranda. *Epistemic Injustice: Power and the Ethics of Knowing*. Oxford: Oxford University Press, 2007.

Gerstein, Robert. "Intimacy and Privacy." In *Philosophical Dimensions of Privacy: An Anthology*, ed. Ferdinand David Schoeman, 265–271. Cambridge: Cambridge University Press, 1984.

Gettier, Edmund L. "Is Justified True Belief Knowledge?" *Analysis* 23, no. 6 (1963): 121–123.

Gilson, Erinn. "Vulnerability, Ignorance, and Oppression." *Hypatia* 26, no. 2 (2012): 308–332.

Glantz, S. A., J. Slade, L. A. Bero, P. Hanauer, and D. E. Barnes, eds. *The Cigarette Papers*. Berkeley, CA: University of California Press, 1998.

Gödel, Kurt. "On Formally Undecidable Propositions of *Principia Mathematica* and Related Systems" (1931). In *The Undecidable: Basic Papers on Undecidable Propositions, Unsolvable Problems, and Computable Functions*, ed. Martin Davis. Hewlett, NY: Raven Press, 1965.

Goldman, Alvin I. *Knowledge in a Social World*. Oxford: Oxford University Press, 1999.

Graham, David A. "Rumsfeld's Knowns and Unknowns: The Intellectual History of a Quip." *Atlantic*, March 27, 2004. http://www.theatlantic.com/politics/archive/2014/03/rumsfelds-knowns-and-unknowns-the-intellectual-history-of-a-quip/359719/.

Gray, Richard. "Does the Future Affect the Past? Physicists Demonstrate How Time Can Seem to Run Backwards." *Daily Mail*, June 9, 2015. http://www.dailymail.co.uk/sciencetech/article-3116792/Does-future-affect-PAST-Physicists-demonstrate-time-run-backwards.html.

Greely, Hank. "Of Science, CRISPR-Cas9, and Asilomar." Stanford Law School, *Law and Biosciences Blog*, April 4, 2015. https://law.stanford.edu/2015/04/04/of-science-crispr-cas9-and-asilomar/.

Grim, Patrick. "Against Omniscience: The Case from Essential Indexicals." *Noûs* 19 (1985): 151–180.

Gross, M., and L. McGoey, eds. *Routledge International Handbook of Ignorance Studies.* London: Routledge, 2015.

Haas, Peter. "Epistemic Communities and International Policy Coordination." *International Organization* 46, no. 1 (1992): 1–35.

Hájek, Alan. "Interpretations of Probability." In *Stanford Encyclopedia of Philosophy* (winter 2011 ed.), ed. Edward N. Zalta. https://plato.stanford.edu/entries/probability -interpret/.

Halper, Stefan, and Jonathan Clarke. *The Silence of the Rational Center.* New York: Basic Books, 2007.

Hecht, Jennifer Michael. *Stay: A History of Suicide and the Arguments against It.* New Haven, CT: Yale University Press, 2013.

Heidegger, Martin. *Letter on Humanism* (1947). Trans. F. A. Capuzzi. In *Martin Heidegger: Basic Writings,* ed. David Farrell Krell. New York: Harper & Row, 1977.

Heldke, Lisa M. "Farming Made Her Stupid." *Hypatia* 21, no. 3 (2006): 151–165.

Helvétius, Claude Adrien. *Treatise on Man,* 2 vols. New York: Burt Franklin, 1969. First published in 1810.

Herzog, Don. *Cunning.* Princeton, NJ: Princeton University Press, 2006.

Horgan, John. *The End of Science: Facing the Limits of Knowledge in the Twilight of the Scientific Age.* New ed. New York: Basic Books, 2015.

Huebner, Dwayne. *The Lure of the Transcendent: Collected Essays.* Mahwah, NJ: Erlbaum, 1999.

Hume, David. *A Treatise of Human Nature.* 2nd ed. Ed. L. A. Selby-Bigge and P. H. Nidditch. Oxford: Oxford University Press, 1978. First published in 1739.

Israilidis, John, Russell Lock, and Louise Cook. "Ignorance Management." *Management Dynamics in the Knowledge Economy* 1, no. 1 (2013): 71–85, http:// www.managementdynamics.ro/index.php/journal/article/view/4.

Jackson, Frank. "Epiphenomenal Qualia." *Philosophical Quarterly* 32 (1982): 127–136.

Jacoby, Susan. *The Age of American Unreason.* New York: Pantheon Books, 2008.

James, William. "The Will to Believe." In *William James: Writings 1878–1899,* 457–479. New York: The Library of America, 1992. First published in 1896.

Joy, Bill. "Why the Future Doesn't Need Us." *Wired Magazine,* April 2000. Reprinted in *Nanoethics: The Ethical and Social Implications of Nanotechnology,* ed. Fritz Allhoff et al. (Hoboken, NJ: Wiley, 2007).

Kant, Immanuel. *Prolegomena to Any Future Metaphysics*. Indianapolis: Bobbs-Merrill, 1951. First published in 1783.

Katzner, Donald W. *Time, Ignorance, and Uncertainty in Economic Models*. Ann Arbor: University of Michigan Press, 1999.

Kerwin, Ann. "None Too Solid: Medical Ignorance." *Science Communication* 15 (1993): 166–185.

Kretzmann, Norman. "Omniscience and Immutability." *Journal of Philosophy* 63 (1966): 409–421.

Kvanvig, Jonathan L. *The Value of Knowledge and the Pursuit of Understanding*. Cambridge: Cambridge University Press, 2003.

Kvanvig, Jonathan L. *The Knowability Paradox*. Oxford: Oxford University Press, 2006.

Laertius, Diogenes. "Life of Pyrrho." In *Hellenistic Philosophy: Introductory Readings*, ed. and trans. B. Inwood and L. P. Gerson. Indianapolis, IN: Hackett, 1988.

Laplace, P. S. *A Philosophical Essay on Probabilities*. New York: Dover, 1951. First published in 1814.

Lewis, D. K., and S. R. Lewis. "Holes." *Australasian Journal of Philosophy* 48 (1970): 206–212. Reprinted in D. K. Lewis, *Philosophical Papers*, vol. 1 (New York: Oxford University Press, 1983).

Lockridge, Kenneth A. *Literacy in Colonial New England: An Enquiry into the Social Context of Literacy in the Early Modern West*. New York: W. W. Norton, 1975.

Logue, Jennifer. "The Unbelievable Truth and the Dilemmas of Ignorance." *Philosophy of Education Archive* (2008): 54–62.

Lowry, George G. *Lowrys' Handbook of Right-to-Know and Emergency Planning*. Chelsea, MI: Lewis Publications, 1989.

Ludlow, P., Y. Nagasawa, and D. Stoljar, eds. *There's Something About Mary: Essays on Phenomenal Consciousness and Frank Jackson's Knowledge Argument*. Cambridge, MA: MIT Press, 2004.

Luhmann, Niklas. *Social Systems*. Trans. J. Bednarz Jr. and D. Baecker. Stanford, CA: Stanford University Press, 1996.

Lynch, J., ed. *Samuel Johnson's Dictionary: From the 1755 Work That Defined the English Language*. Delray Beach, FL: Levinger Press, 2004.

Lyons, William E. *The Disappearance of Introspection*. Cambridge, MA: MIT Press, 1986.

MacDonough, Glen, and Victor Herbert. *Babes in Toyland*. New York: M. Witmark, 1903.

Mair, J., A. H. Kelly, and C. High, eds. *The Anthropology of Ignorance: An Ethnographic Approach*. New York: Palgrave Macmillan, 2012.

Malewski, E., and N. Jaramillo, eds. *Epistemologies of Ignorance in Education*. Charlotte, NC: Information Age Publishing, 2011.

Manning, A. G., R. I. Khakimov, R. G. Dall, and A. G. Truscott. "Wheeler's Delayed-Choice Gedanken Experiment with a Single Atom." *Nature Physics* 11 (2015): 539–542, http://www.nature.com/nphys/journal/v11/n7/full/nphys3343.html.

Manson, Neil C. "Epistemic Restraint and the Vice of Curiosity." *Philosophy* 87, no. 2 (April 2012): 239–259.

Mason, Richard. *Understanding Understanding*. Albany, NY: SUNY Press, 2003.

Mayer, Andre. "Soft-drink Makers Accused of Using 'Big Tobacco Playbook.'" CBC News, http://www.cbc.ca/news/health/soft-drink-makers-accused-of-using-big -tobacco-playbook-1.1362598 (accessed October 2016).

Mayer-Schönberger, Viktor. *Delete: The Virtue of Forgetting in the Digital Age*. Princeton, NJ: Princeton University Press, 2011.

McIntyre, Lee. *Respecting Truth: Willful Ignorance in the Internet Age*. New York: Routledge, 2015.

Medina, José. *The Epistemology of Resistance: Gender and Racial Oppression, Epistemic Injustice, and Resistant Imaginations*. Oxford: Oxford University Press, 2013.

Melzer, Arthur M. *Philosophy between the Lines: The Lost History of Esoteric Writing*. Chicago: University of Chicago Press, 2014.

Michaels, David. "Manufactured Uncertainty: Contested Science and the Protection of the Public's Health and Environment." In *Agnotology*, ed. Robert N. Proctor and Londa Schiebinger. Stanford, CA: Stanford University Press, 2008.

Mills, Charles W. *The Racial Contract*. Ithaca, NY: Cornell University Press, 1997.

Mills, Charles W. "White Ignorance." In *Race and Epistemologies of Ignorance*, ed. Shannon Sullivan and Nancy Tuana. Albany, NY: SUNY Press, 2007.

Milton, John. *Paradise Lost*. Project Gutenberg, 2011. http://www.gutenberg.org/ cache/epub/20/pg20.html (accessed October 2016). First published in 1667.

Moore, G. E. "Moore's Paradox." In *G. E. Moore: Selected Writings*, ed. Thomas Baldwin. 207–212. London: Routledge, 1993.

Morris, Herbert. "Lost Innocence." In Herbert Morris, *On Guilt and Innocence: Essays in Legal Philosophy and Moral Psychology*. Berkeley, CA: University of California Press, 1976.

National Weather Service. "Explaining Probability of Precipitation." National Weather Center Weather Forecast Office, August 2009. http://www.weather.gov/ffc/pop (accessed October 2016).

Nicholas of Cusa (Cusanus). *On Learned Ignorance (De docta ignorantia)*. In *Renaissance Philosophy*, vol. 2: *The Transalpine Thinkers*, ed. and trans. Herman Shapiro and Arturo B. Fallico. New York: The Modern Library, 1969.

Nussbaum, Martha C. *Love's Knowledge: Essays on Philosophy and Literature*. Oxford: Oxford University Press, 1990.

Nuyen, A. T. "Just Modesty." *American Philosophical Quarterly* 35, no. 1 (1998): 101–109.

Oreskes, Naomi, and Erik M. Conway. *Merchants of Doubt: How a Handful of Scientists Obscured the Truth on Issues from Tobacco Smoke to Global Warming*. New York: Bloomsbury Press, 2010.

Pascal, Blaise. *Pensées*. Trans. W. F. Trotter. New York: E. P. Dutton, 1958. First published in 1670.

Paul, L. A. *Transformative Experience*. Oxford: Oxford University Press, 2014.

Peels, Rik. "What Is Ignorance?" *Philosophia* 38 (2010): 57–67.

Peels, Rik. "Ignorance Is Lack of True Belief: A Rejoinder to Le Morvan." *Philosophia* 39 (2011): 345–355.

Peels, Rik. "The New View on Ignorance Undefeated." *Philosophia* 40 (2012): 741–750.

Pieper, Josef. *Leisure, the Basis of Culture*. Trans. G. Malsbary. South Bend, IN: St. Augustine's Press, 1998. First published in 1948.

Pinnock, Charles, Richard Rice, John Sanders, William Hasker, and David Basinger. *The Openness of God: A Biblical Challenge to the Traditional Understanding of God*. Downers Grove, IL: InterVarsity Press, 1994.

Plato. *Republic*. 3rd ed. Ed. and trans. C. D. C. Greeve. Indianapolis, IN: Hackett, 2004.

Plato. *Theaetetus*. In *Plato, Complete Works*, ed. John Cooper and D. S. Hutchinson. Indianapolis, IN: Hackett, 1997.

Polanyi, Michael. *Personal Knowledge: Towards a Post Critical Epistemology*. Chicago: University of Chicago Press, 1958.

Polanyi, Michael. *The Tacit Dimension*. New York: Anchor Books, 1967.

PoliTech, Texas Tech University. "Politically-Challenged: Texas Tech Edition." Video. YouTube, October 28, 2014. https://www.youtube.com/watch?v=yRZZpk_9k8E (accessed October 2016).

Pritchard, Duncan. *Epistemic Luck*. Oxford: Oxford University Press, 2005.

Proctor, Robert N. "Agnotology: A Missing Term to Describe the Cultural Production of Ignorance (and Its Study)." In *Agnotology: The Making and Unmaking of Ignorance*, ed. Robert N. Proctor and Londa Schiebinger. Stanford, CA: Stanford University Press, 2008.

Proctor, Robert N., and Londa Schiebinger, eds. *Agnotology: The Making and Unmaking of Ignorance*. Stanford, CA: Stanford University Press, 2008.

Rancière, Jacques. *The Ignorant Schoolmaster: Five Lessons in Intellectual Emancipation*. Trans. Kristin Ross. Stanford, CA: Stanford University Press, 1991.

Rancière, Jacques. "On Ignorant Schoolmasters." In *Jacques Rancière: Education, Truth, Emancipation*, ed. Charles Bingham and Gert Biesta. New York: Bloomsbury, 2010.

Rawls, John. *A Theory of Justice*. Cambridge, MA: Harvard University Press, 1971.

Reichenbach, Hans. *Experience and Prediction: An Analysis of the Foundations and Structure of Knowledge*. Chicago: University of Chicago Press, 1938.

Rescher, Nicholas. *Error (On Our Predicament When Things Go Wrong)*. Pittsburgh: University of Pittsburgh Press, 2009.

Rescher, Nicholas. *Ignorance (On the Wider Implications of Deficient Knowledge)*. Pittsburgh: University of Pittsburgh Press, 2009.

Rescher, Nicholas. *Scientific Progress: A Philosophical Essay on the Economics of Research in Natural Science*. Pittsburgh: University of Pittsburgh Press, 1978.

Rescher, Nicholas. *Unknowability: An Inquiry into the Limits of Knowledge*. Lanham, MD: Rowman & Littlefield, 2010.

Roberts, Robert C., and W. Jay Wood. *Intellectual Virtues: An Essay in Regulative Epistemology*. Oxford: Oxford University Press, 2007.

Ronell, Avital. *Stupidity*. Urbana: University of Illinois Press, 2002.

Rorty, Richard. "Education as Socialization and Individualization." In Richard Rorty, *Philosophy and Social Hope*. London: Penguin Books, 1999.

Rorty, Richard, and Eduardo Mendieta. *Take Care of Freedom and Truth Will Take Care of Itself: Interviews with Richard Rorty*. Palo Alto, CA: Stanford University Press, 2005.

Rousseau, Jean-Jacques. *Emile, or On Education*. Ed. R. L. Archer. New York: Barron's Educational Series, 1964.

Rubenstein, Mary-Jane. *Strange Wonder: The Closure of Metaphysics and the Opening of Awe*. New York: Columbia University Press, 2008.

Ryle, Gilbert. *The Concept of Mind*. New York: Barnes & Noble, 1949.

Sartre, Jean-Paul. *Being and Nothingness*. Trans. H. E. Barnes. London: Methuen, 1957.

Scheffler, Israel. *Science and Subjectivity*. 2nd ed. Indianapolis, IN: Hackett, 1982.

Schoeman, F. D., ed. *Philosophical Dimensions of Privacy: An Anthology*. Cambridge: Cambridge University Press, 1984.

Schoen, Donald. *The Reflective Practitioner: How Professionals Think in Action*. New York: Basic Books, 1984.

Schueler, G. F. "Why IS Modesty a Virtue?" *Ethics* 109, no. 4 (July 1999): 835–841.

Schueler, G. F. "Why Modesty Is a Virtue." *Ethics* 107, no. 3 (April 1997): 467–485.

Searle, John R. "Minds, Brains, and Programs." *Behavioral and Brain Sciences* 3, no. 3 (1980): 417–457.

Searle, John R. "The Chinese Room." In *The MIT Encyclopedia of the Cognitive Sciences*, ed. R. A. Wilson and F. Keil. Cambridge, MA: MIT Press, 1999.

Serres, Michel. *Genesis*. Trans. Genevieve and James Nielson. Ann Arbor: University of Michigan Press, 1997.

Shattuck, Roger. *Forbidden Knowledge: From Prometheus to Pornography*. New York: St. Martin's Press, 1996.

Sher, George. *Who Knew? Responsibility without Awareness*. Oxford: Oxford University Press, 2009.

Sloterdijk, Peter. *Spheres*, vol. 1: *Bubbles: Microspherology*. Trans. Wieland Hoban. Los Angeles, CA: Semiotext(e), 2011.

Smith, Adam. *The Theory of Moral Sentiments*. Ed. D. D. Raphael. Oxford: Oxford University Press, 1976. First published in 1759.

Smithson, Michael. *Ignorance and Uncertainty: Emerging Paradigms*. New York: Springer Science & Business Media, 2012. First published in 1989.

Somin, Ilya. *Democracy and Political Ignorance: Why Smaller Government Is Smarter*. Stanford, CA: Stanford University Press, 2013.

Sosa, Ernest. *Knowledge in Perspective*. Cambridge: Cambridge University Press, 1991.

Sosa, Ernest. *Reflective Knowledge: Apt Belief and Reflective Knowledge*, vol. 2. Oxford: Oxford University Press, 2011.

Sosa, Ernest. *A Virtue Epistemology: Apt Belief and Reflective Knowledge*, vol. 1. Oxford: Oxford University Press, 2009.

Stanley, Jason. *Know How*. Oxford: Oxford University Press, 2011.

Sullivan, S., and N. Tuana, eds. *Race and Epistemologies of Ignorance*. Albany, NY: SUNY Press, 2007.

Symonds, John Addington. *On a Problem in Greek Ethics: Being an Inquiry into the Phenomenon of Sexual Inversion Addressed Especially to Medical Psychologists and Jurists*. London: privately printed, 1901.

Tillich, Paul. *Systematic Theology*, vol. 2: *Existence and the Christ*. Chicago: University of Chicago Press, 1963.

Townley, Cynthia. *A Defense of Ignorance: Its Value for Knowers in Feminist and Social Epistemologies*. Lanham, MD: Roman & Littlefield, 2011.

Travers, Frank J. *Hedge Fund Analysis: An In-Depth Guide to Evaluating Return Potential and Assessing Risks*. Hoboken, NJ: Wiley, 2012.

Tuana, Nancy. "Coming to Understand: Orgasm and the Epistemology of Ignorance." *Hypatia* 19, no. 1 (2004): 194–232.

Ungar, Sheldon. "Ignorance as an Under-Identified Social Problem." *British Journal of Sociology* 59, no. 2 (2008): 301–326.

Unger, Peter. *Ignorance: A Case for Scepticism*. Oxford: Clarendon Press of Oxford University Press, 1979.

University of Arizona. *Q-Cubed: College of Medicine's Curriculum on Medical Ignorance* (CMI). http://ignorance.medicine.arizona.edu/about-us/home (accessed October 2016).

Unknown Known, The: The Life and Times of Donald Rumsfeld. Directed by Errol Morris. Film. Los Angeles, CA: The Weinstein Company, 2013.

Vitek, B., and W. Jackson, eds. *The Virtues of Ignorance: Complexity, Sustainability, and the Limits of Knowledge*. Lexington: The University Press of Kentucky, 2008.

Walsh, P. G. "The Rights and Wrongs of Curiosity (Plato to Augustine)." *Greece and Rome* 35, no. 1 (April 1988): 73–85.

Walters, John. "No Good Deed Goes Unpunished." *Vermont Political Observer*, January 19, 2015, https://thevpo.org/2015/01/19/no-good-deed-goes-unpunished/.

Walton, Douglas. *Arguments from Ignorance*. University Park: The Pennsylvania State University Press, 1996.

Weisberg, Herbert I. *Willful Ignorance: The Mismeasure of Uncertainty*. Hoboken, NJ: Wiley, 2014.

Whatham, A. E. "The Polytheism of Gen., Chap. 1." *Biblical World* 37, no. 1 (January 1911): 40–47.

Whitehead, Alfred North. *The Aims of Education*. New York: Free Press, 1967. First published in 1929.

Whitehead, Alfred North. *Process and Reality: An Essay on Cosmology*. New York: Harper & Row, 1960. First published in 1929.

Wierenga, Edward. "Omniscience." In *The Stanford Encyclopedia of Philosophy* (winter 2013 ed.), ed. Edward N. Zalta, https://plato.stanford.edu/archives/win2013/entries/omniscience/.

Wilde, Oscar. *The Importance of Being Earnest*. N.p., 1895; Project Gutenberg, 1997, https://www.gutenberg.org/files/844/844-h/844-h.htm.

Williamson, Timothy. *Knowledge and Its Limits*. Oxford: Oxford University Press, 2000.

Wittgenstein, Ludwig. *Tractatus Logic-Philosophicus*. Trans. C. K. Ogden, with an introduction by Bertrand Russell. London: Routledge & Kegan Paul, 1981. First published in 1922.

Wood, Terry. "11 of the Most Unusual Things People Have Ever Insured." US Insurance Agents, n.d., https://usinsuranceagents.com/unusual-insurance-policies (accessed October 2016).

Zagzebski, Linda. *Epistemic Authority: A Theory of Trust, Authority, and Autonomy in Belief*. Oxford: Oxford University Press, 2012.

Zagzebski, Linda. *Virtues of the Mind: An Inquiry into the Nature of Virtue and the Ethical Foundations of Knowledge*. Cambridge: Cambridge University, 1996.

Zimmerman, Michael J. *Ignorance and Moral Obligation*. Oxford: Oxford University Press, 2014.

Žižek, Slavoj. "What Rumsfeld Doesn't Know That He Knows about Abu Ghraib." *In These Times*, May 21, 2004, http://www.lacan.com/zizekrumsfeld.htm.

Index

Acting from ignorance (vs. acting in ignorance), 112, 224n20

Adams, Scott, 9, 210n13

Agnoiology, 13, 211n20

Agnosognosia, 43

Agnotology, 13, 211n19

Aleatoric art, 186–187

Al-Ghazzali, Abū Ḥāmid Muḥammad ibn Muḥammad, 36

al-Shābbī, Abū al-Qāsim, 29

Amnesia, 43, 60

Amousos, 26

Anosognosia. *See* Agnosognosia

Applebaum, Barbara, 113

Aquinas, Thomas, 119, 121, 151

Arguments from ignorance, 153–155, 215n13

Aristotle, 79, 111–112, 116, 126, 140, 191

Asilomar Conference of 1975, 93–94, 221n26

Autonomy, 49, 105, 110
  epistemic, 204–205

Belief, 12, 37–38, 42, 44, 58, 72–73, 151–152, 199–200. *See also* False beliefs (false knowledge)
  degree of, 171–174
  ethics of, 98–100
  factors affecting, 95–98, 122
  immoral, 99

Birdman: Or (The Unexpected Virtue of Ignorance), 131, 225n31

Bivalent (vs. scalar conception of epistemic states), 71–72, 197, 202–203

Bliss (ignorance as), 10, 23, 47–49, 51, 56

Bok, Sissela, 91, 123

Bommarito, Nicolas, 128

Borders, 32, 66–67, 70–74, 92, 101, 137

Boundaries, epistemic, 28, 62, 66–68, 70–73, 88, 137, 179, 202
  natural vs. constructed, 70, 79–80, 90–91

Bullshit, 86, 90

Butler, Judith, 179

Category mistake, 17–18

Cave Allegory, 33–40, 42, 50–51, 57–58, 120, 130. *See also* Plato

Censorship. *See* Forbidden knowledge

Certainty, 12, 42, 45, 171, 173, 193, 196, 203. *See also* Uncertainty

Chance, 140, 164–165, 168–176. *See also* Luck; Probability

Cherimoya, 93

Chinese Room, 60–61

Clifford, William K., 99–100, 205

Coady, C. A. J., 205

Coincidences, 164–165, 181, 200